How To Succeed In Commercial Real Estate

MESA HOUSE

Related titles by
Mesa House Publishing

Readers of this book may be interested in the following titles also published by Mesa House Publishing. Visit **www.mesahouse.com** for more details.

Negotiating Commercial Real Estate Leases
by Martin I. Zankel.

One of the few books that examines the essential business issues underlying each clause of the commercial lease (retail, office, and industrial) from both sides of the negotiating table — tenant and landlord alike. The book examines the critical economic and legal issues at stake in each clause of the lease; identifies which points are most easily negotiated; and what alternative clauses and solutions can be offered to create a deal that works for both parties.

The Site Book: A Field Guide to
Commercial Real Estate Leases
by Richard M. Fenker.

This easy-to-read, straightforward book explores the dynamic and sometimes complex relationship between a piece of real estate, site features, and the other factors that will ultimately determine the success of any restaurant or retail location. The Site Book includes in-depth discussion of the major areas affecting a site evaluation including customer sources, usage patterns, demographic reports, day parts, linkages, drop-in features, physical surroundings, image, trade area, growth strategies, competition, and cannibalism.

How To Succeed In Commercial Real Estate

John L. Bowman

MESA HOUSE

Mesa House Publishing
Fort Worth, Texas

Cover and book design by Scott Anderson

Library of Congress Card Number: 2004112286

© 2005 by John L. Bowman

Editorial correspondence and requests for permission to reprint should be mailed to Mesa House Publishing, c/o Two Coyotes, Inc., 3228 College Avenue, Fort Worth, TX 76110. E-mail should be addressed to books@mesahouse.com.

This publication is intended to provide accurate information in regard to the subject matter presented. It is sold with the understanding that the publisher is not engaged in rendering legal, financial, medical, or other professional services.

ISBN: 0-940352-16-8

Printed in the United States of America

I dedicate this book to my wife, Kathy Ileen McCoy Bowman. Commercial real estate can be a tumultuous and stressful business. She is an honorable and noble soul who has patiently stood by my side throughout my career.

About the Author

The author has been active in commercial real estate for most of his adult life. He was born in Portland, Oregon, in 1950. He graduated from Whitman College in 1973 with a Bachelor of Arts. After college he entered the commercial real estate field where he has been active as a salesman, broker, or manager for more than 30 years. He started in his family's commercial real estate company, Bowman Company, located in Portland, Oregon, where he became sales manager, president, and a part owner. He also has a Bachelor of Arts in Philosophy from Portland State University.

In 1983 Bowman Company joined forces with Portland's largest commercial firm, Norris, Beggs and Simpson, where the author spent 10 years as an industrial broker. He started his own commercial real estate company, John L. Bowman, Realtor® in 1992. He was a member of the Society of Industrial and Office Realtors®, president of the SIOR Oregon Chapter, member of the SIOR national board of directors, and board member of the Oregon and Southwest Washington Commercial Association of Realtors®. He has also served on various association committees including professional standards.

The author specialized in industrial real estate, but has had experience in all areas of the business. He has done real estate deals in office, retail, and investments and is also experienced in land sales, high-tech, and exchanges. He has also had experience managing commercial real estate sales people and operating a commercial real estate office. The author has represented many national companies in their real estate dealings including General Electric, Westinghouse, Coca-Cola, and Goodyear Tire and Rubber Co.

Table of Contents

Acknowledgments

Commercial real estate is an involved and sometimes complicated subject. In addition to the practical aspects of the business, there are many technical areas that commercial real estate agents encounter. These technical areas require experts. In order to make this book as accurate as possible, I asked many of these experts to review the parts of this book that deal with their area of expertise. I also asked other commercial brokers, whom I considered most knowledgeable and professional, to review parts of the manuscript. I tried to have these brokers evaluate the areas they are most familiar with. Everyone responded in a very positive and helpful manner. I would like to thank all of them for their time and willingness to help. It has been a real pleasure working with them and discussing the various aspects of their areas of knowledge. If I had not dedicated this book to my wife, I would have dedicated it to them.

I would like to thank the following people. Gene Bentley of Norris, Beggs and Simpson, Realtors® for investment and technology; Scott Napier of Napier's Multiple Listing Service for multiple listing services; Marlene McCartney of H&R Block for taxation; Dave Andersen of Andersen Construction Company for construction and architecture; Roger Anderson, M.A.I., of R. D. Anderson and Associates for appraisal; Harold Cox of Morgan, Cox and Slater for financing; Dave Samples of Evergreen Environmental for environmental; Kathy Bork and Bob Brandon of Ticor Title Insurance Company for title; Dave Parr of Drax Corporation for development; and John Guinasso of Schwabe, Williamson and Wyatt, Attorneys at Law, for his contribution to law. A special thanks to Barbara Radler of Ball, Janik LLP, for her contributions to contracts because of the volume of material; Michael Harrison for his comments on zoning and land use; Gary Cheel of Weddle and Associates for surveys; George Macoubray of HSM Pacific for his comments on the retail end of the profession; and Doug Bean of Doug Bean and Associates for his comments on the office end. George Macoubray also looked at the Rent Quote Diagram in Chapter 1. I would like to thank Bob Stutte of Norris and Stevens, Realtors® for office management; John Mitchell, economist for the U.S. Bank, for comments on the economy; Ron Timmerman of Timmerman Realty Advisors for investments; Jay Jacobsmuhlen of Lance Denning Properties for reviewing the parts of the book dealing with high-tech and investments; Neil Morfitt of Morfitt

Real Estate Services for looking at "Things to Avoid"; Bill Wright of Bill Wright and Associates for looking at "Helpful Hints and Things to Know"; Robin White of the Builders Owners and Managers Association for reviewing organizations; Paul Gold of ProSchools for state licensing and brokerage requirements; Jack McConnell of Norris, Beggs and Simpson for comments on sales points; and Cathy Munson of Schnitzer Northwest for property management.

In addition, I would like to acknowledge the contributions of MaryAnn Gray of Westside Secretarial Service, Portland, Oregon, for her work editing earlier versions of this manuscript.

Thank you all.

INTRODUCTION

Commercial real estate is one of the last bastions of free enterprise in business. It is one of the few remaining areas where the amount of money individuals can make is limited only by their talent and how hard they work. It is comprised of smart, motivated, and talented people imbued with the entrepreneurial spirit. It is a wonderful business with endless opportunities that include money, material possessions (if that is what you want), recognition, fulfillment, and access to a multitude of allied fields, to name a few. It can be fun and exciting. It is a business that rewards effort. It is a tremendous thrill to go to the title company after a closing and pick up a $150,000 commission check. Because of this, however, it is an intense and competitive business full of intense and competitive people.

The purpose of this book is to help you navigate that competition in order to be successful. There seem to be certain principles that succor success. Good character, knowledge, effort, and creativity are a few examples. In commercial real estate these principles translate to ethics and integrity, knowledge of the business and practices, a strong work ethic, and the ability to figure out how to do things that others cannot. This book endeavors to translate these general principles of success into practical advice for the commercial real estate profession in the hope that they will help you succeed.

Success is a very subjective word. It means different things to different people. To some, it is just money. To others, it may mean happiness. And to yet another, it may just mean to have achieved more than someone else. In the end, success is personal. On one level, the purpose of this book is prosaic. It is about selling and leasing as much commercial property as you can in order to earn commissions. On another level, it is about getting to a place in life where you no longer have to worry everyday about making the mortgage payment. At that point, you can then go do what you want to do. You are free to pursue your personal concept of what it means to be successful.

This book is intended to be a practical guide full of practical information that may help you succeed. It is intended to be comprehensive enough to provide some general and introductory information to most areas of commercial real estate. It is intended to give you an overview and a summary of what you should know about the business in order to succeed. It is hoped that this book will help point you in the right direction. It will give you some basic information and discuss some issues and problems in the industry that affect most brokers. It is not intended to be a textbook. Commercial real estate is too big an industry to be covered in one book. Technical books have literally been written on paragraphs of this book. This book's purpose is analogous to the function of a liberal arts education as opposed to a technical one. It is a broad overview of the commercial real estate industry and its everyday practices — not a tightly focused and highly technical treatise. In an effort to ensure accuracy, portions of this book have been reviewed by specialists in commercial real estate as well as allied areas.

There is a logical sequence to this book. Generally, the first half deals with the technical aspects of the business and, the last half, with the practical ones. It begins with a discussion of whether the business is suited to you. If you decide that it is, then it raises some issues that you should think about such as the type of firm to work for and what area to specialize in. The importance of integrity and ethics is offered early on because they are prerequisites to success. The early part of the book then covers the fundamentals of the business and what you need to do to prepare yourself. Considerable time is spent on the technical knowledge that you need to master. This encompasses contracts and allied areas of knowledge that affect commercial real estate such as law, taxation, construction, and surveys. A full chapter is devoted to salesmanship and its importance to success. This part of the book then concludes with some ideas about organizing yourself. If you are already familiar with the nuts and bolts of the business, you may want to consider skipping the first part of the book and starting with Chapter 5, Salesmanship.

The middle part of the book covers the practical aspect of the business. This is the part that involves making deals. How to get prospects, how to market property, and the deal itself are the core of this section. A chapter is then devoted to some practical information about the business that one does not usually find in books. The section in this chapter dealing with listings is probably the core to the book. The last part of the book deals with your relations with other brokers, the public, and clients as well as those in similar professions. At the end, information on the various organizations found in commercial real estate is presented along with a final chapter about what to consider once you have gained success.

If this book were distilled, the most important chapters would probably be Chapter 5, Salesmanship, and Chapter 10, Practical Knowledge. This is because they deal with the issues the author believes lead directly to success in the business. The formula for success could be condensed as follows: learn to sell so you can get listings and make deals. It may be a simple formula, but it is an effective one. There are many routes to success, and this book presents one person's methods of achieving it. There are other ways. If other ways work for you, use them.

This book is not a "how to make a million dollars in real estate" book. It is not a shortcut to success and money. It is, rather, a conservative, straightforward approach on how to succeed in commercial real estate. It treats and respects commercial real estate as a profession and deals with how to become a professional. Commercial brokers are professionals because they represent other people on a fiduciary basis, which carries certain obligations and responsibilities. In this respect, it is hoped that this book furthers the commercial real estate industry in that direction. This is why considerable time is spent discussing brokers relations, ethics, and conduct. This book assumes that if you do a good job for your clients, the fruits of success will follow.

This book is targeted to those who want to succeed in commercial real estate. These could include those outside real estate who are considering entering the field, those in allied fields (such as residential real estate) who want to switch to commercial, and those who are already commercial brokers who want to do better. This book should help you decide if you want to enter the field and, if you do, help you succeed.

A few personal comments: This book explains the way I managed to succeed in commercial real estate. As mentioned before, it is not the only way. I am assuming that if it worked for me, it will work for you. A problem in writing this book was that making personal experience universal can be problematic. Much of the information in this book is based on the practices where I live, which is Portland, Oregon. Practices and laws vary from place to place and things change. What works in one place may not work in another, and what works today may not work tomorrow. Also, many of the technical aspects of commercial real estate change rapidly. These include such things as the law, technology, contracts, and taxation. It may also be true that some of the advice in one area, such as industrial, may not apply to another, such as office. For these reasons, the author and the publisher do not guarantee the accuracy of all information in this book. Some advice or information may simply not be applicable to commercial real estate in your area. You should always seek competent expert advice in all of the technical areas this book describes.

Please also excuse me if some of the advice is limited or parochial. I tried to make the advice up to date, and universal, so it could be applied in most circumstances. For example, if you can get good listings, which is one of my themes, it is pretty hard to fail. It also seems that integrity and the acquisition of knowledge are timeless and universal formulas for success. This is what I know, and it worked. I just hope it works for you.

Because one of the central themes of this book is getting listings, much of the advice and many of the examples are from the owner's and listing broker's perspective. This is especially true in Chapter 10 under "Things to Avoid." There are other ways to look at things, but I have found that doing so from the owner's perspective is the most productive in the long run. An effort was made, however, to make the advice balanced. Also, you should know that I am an industrial broker. I have specialized in that area for most of my career. Consequently, many of the examples and situations in this book deal with industrial real estate and the information on other specialty areas may be limited. I have, however, done deals in all areas including office, retail, investments, and land. I have tried to focus on the principles that apply across the board and include information on each field.

Finally, let me say that this book contains many of my own biases and prejudices. I did not want to write a dry, boring textbook. I wanted a book with a little 'edge,' not pabulum. I suppose my only defense in this matter is that my biases and prejudices have come as a result of experience gained from being in the business for 30 years. I suppose others with equal experience could have different biases, so please take mine with a grain of salt. Anyhow, I had fun putting a little of my personality in the book.

Some final comments on vocabulary: My vocabulary in this book is not always precise. Some words that are used generically have very specific legal or real estate definitions. Company, brokerage house, and firm are examples of entities a broker can work for. I use them interchangeably. Other words are used because they condense a meaning quickly and avoid redundant explanations. For example, the words buyer, seller, lessee, and lessor are specific, but often I needed to refer to them in general because they are the principals doing the deals. So I often collectively call them "principals" in the book. I tried to avoid the use of slang words, but they are so common and expressive a few crept in.

Additional comments on vocabulary are as follows:

- Broker, agent, Realtor® and salesperson are used interchangeably. Realtor® is a registered trademark term used only for members of the National Association of Realtors®; therefore, not all brokers, agents, and salespeople are Realtors®. The term broker is sometimes used to connote a senior salesperson.

- Business, profession, field, and industry all refer to commercial real estate.

- The word "move" is sometimes used to mean sold or leased.

- The word employment is sometimes used for a broker who gets a listing. The broker has been "employed" in a sense to "move" the property.

- The words prospect and suspect have different meanings. A suspect is someone who might be interested in property. They are a "suspected" prospect. A prospect is someone who is interested in the property. They have, for example, seen a brochure or had a tour and have expressed some interest. Prospects are buyers and tenants.

- Deal and transaction are used to mean the process of buying, selling, exchanging, or leasing property. Nobody seems to like the word deal, but everyone uses it. I use it because it is descriptive and everyone knows what it means.

- A pitch is a sales presentation or sales comments.

- The word owner is often used to mean a landlord or seller.

- The term price is often used to mean both rental price and sales price. When referring to sales and leases together, it was simpler to refer to the consideration as price, rather than repeatedly say, "lease rental and sales price."

- Tenant and lessee are used interchangeably as well as landlord and lessor.

- Occasionally the words sale and lease will be used in a generic sense. Sometimes, for example, I just needed to refer to some deal.

Finally, it is my intention to improve each edition of this book. If you have any suggestions on the book's contents, ideas on things that were not covered, or corrections, I would appreciate hearing from you. I can be reached at jlbrealtor@uswest.net or by contacting the publisher.

CHAPTER 1
Where to Start

There are many things to consider before entering the field of commercial real estate. It is a very big industry with many of its own particularities. You should first consider honestly whether it is for you and, knowing yourself, what your chances are for success. Once you have made the decision to enter the business, you will want to think about whom to work for, what field you want to work in (office, industrial, retail, investments, etc.), and your territory, if appropriate. You should ask yourself if there is someone who might take a special interest in your career and could act as a mentor. There are also some books you might want to read that could help you succeed in the business.

One of the most often asked questions is whether you should start in residential real estate or some other branch of real estate, before entering commercial. The answer is simple: The sooner you get into commercial real estate the better. Certainly, there are some similarities between residential and commercial real estate, and there may be some residual value in starting in residential first. However, it is also true that many of the things you learn in residential real estate are unlikely to apply at all to commercial real estate, and, in addition, most of the prospects you encounter in residential real estate are not transferable to commercial. So why learn two things? If you want to learn something specific, learn it.

Don't waste your time on something else. The sooner you can start talking to commercial prospects, getting commercial listings, and making commercial deals, the sooner you will learn the business.

Is Commercial Real Estate for You?

Is commercial real estate for you? As mentioned in the introduction, commercial real estate is one of the truly pure entrepreneurial businesses remaining in America today. It is one of the few areas left where an individual can actually go out into the world and achieve fabulous success on his or her own. Perhaps more than any other business endeavor, it rewards effort and punishes indolence. There are no regular paychecks in commercial real estate, and there is no safety net. It is the kind of field that attracts the ambitious, calculating, risk-taking extrovert. Unlike residential real estate, it involves dealing with other business people who tend to be more objective, rather than emotional, in their decision making.

There is a tremendous amount of money to be made in commercial real estate. How much you make really depends on how hard you work. Consequently, commercial real estate attracts hard working and aggressive people — people who want to get ahead in the world, not people looking for a safe place and a steady paycheck. It comes as no surprise then that it is a highly competitive business in which many fail. The old adage in commercial real estate is that 10 percent of the brokers make 90 percent of the money.

The profession of commercial real estate essentially involves selling and leasing commercial property. In order to accomplish this, a commercial broker must engage in a wide range of activities including listing and marketing property; providing real estate advice; representing principals to find suitable property; evaluating property for listing purposes; writing up offers to lease or sell; and negotiating deals. Most of these activities require significant interpersonal skills as well as skills in financial analysis, sales, research, and problem solving. During a typical day, a commercial broker might

- Prepare an ad or brochure.
- Write up an earnest money offer.
- Order a preliminary title report.

- Show property.

- Answer prospect Inquiries on listings.

- Inquire about other listings for a client.

- Deliver documents.

- Make a listing sales pitch.

- Obtain information from a governmental agency on a property.

- Negotiate the terms of an offer to lease with a lessee and lessor.

- Deal with an attorney regarding the title exceptions in a preliminary title report.

- Arrange for an environmental report for a property being sold.

- Deal with an architect or space planner on the tenant improvements for a lease.

- Analyze an investment property for a client.

- Arrange for credit information from a lessee on a lease.

- Make cold calls on prospects.

- Write status reports to clients.

- Update the list of contacts.

- And, hopefully, pick up a commission check from the escrow company.

A broker's life is often hectic with phones ringing, offers to write, calls to return, things to get done, deadlines to meet, appointments to attend, and properties to show.

Brokers earn a living by collecting fees on the sales and leases they complete or by charging set hourly fees for counseling. There are no regular paychecks, which makes for an uneven and uncertain income. Since commercial transactions take time to complete (it's not unusual for a deal to stretch anywhere from two to six months beginning to end), there can be extended periods of time when there is no money coming in. Consequently, it is important to be able to budget. It is also helpful if you can muster enough cash up front to get you through the first year or so of the business.

Incomes vary from year to year and from broker to broker depending on the market, the level of competition, sheer luck, and so forth. While firm income statistics are difficult to come by, it's safe to say that overall, good commercial brokers make a good living. An educated guess would be that many commercial brokers earn between $30,000 and $60,000 per year, while quite a few make more than $100,000 on a regular basis, and a surprising number (mostly long-time, experienced brokers) make between $150,000 and $500,000 annually. And then there are always those few star brokers who make lots of money, sometimes in excess of $1,000,000 per year. It's not uncommon for an experienced broker, earning $200,000 per year, to make a few unusually large deals and reach the top category for one year.

Do you possess the characteristics to make it in such a field? An honest self-appraisal can help you decide and perhaps avoid future disappointments. The following personal qualities are some of the predictors of success in the business.

Self-motivated — As in life, you either act or are acted upon. To be a self-starter is to act. Even those on the right path get run over if they stand still too long. In commercial real estate, you must be able to motivate yourself without help and without direction. Every day, you must make yourself do what needs to be done to find a prospect, get a listing, close a deal, etc.

Aggressive — Commercial real estate is among the most competitive of businesses, and such a level of competition can either elevate the participants to a higher level of achievement or, as Sarnoff once said, "it can bring out the worst in man" (and the best in products). Successful brokers must be forceful and aggressive when the situation calls for it.

Hard working — Success in a competitive business like commercial real estate often boils down to applying yourself to the task more than others do. You must stay with a task through thick and thin and remain consistent in all of your efforts, from finding a listing to closing a deal.

Honest — To be honest and fair is a prerequisite to success. Good brokers rely on a reputation of integrity to gain repeat business and new prospects.

Intelligent — Intelligence and ability are definitely helpful, but are not necessarily prerequisites of success. The lack of these qualities can be overcome by persistence.

Influential — A good broker must have the ability to sell and inspire confidence and trust. In addition to a firm grasp on the real estate situation, it is equally important to have an understanding of human nature.

Competent — A good broker must possess a willingness to study the profession and learn what is necessary in order to become proficient and knowledgeable about the field. In addition, a good broker will be able to change past behavior and ideas, if necessary, in order to conform with what is needed to succeed. Knowledge of your craft (along with success) will give you confidence in your judgment.

Tough — This business is not for those weak at heart. It requires a certain toughness, for as Shakespeare said in Henry V "...successful men display a certain hardness of character." Be aware however that while this "hardness of character" may work for you at the office, it is not a quality that helps a marriage. Perhaps this is why successful brokers who remain married tend to be somewhat schizophrenic.

And, in the end, even if you do possess all these qualities, success is not a guarantee. Because the truth of the matter is that a lot of success is just luck. Perhaps a career in commercial real estate can best be captured by Sir Walter Scott's remarks about business in *Rob Roy:*

> *"Yet, in the fluctuations of mercantile speculation, there is something captivating to the adventurer, even independent of the hope of gain. He who embarks on that fickle sea, requires to possess the skill of the pilot and the fortitude of the navigator, and after all may be wrecked and lost, unless the gales of fortune breathe in his favor. This mixture of necessary attention and inevitable hazard, the frequent and awful uncertainty whether prudence shall overcome fortune, or fortune baffle the schemes of prudence, affords full occupation for the powers, as well as for the feelings of the mind, and trade has all the fascination of gambling without its moral guilt."*

Choosing a Firm

Once you have made the decision to enter the field, the next critical issue is deciding where to work. There are many options, from large multi-national firms, to small one-person shops, and each type has its own set of advantages and disadvantages. Obviously you want to pick a company where you can learn the business and make money. You should interview a variety of firms and ask a lot of questions. Some of the issues to consider and questions to ask when considering a company are discussed below.

Company Size

A large company can offer many advantages to the beginner. Large companies typically offer a stimulating environment of brokers actively doing what you want to learn. They may have a training program, listings that you can start work on immediately, and sometimes will provide a mentor. However, large firms are not without pitfalls. They often are pressure cooker environments where production is more important than understanding the business. All too often, large firms focus on making money rather than representing clients. The beginner often falls through the cracks because everyone is too busy working on projects. Large firms also tend to have more brokers who do not want you to call on their long-term clients or to prospect a certain territory. These factors tend to diminish your ability to flourish as a prospective commercial real estate broker.

Occasionally, a small company may offer a better training ground. It may take longer to get up and running as a broker, but you may ultimately become a better one in the end. Many brokers from large firms make money, but never fully understand the business. They are like a plow that goes only an inch or two deep — it may plow a lot of the field, but whenever it hits a rock it has to go around.

Fee Splits

Different companies have different fee split arrangements with brokers that will affect your earnings. Most start off with a 50-50 split and then increase your percentage as you make more money. Ask about the split and compare.

Listings and Projects

Often companies have properties they manage, listings, assignments, or long-term clients that you can be assigned to. This is very helpful because it lets you hit the ground running, so to speak. You immediately start working a listing, talking to clients, and getting new prospects.

Management

What is the management like? Will they actually take the time to help you get started? Are they fair, reasonable, and firm? Do they spoon feed all good leads to a select few brokers or do they share them? Because of the competition and dynamics inherent in the brokerage business, a capricious management can destroy good will and a company's effectiveness.

Broker Experience

What are the company's other brokers like? Are they reputable, successful, and cooperative? These are the people you will be working with, and what they know and how they conduct themselves will largely determine how you do business.

Reputation

Does the company have a good reputation? This is very important because the name will precede you into every sales meeting and pitch. It can either help you or hurt you.

Area of Experience

Some brokerages have more experience in some areas than others. If you want to learn office brokerage it does little good to pick a company that specializes in investments. Generally, the broad areas of specialization are industrial, office, retail, and investments. Pick the company that is experienced in the area that interests you. Sometimes a company does not have an opening in the specialty area, or farm area, you want. Consequently, some

13

\hole you into another specialty or farm area. Try
has openings for the specialty area you want.

...ng

Some companies offer formal training and others just turn
you loose. Others assign you to another broker and, in some,
management is actively involved in training. The straight fact is
that the best training comes from doing it. There is no substitute
for experience.

Salary or Draw

Does the company pay you a salary or draw while you are getting started? Salaries are nice, but should not be the determining
factor in deciding where to go. Salary draws put you in the hole
and are often hard to pay back, but they are better than nothing if
you need help staying afloat until you can make a few sales.

Connections

Some companies have better connections with property owners, the community, and other brokers. The more and better the
connections, the better your chance to succeed. Do not overlook
a company's reputation among other brokers. If a company has a
poor track record or a history of treating outside brokers unfairly,
it will make it harder on you.

Benefits

The obvious questions concerning retirement plans, health
insurance, vacation, sick policies, and even parking space should
be asked.

Personalities

Brokerages are like families and, as the old adage goes, show
me a family and I will show you problems. They have their share
of personality conflicts. The commercial real estate business seems

to attract many big egos, which are barely restrained in some firms. This can be either negative or positive. Negative competition can be destructive. Conversely, competition between two good brokers who have integrity and respect for one another can raise the level of success for each.

Staff Support

Is there enough support staff to handle your needs? It can be very frustrating to have to wait two days to get an earnest money agreement or letter typed. Sometimes senior brokers will demand that their business be taken care of first, which puts you at a disadvantage. Sometimes other brokers are just so disorganized everything is a rush, which may delay your work. In some larger companies, there is also support staff for marketing and sometimes assistants. These people prepare brochures, collect information, keep track of the market, assemble a listing database and, if qualified, prepare documents and handle calls. They can be very helpful.

National Company vs. Local Company

There is considerable debate over whether a national company or a local company is best. They both have their pros and cons. National companies offer name recognition and often more leads (including national companies), but often leave you feeling like a small insignificant cog in a huge machine. Occasionally, a few long-time brokers in large firms will garner the best prospects; however, you often may be included in the business as a co-broker. They often are pressure cooker and cutthroat environments that try and pit you against your fellow brokers. Many seem to emphasize money over professionalism.

National companies sometimes offer formal training programs, which are helpful. Some may just attach you to one of the experienced brokers, which can be a blessing or curse, depending on the quality of the broker to whom you are attached. Often, in large companies, there will be many brokers on one listing or deal, which translates to less commission for you. If the commission, for example, was $30,000, the company may take half with the balance split between three brokers. This means you make $5,000 or 16.67% of the total. This would be reduced to $2,500, or 8.3%, if there was a cooperating, outside broker. In smaller companies, there usually are fewer splits. If you were on your own, you could have made the entire $30,000, if there were no cooperating broker.

Local companies often have deep roots in the community, which translates to name recognition and leads. They sometimes, however, have difficulty doing business with national company prospects because those prospects often prefer the name recognition of national real estate firms or their affiliations. Brokers from smaller companies have to overcome the size issue when competing for listings. Small or medium-sized companies often offer a more personal atmosphere and personal attention, but not the volume of business. Size of a company, however, is not necessarily the determining factor for success in commercial real estate. This is because the quality of firms varies so much. There are many struggling large firms and highly successful, competitive, small to medium-sized ones. Because more business is usually generated by more people working together, your decision should be based more on whether the company has many active brokers rather than size.

Employment Agreements

Most real estate companies will have you sign an employment agreement that specifies the terms of your employment. Most of these are pretty generic but you should read the agreement carefully. Most employment agreements include the following:

- The obligation to abide by the Code of Ethics (see Appendix).

- The employer's rights to control advertising.

- The employer's right to control any litigation and keep any awards.

- The employer's right to control all transactions. (This means they can take a deal or listing away from you if they want.)

- The right to control all publicity.
- The salesperson's obligations to do the following:
  » To work full time.
  » Abide by the firm's fee schedule and commission split policies, which should be attached to the employment agreement.
  » Submit to the firm's decisions on any fee issues or commission disputes.
  » Furnish his or her own transportation.
  » Remain licensed by the state.
  » Use only the company's real estate forms.
  » Deliver any compensation to the firm. This means that prizes and gifts are subject to the same commission split arrangements as fees.
  » Make all listings in the name of the firm.
  » Keep all information about the firm confidential.
- A provision that all listings, files and records remain with the firm if the broker is terminated or leaves and that the broker give the firm a list of all deals in progress upon termination. (This is an important consideration because you may lose all income from your deals in progress if you leave the firm. You will also probably earn nothing on your listings.)

In addition, employment agreements sometimes include a non-compete clause that says if you leave, you cannot compete with the company for a period of time.

Perhaps the important thing to keep in mind about employment agreements is that everything you do is in the name of the firm. All of your listing and site search agreements are between the principals and the firm, not the principals and you. Also, all documents and files are the property of the firm. This, along with the non-compete clause, are significant matters if you ever decide to leave.

Intuition

After you have gone through your checklist of things to ask and consider, you should ask yourself one last question: How does the place feel? Intuition is often a better judge than reason because reason is based on incomplete premises. You may simply have not considered all the questions or perhaps you did not ask the right questions. Intuition draws on our vast experiences, which often is a more reliable guide to what you really want and need.

Finding a Mentor

As in life, it is helpful if someone will take you under his or her wing and help you out once and awhile. Many brokers peak well below their potential because they never thoroughly learned the fundamentals of the business. So get a good mentor.

How do you find a good mentor? The best and surest way to succeed is to learn from someone who is successful. When selecting a mentor, ask yourself: Is he or she making money? Does he have a good reputation? Does he do a lot of business? Does she have a reputation for honesty?

Be aware that the top producers in most companies resist taking on neophytes because they gain little from the relationship. (A runner is nice, but not when you have to split your commission with him or her.) Some companies will automatically assign a newcomer to an experienced broker, which can be a blessing or a curse. If you're assigned to an incompetent broker, you may end up learning a lot of the wrong things. It is better to learn things right the first time than have to go back and correct misinformation.

Choosing an Area of Specialty

Once you decide that commercial real estate is for you, you need to start thinking about an area of specialization. While you may be able to work in more than one area in a smaller market, in larger markets, there are no more generalists. The business has just become too complex and the markets so large, that one simply cannot know it all. The main areas of specialization are industrial, office, retail, and investments. In addition, there are other allied, sub-areas such as multi-family (apartments), land, development, finance, property management, office management, business chance brokerage, hotel or hospitality brokerage, and securities (limited partnerships, syndication, real estate investment trusts, etc.), but the four listed above are the main ones. For example, multi-family (apartments) is typically treated as a branch or sub-area under the specialty of investment, while land and development are treated as sub-areas of the specific specialty the deal falls under (i.e. development of industrial, retail, office, etc.).

Not everyone will agree with these characterizations. Certainly, markets and practices vary from location to location and time to time. These summaries are only intended to give the beginner a broad view of each area without boring them too much.

Industrial

Historically, industrial has been where the "real men" go, although that has changed somewhat since more women are entering the specialty. Industrial brokers usually have dirty shoes. They deal with industrial land, warehouses, manufacturing plants, and high-tech buildings. Most of the people you deal with in industrial tend to be down to earth and practical. The market for industrial real estate tends to be more spread out in the community because of distribution, transportation, and labor considerations. The clients are usually local companies, although it's not unusual to have a national client. It is probably one of the easier areas to get started in because there is such a variety of industrial product and numerous buyers and sellers. The products vary from warehouses, to crane-way buildings, to low-ceiling, high-tech/office-type incubator buildings. The industrial market tends to remain relatively constant over time, and there usually is an equal amount of leasing and selling going on. Leasing is generally easier than selling because of the many issues like taxation and environmental regulation that are involved in selling and buying. Most deals tend to be small to mid-size, with few large sales and leases.

The high-tech end of the industrial area tends to be a specialty within itself. High-tech industrial is a cross between office and industrial real estate, with lower ceiling buildings, higher tenant improvements, higher rents, more campus-like environments, and often smaller sizes. Over the last 10 to 15 years, as our economy has transformed from a product-based market to an information-based one, high-tech has been the fastest growing and hottest area in commercial real estate. It is also one of the most volatile specialties, where vacancies skyrocket in recessions. High-tech brokers are a little schizophrenic. They are not quite industrial brokers and not quite office brokers. They occupy a never-never land between those two specialties, but they probably represent the future of the business.

Office

Office brokers wear nice suits with a hanky in the pocket. They typically are smoother than industrial brokers. They tend to deal with local and some national companies in compact market areas, usually downtown. Office real estate varies considerably, but it is generally congregated into areas (downtown or suburban) where the market and product tend to be more uniform. Some believe that this uniformity makes office brokerage one of the easier specialties to master. Offices can be classified by age or construction (concrete and glass, masonry or brick, or wood frame). Issues related to tenant improvements and space planning occupy a lot of the broker's time. The clients and prospects tend to be more professional, upscale, and sophisticated. Prestige and status are often factors in the principals' decision-making process. The product and market for office real estate tend to remain relatively constant over time with a steady demand, except in severe recessions. Office real estate involves more leasing than selling, but the sales, when they occur, can be very large. Office real estate is one of the more difficult areas to get started in if you do not work for a firm that has a large office property management portfolio and contacts within the office market.

Retail

Retail is fast and loose with quick-talking brokers with a flair for flashy and stylish dress. Rapid change is the nature of the retail area. Clients come and go with the change of styles, fads, buying habits, and so forth. Clients may be a national chain, like a "big box" retailer, or a local mom and pop store. Many clients are large property owners with shopping centers, whose retail spaces must then be leased. Retail areas tend to be spread out geographically, but are then tightly packed in shopping districts close to transportation. These areas are often found near freeway interchanges or in strip development along heavily trafficked arterial roads. Brokers spend a lot of time studying traffic counts, demographics, and shopping patterns. Location is often the most important consideration in retail because a retailer's business success is so closely tied to the location. A good retailer will not be successful in a bad location. A retail broker not only needs to know about the physical characteristics of a site, but also the economic and competitive environment surrounding the site as well as the nature of the retailer's business itself. Even though the prices per square foot are some of the highest, the areas leased tend to be small, which translates into smaller deals. Often the larger deals involve national chains or large property owners. Like office real estate, it helps in retail to work for a firm that manages or has relations with large retail property owners and retail chains. It is also important to be a member of a national network of retail brokers because they track movements, such as expansion patterns, of national tenants.

Investment

Investments are a world unto themselves. Investment brokers are the computer hackers of the commercial real estate business. They spend much of their time hunched over computers, manipulating numbers and working on investment analyses or spreadsheets. Their clientele often includes insurance companies and pension funds, but in reality, can be anyone with some money who wants to buy some real estate. Some clients can be speculators. Unlike industrial, office, and retail, the only real prospects are investors, not users, which limits the market. Investment specialists often struggle with the problem of limited and overpriced product. Getting the buyer or investor is the easy part; the hard part is finding something to buy. It helps to be in a firm that has contacts with large investment property owners; however, this is not absolutely necessary, because there are many individual owners and investors that a broker can work with. Sophisticated investment analysis can be one of the more challenging areas to learn. Investment analysis deals with such things as discounted cash flow, net operating income, and internal rate of return.

Investment deals are some of the largest in real estate. The investment market tends to remain constant, and the product is everywhere. One specialized sub-area of investments is apartment sales,
which involves some special issues surrounding apartments.

Cross Overs and Special Considerations

While specializing is more of a rule than an exception, the
truth of the matter is that specialty areas are not as rigid as they
sound. Commercial brokers will often "cross over" to facilitate
deals in areas other than their specialty. Office brokers sometimes
do industrial deals; industrial brokers sometimes do retail deals;
and everyone does investment deals. The real factors that determine whether a broker does a deal in another area are the nature
of the client and the time involved. A broker will be reluctant to
pass on a very good client with a juicy requirement to another
broker. Usually, they will attempt to learn what they need to know
in order to make the deal or work with another broker in that
specialty area as partners. The real question for brokers who are
considering crossing over is how much time they want to spend
learning what they need to know in order to do the deal properly.
If it is a big deal, the answer is often lots of time.

A couple of final comments regarding areas of specialty: The
first concerns land sales and the development of commercial real
estate, which involves industrial, office, retail and investment
(apartments mostly). With increasing governmental regulation in
zoning and the environment, to name just a few, this has become
one of the toughest areas to deal in. Many brokers and principals
have made a lot of money over the years in land sales and development, but it is becoming increasingly difficult to do so. It is
important to understand issues related to land and development,
but probably wise to keep it as ancillary to one of the four main
areas of specialty.

Business Brokerage

Many brokers make successful careers in business opportunities. This is a highly specialized area of the business that involves
the sale of businesses as well as their real estate. It can be very com-

plex because it involves valuing and selling businesses, machinery, equipment, and inventory, in addition to the real estate. Many of the largest sales of businesses occur directly, without the involvement of a broker. When an owner is thinking of selling a business, he or she usually first calls a main competitor, who is often the best prospect. It is usually only after a few unsuccessful attempts that an owner looking to sell engages a broker. For this reason, business chance brokers often end up handling smaller businesses like taverns and small retail businesses.

Books to Read

Most of commercial real estate is learned by doing. There is no substitute for observing others, talking to prospects and potential clients, working to get listings, and just trying to make deals. There is an abundance of books available — some technical in nature and some general — to help you get started and, once you've started, to continue to help you learn the trade. The general books will give you a more comprehensive view of what you are doing, while the technical books explain the mechanics of commercial real estate. A beginner should make an effort to read both. Beginners should also make an effort to read technical books that relate to the mechanics of commercial real estate in their specialty area. Such books can be obtained from various sources including real estate associations such as the National Association of Realtors® and its affiliates such as the Society of Industrial and Office Realtors®, local boards such as the Commercial Association of Realtors® (if you have one in your area), or from a bookstore. There are also books for state licensing requirements, for educational seminars, and real estate schools. The latter are important because they keep you informed about what's new in the industry.

The books listed below generally deal with some particular aspect of the business — how to sell, how to deal with people successfully, how to negotiate a lease, how to conduct a transaction in a legal and ethical manner, and how to handle money. Some are not directly related to commercial real estate but, rather, with how to manage the fruits of your labors. Some of these books are broad based and general in nature. They will help you succeed by helping you deal with the people in the business. Many of the lessons in these books also pertain to life.

How I Raised Myself from Failure to Success in Selling by Frank Bettger is, in spite of its prosaic title, one of the best books ever written on selling. As we will discuss later, the ability to sell is one of the key elements that separate those that succeed and those that fail. The book was written by a man who failed at business until he discovered the time-tested ways of selling. Selling is not a dirty word; it is simply a way to help people get what they want and then profiting from the process.

How to Win Friends and Influence People by Dale Carnegie. This classic book deals with how to understand and deal with people. Much of the emphasis is on how you conduct yourself and your attitudes.

The Code of Ethics and Standards and Practices of the National Association of REALTORS. This is found in Appendix A.

Negotiating Commercial Real Estate Leases by Martin I. Zankel. One of the few books that examines the essential business issues underlying each clause of the lease from both sides of the negotiating table — tenant and landlord alike.

The Site Book: A Field Guide to Commercial Real Estate Evaluation by Richard M. Fenker. This easy-to-read, straightforward book explores the dynamic and sometimes complex relationship between a piece of real estate, site features, and other factors that will ultimately determine the success of any restaurant or retail location. If you are planning to specialize in retail, this book will help you impress any prospect you meet.

The Valuation of Real Estate by Alfred A. Ring and James H. Boykin. This industry standard has been around for years and provides an excellent and detailed explanation of how property is valued.

Real Estate Market Analysis by John M. Clapp and Stephen D. Messner. This book covers a wide range of property types, including office, retail, industrial, and housing. The various chapters lucidly discuss forecasting and investment selections; the impact of inflation; estimating risks in real estate investment; trade-offs in the office market, and many other issues.

Real Estate Finance and Investment by William B. Brueggeman and Jeffrey Fisher. Now in its 11ᵗʰ edition, this book has truly stood the test of time. The author provides step-by-step help for understanding mortgages, internal rates of return, net present value calculations, etc. The book also discusses real estate development and secondary markets.

A Practical Guide to Commercial Real Estate Transactions: From Contract to Closing by Gregory M. Stein, Morton P. Fisher, and Gail M. Stern. Though written primarily for real estate lawyers, this book is a valuable aid for anyone who needs to navigate and better understand the maze of steps involved in a commercial real estate transaction. The book follows each of the steps of a commercial real estate transaction in the order in which they generally arise.

The Richest Man in Babylon by George S. Clason. This fun little book deals with the timeless laws of money and will help you with your financial affairs. The book you are reading now, *How to Succeed in Commercial Real Estate*, will help you get money. This book, *The Richest Man in Babylon*, will help you keep it.

Farm Areas

In some specialty areas, such as industrial, office and retail, it is a good idea to establish a farm area. A farm area is the territory you work. This gives you a place to start and makes your efforts cumulative. The more you work your farm, the more you come to know the area and the more you become known as the expert in the area, which leads to more business. You should make it your business to know everything that is going on in your farm area. You should get to know the properties, tenants, and owners in the area. You should know when significant leases expire and when key owners are considering selling or leasing. You should know every prospect that enters your farm area and every business that leaves. Who is growing and needs more space? Whose business is not doing well and may be looking to downsize? Conversely, owners and prospects come to know you and your expertise in the area, so when it comes time to pick a broker, they naturally think of you. Also, when your business activity slows down, you can always go back and work the farm. It becomes the source of much of your business and the foundation on which you build your clientele.

You should pick an area that is vital and has a future. Areas in the path of growth or with excellent transportation are factors that make some areas more attractive than others. You should apply the old real estate saw, "location, location, location" to your evaluation of which farm area you choose. Who will be doing business there and why? You should endeavor to learn everything about your farm area including such things as zoning and land use trends, transportation, and prices. You should be knowledgeable on all recent deals, prospects, and market trends in your farm area. Are rates going up? What is the vacancy? Are landlords giving free rent? You should know what is available at any time. In short, you want to know more about the area than anybody else and to gain the reputation for that knowledge.

One caution: You do not want to be cast by your competition as only working one area. When competing for listings, competitors may say that you only work another area if the listing is outside your farm. Counter this by saying you work all areas and give examples of deals you or your company has done in other areas.

CHAPTER 2
Integrity And Ethics

Some, no doubt, think it a contradiction to associate commercial real estate brokers with integrity and ethics. On the contrary, integrity and ethics are prerequisites to long-term success in the business. Certainly some unethical brokers have survived, but once they gain a reputation as untrustworthy, their business suffers. Other brokers and potential clients avoid them, and, in time, most leave the business. Commercial real estate is truly an industry where what goes around comes around. If you treat other brokers, clients, and the public dishonestly or unfairly, you gain a reputation for such, and they will be wary of any involvement with you. Good reputations, which are worth their weight in gold, are hard to establish and easy to tarnish. Once tarnished, they are difficult to regain.

Central to succeeding in the business is the ability to establish a sense of trust with those whom you deal. One accomplishes this by having integrity and adhering to a code of ethics. This is not always easy to do because you will often find yourself in situations where ethics demand that you act counter to your personal interests. Commercial real estate is especially prone to such situations for a number of reasons, including the unusually large sums of money involved, the nature of the broker's role, the level of pressure to complete a deal, and the compensation structure. The best brokers avoid allowing their personal interests to be confused with their clients' interests. The best brokers always keep their clients' interests supreme. When all is said and done, one key measure of a person's character is his or her ability to compete fairly when under pressure.

Many brokers and companies prefer to think of commercial real estate as an industry or business, rather than a profession. There exists a kind of tug of war between those who are primarily motivated by profit and those who welcome the responsibility that comes with a profession. Many would prefer not to have the ethical restraints of a profession. However, it's difficult to deny that commercial real estate is much more of a profession — in the same way that law and medicine are — than a business. For example, commercial real estate is based on technical knowledge unknown to laymen; the establishment of fiduciary relationships with clients; and the completion of certain educational requirements in order to enter the profession. Because of this, brokers who are members of the National Association of Realtors® and their affiliates abide by a Code of Ethics. This code will be discussed later in this chapter.

Integrity

Being square with the world lets you live a better life. In both your personal and business life, you will have better relationships, more success, and peace of mind. If you always tell the truth, for example, you never need to worry about getting caught in a lie. Brokers with integrity are sought out and respected by their colleagues, clients, and the public. They are the ones everyone looks up to. They are the ones who set and maintain the standards by which others are judged. They are also the ones who get the recommendations, referrals, and long-term clients. Integrity is more important than money.

Integrity includes adhering to the following qualities:

Honesty — Always be honest and truthful regardless of the consequences. You must have the ability to recommend what is not in your best interest. You must not shade the truth or give out only partial information.

Fairness — You should always treat clients, the public, and other brokers with fairness and evenhandedness. You should ask yourself what is the right and just thing to do in difficult situations.

Reliability — Do what you say you are going to do. Make your word good. Always follow through and complete the task.

Forthrightness — Tell others the things that don't necessarily *have* to be said — the things that you know that may influence their decisions. Give all the facts and your honest opinion.

Consistency — Be consistent in what you do. Consistency in action builds predictable results that enable others to depend on you.

Though they may seem simplistic, these important qualities will allow others to gain trust in you. And trust is a cornerstone to success in commercial real estate. Once others come to know you, they will continue to use your services. Your opinion will be valued, which will help you make deals. People will know that they can rely on you for accurate information and results. Your own honesty and forthrightness will in turn encourage others to be honest and forthright with you, which is critical in making a deal. When you do not know what others are thinking, you are working in a vacuum. In the end, without the above characteristics, potential clients and other brokers will tend to avoid you. These qualities are especially important in commercial real estate because there is often a large amount of money at stake, which causes people to be especially careful with whom they deal. They tend to seek out only those brokers who are not only the most qualified, but those with the highest integrity as well.

Code of Ethics

If you ask five different commercial brokers the same question about an ethical situation, you are likely to get five different explanations. Everyone seems to have his or her own interpretation of what the right thing to do is. This is because most brokers have never taken the time to read the Code of Ethics. Most situations and circumstances that you will encounter have most likely already been thought through by knowledgeable people. Their thinking and solutions are embodied in the Code of Ethics.

The Code of Ethics embodies the rules by which a commercial Realtor® should act in order to have integrity. They guide us in behavior, conduct and practice. They include 14 articles with associated standards of practice. Some of them are obvious, such as not to mislead an owner when attempting to secure a listing (Article 3, Standard of Practice 1-3), while others are less obvious, such as to avoid exaggeration (Article 2). They cover many subjects such as cooperation, representation, conflict of interest, and discrimination. What follows is an abbreviated summary of each of the articles of the National Association of Realtors® Code of Ethics. A complete reproduction of the code is found in Appendix A along with the standards of practice. Be sure to take the time to read it.

Article 1   — Promote the interests of your client and always be honest and fair.

Article 2   — Avoid exaggeration, misrepresentation, and concealment.

Article 3   — Cooperate with other brokers.

Article 4   — Disclose any interests you may have in all your real estate dealings.

Article 5   — Disclose any interests when providing professional services or valuations.

Article 6   — Disclose to clients any commissions, rebates, profits, benefits, or fees earned.

Article 7   — Disclose any fees earned from more than one party in a transaction.

Article 8   — Keep an account, separate from your own, in trust, for other people's money.

Article 9   — Be sure all agreements are clear, understandable, comprehensive, and in writing. A copy should be given to each party to the contract.

Article 10 — Do not discriminate.

Article 11 — Be competent and adhere to the Code of Ethics.

Article 12 — Make all representations clear and true and disclose your professional status.

Article 13 — Do not practice law and always recommend an attorney.

Article 14 — Cooperate with any Code of Ethics proceedings.

Article 15 — Do not make reckless or misleading comments about competitors.

Article 16 — Respect the exclusive agencies and relationships of other Realtors®.

Article 17 — Arbitrate rather than litigate disputes.

The Preamble to the Code of Ethics probably best summarizes the ideals and spirit of professionalism in the commercial real estate industry, as well as the obligations of Realtors®. It urges the wise utilization and wide ownership of the land because these things are necessary for freedom. It imposes social responsibilities and patriotic duty on all Realtors®. Freedom truly does entail responsibility. It admonishes Realtors® to be informed of matters affecting real estate and to share their knowledge with others. It urges exclusive representation, that Realtors® not take unfair advantage of other competitors, and for Realtors® to refrain from unsolicited comments about other practitioners. It mandates competency, fairness, and integrity in all business relations. It states that all Realtors® should be guided by the golden rule, "Whatsoever ye would that others should do to you, do ye even so to them."

A central theme of the code, and perhaps one of the most important things to remember in commercial real estate, is to always put your client's interests ahead of your own. This is a major mistake made by some brokers. They all too often confuse their interests with their clients. Some brokers, for example, contrive to sell listings without other brokers in order to collect the full commission. They may withhold information, market a property selectively, or shade the truth to avoid cooperation. This may be in the broker's immediate interests, but not the client's or the profession's.

This example, however, also illustrates a difficulty with the Code of Ethics. Sometimes the code is contradictory, and the right course of action is not so clear. In the above example, if you were the non-listing salesperson, you may not be able to get information for your client from such a broker, but the code still requires you to cooperate. In situations like this, it is often better to follow the spirit of the Code of Ethics, rather than the letter. In the above example, you may have to go around the non-cooperative broker either to his broker, or the owner directly, because you have an obligation to your client to get the information.

One final point regarding ethics in commercial real estate: Do not confuse ethics with tough competition. Good brokers will adhere to the spirit of the code, but not give you any breaks. Another broker may call on your exclusive client for other legitimate purposes or persuade a nonexclusive prospect of yours, for whom you have done a lot of work, to work with him or her. This isn't unethical. It's just tough competition.

CHAPTER 3

Contracts And Forms

Contracts are the tools of the commercial real estate business. They are like the carpenter's hammer or the surgeon's scalpel. You must become intimately familiar with them, understand them, and know how to use them. Because practices and laws vary so much from place to place, and because there are so many variations of the same agreement, you need to also understand the concepts and principles behind the parts of each contract. You should be familiar with the contracts (or forms) most commonly used in your particular area in order to communicate with other brokers, as well as others, such as attorneys and escrow agents, who also use the forms. You also need to be able to explain, in plain English, the meaning of each sentence and phrase to principals. If you cannot explain it, you probably do not understand it.

There are many different forms. Some are preprinted association forms like the ones used by the American Industrial Real Estate Association or National Association of Industrial and Office Properties (NAIOP); some forms are generated by attorneys and revised on computer; some forms are obtained from private publishing companies like Stevens Ness; some are forms particular to individual real estate companies; some forms are provided by private owners; etc. In addition, there are different forms for different purposes such as selling, leasing, offering to sell or lease, options, trades, escrow, listing, and so forth. For simplicity, this chapter will not attempt to explain everything in each form, but rather will address some important terms of the basic forms that a novice commercial real estate professional should be familiar with. It is assumed that you will gain a more complete understanding of these forms in the educational process required to obtain a real estate license. It is also assumed that you will know the applicable requirements of the laws of your state. The major forms that will be discussed in this chapter include the Earnest Money Agreement or Purchase and Sale Agreement, Offer to Lease, Lease, Option, Listing for Sale and Lease, and Counter Offer. The nature and function of each contract, the most important elements in each one, and the critical things you should know that make them work, will be discussed. This chapter will also review the way rent is quoted in commercial real estate. Fee schedules for listings will be discussed at the end of the chapter

Lawyers view contracts as legal agreements. For brokers, they have the additional, practical function as tools to make a deal. They act as "commitment getters" that secure one side or party to a deal, which allows a broker to narrow the areas of disagreement and eventually achieve a meeting of the minds, as the contract is negotiated. Given the complicated legal aspects of these contracts, this book is not intended to provide a legal analysis, but rather a practical, common sense, guide on how a typical commercial real estate broker can use them. The issues presented in this book are general in nature. Each real estate transaction presents its own unique issues and circumstances that no one book can cover. You and your principals should always seek competent legal advice when using these contracts.

One last comment about all agreements: If you do not understand something, get help. Commercial real estate is no place to "fake it." You need to understand what is going on and how to do things the right way. Money, your client's interests, and your reputation are at stake. You should always endeavor to be a competent professional.

Earnest Money Agreement

The earnest money agreement is a document that reduces to writing the terms of an agreement between a buyer and seller for the sale of property. It covers both the business and legal terms of the agreement and is usually a preprinted or computer-generated form with blanks to be filled in by you. Earnest money agreements often require an addendum and/or exhibits to cover additional terms. They are used as a tool to commit a buyer in writing to an offer on property and, hopefully, to confirm receipt for money that the buyer puts up to show that he or she means business.

Standard Parts of Earnest Money Agreements

The most important parts of the agreement you should think about, understand, and get right, are listed below.

- The complete and proper names of the buyer and seller. Identify whether they are individuals, corporations, LLCs (limited liability companies), partnerships, etc. Entity names should include their state of formation.

- A proper and complete description of the property.

- The purchase price.

- The financial terms of the purchase whether it be by cash, contract, trust deed or mortgage, assumption, or exchange.

- The amount and form of earnest money receipted for, whether it be cash or note. Unsecured promissory notes are commonly used instead of money in commercial real estate. Promissory notes should include the payer and payee, date, amount, signature of payee, and description of the terms of the note (which is usually in accordance with the terms of the earnest money agreement). Typically, the notes are payable when certain contingencies are satisfied.

- The conditions to purchase and contingencies. A condition is a requirement of the sale. For example, a condition to the seller's obligation to sell is the buyer's payment of the purchase price. A contingency allows the buyer or seller to terminate the deal if the condition is not satisfied or the contingency is not waived. Typically, a buyer's obligation to purchase is contingent on the buyer's inspection of the property. It is important to specify which party has the benefit of the condition or contingency, what the condition or contingency is, and how long the buyer or seller has to determine whether or not the party will either satisfy the condition or contingency or waive it. The contract should state that the agreement and the transaction terminate if a condition or contingency is not satisfied.

- Title review and title insurance.

- The closing date and time of delivery. Specify if rights to possession are subject to any existing leases.

- Whether closing will be through escrow and who will act as escrow agent.

- Proration of such things as taxes, rents, security deposits, and utilities.

- The condition the property is to be in when delivered at closing. When there are no tenants, this usually is "broom clean" condition. Sometimes, however, a seller is required to make some repairs.

- Specify the personal property that is to be transferred with the real property at closing, if any.

- Agency disclosure, if required by applicable state law.

- How much time the seller has to accept the buyer's offer.

- Agreement regarding the real estate fee and its division with cooperative brokers.

- Addendums or exhibits. Earnest money agreements will often have these as property descriptions, plats, or additional terms. Be sure to refer to them in the agreement and incorporate them into the agreement by reference.

- All provisions necessary to comply with applicable laws, such as land use disclaimers or statutory liquidated damages provisions.

- Representations and warranties from the seller regarding the condition of the property, or provision that the sale is "as is."

- The requirements, if any, of the seller to give the buyer documents to review such as surveys, existing leases, and environmental reports.

- Whether the buyer has the right to assign the buyer's interest under the agreement to a third party or not.

- Whether the seller or buyer requires the other party to cooperate in a tax-deferred exchange transaction under Section 1031 of the Internal Revenue Code.

Common Points of Negotiation in Earnest Money Agreements

From a sales standpoint, some of the more important things you should do and know about earnest money agreements are summarized below.

- Are you in the ballpark on the price? Setting unrealistically high asking prices and making lowball offers make it hard to make deals.

- Generally, when it comes to purchase price, cash on delivery is best for the seller, while term payments are best for the buyer. This is not always the case, however. The seller, for example, may prefer to receive the purchase price in installments for tax reasons. If the buyer is offering term payments, are they realistic? Low down or nothing down deals, low interest rates, long amortization periods with no balloon payments, and subordination to other financing make deals tough to close.

- Are the contingencies and their time limits realistic? Contingencies are, in effect, free options. They allow a buyer to take a seller's property off the market at no cost. There is good reason for the seller to allow this. Contingencies enable a buyer to spend time and money to evaluate a property, establish price and terms before they do an evaluation, and allow the deal to move forward with all matters being handled contemporarily. They should, however, be realistic and short. Making a deal subject to such things as obtaining financing, checking zoning and code issues, doing an environmental and engineering investigation, checking on credit, obtaining an occupancy permit, or confirming the terms of existing leases are reasonable. Making the purchase subject to the sale of other property or to buyers deciding at a later date whether they want the property are not. Contingencies requiring some governmental approval are especially difficult because they can be very long. It is usually better to try and make such contingencies short and subject to buyers' satisfaction that they can get the necessary approval. Long contingencies with no forfeitable earnest money are tantamount to long, free options. They take the property off the market, and they take the pressure off the buyer to perform.

Contingencies should be short, notes should be converted to cash early on, and there should be a time when the earnest money becomes nonrefundable. It is a good idea to have the buyer put up additional, nonrefundable earnest money for any extended contingency periods. This qualifies the buyer early on because then a buyer won't want to put the money up unless he or she plans on making the deal. All contingencies should have a definite time limit, and the deal should be automatically terminated if they are not satisfied. There are two ways for a buyer to waive, or satisfy, a contingency. One is that they must give notice, usually in writing, that the contingency is satisfied. If they don't, the deal automatically terminates. The other is that the contingency is automatically satisfied if the buyer says nothing. Deals tend to go a little smoother with the latter method.

- It is best to get cash up front as earnest money. Anyone can sign a note. Cash shows that the buyer wants the property and tells the seller that the buyer means business.

- As mentioned earlier, carefully specify what property stays (and will be conveyed at closing) and what goes. Deals have been lost because these terms were not spelled out up front.

- The time for the seller's acceptance of the buyer's offer should be kept as short as possible in order to keep pressure on the seller to act. This is especially true if there are other buyers, because the buyer wants to prevent the seller from using the offer to get a better offer from another buyer (or "shopping the property"). Generally, a time frame of three to five days will keep a sense of urgency in the deal. This clause is often called the scare clause because it is intended to make the seller think they could lose the deal if they do not act in time. In reality, it does not mean much because the buyer can rescind the offer at anytime prior to acceptance.

- If the seller is offering to extend credit to the buyer, there should be a contingency for the seller's approval of the buyer's credit. The buyer should be required to provide current financial statements and/or credit references.

- When selling on a contract it is sometimes a good idea to include a provision that the buyer must obtain the seller's approval before reselling the property. If this is unattainable, provisions that require the buyer to apply the proceeds of a resale to the contract or that the security for repayment of the remaining principal balance owed to the seller on the contract not be impaired, should be considered.

Offer to Lease

The offer to lease is similar to the earnest money agreement in that it reduces to writing an agreement, but this time the agreement is between a lessee and lessor, rather than a buyer and seller. The offer to lease covers the terms by which a tenant may use an owner's property. Like the earnest money agreement, the offer to lease is a tool by which a salesperson makes a lease transaction by obtaining a commitment, in writing, from a tenant to lease a property. The offer is a prelude to a lease document (which is discussed in the following section) and acts as a kind of worksheet that the owner may accept or counter. The goal is to obtain a written meeting of the minds on the important business terms of the lease transaction. Some of the more important aspects to the offer to lease are outlined on the next page.

Standard Parts of an Offer to Lease

- The correct name of the lessee and lessor. Be sure the terms "lessee" and "lessor" are not mixed up. You may want to use the terms "landlord" and "tenant" because they are easier to distinguish.

- A complete and proper description of the leased premises, including sizes. It is a good idea to say somewhere that all sizes and dimensions are approximate.

- The condition in which the landlord is to deliver the premises to the tenant and any tenant improvements to be made. The document should specify what the improvements are, who is to make them, and how they are to be paid for.

- The term of the lease and when the tenant is to take possession.

- Whether the tenant has any option(s) to extend the term of the lease.

- What the property is to be used for.

- The amount of rent, when it is to be paid, and how it is to be adjusted, if needed.

- Who pays for the taxes, insurance (both property and liability), utilities, and any other operating expenses (such as maintenance of common areas in a multi-tenant project).

- Who is responsible for maintaining the property.

- How much time the landlord has to accept the offer.

- What security will be offered (such as a deposit or a letter of credit) and how it will be handled.

- Who will pay the leasing commission, how it will be calculated, and how it will be shared between the landlord's broker and tenant's broker, if applicable.

Common Points of Negotiation in Offers to Lease

Leasing property presents a few unique issues. It is important to understand these issues, be able to explain them to the principals, and provide for them in the offer to lease. Some of these issues are presented below.

- When a lease includes an option to renew the lease, it should be made clear how long the renewed lease will be for and whether the terms and conditions are the same as in the initial lease. If the terms and conditions are different, specify them. The most significant change in options is usually rent because rents tend to increase. If rent is to change, there should be some explanation as to how the new rate will be figured and applied. There are numerous ways to do this, but the three most common are listed below.

  1. Agreeing in advance on a fixed amount.
  2. Making it the then fair market rent (with an arbitration process if the parties do not agree).
  3. Adjusting it based on some index, such as the Consumer Price Index.

The advantage of using fixed amounts is that the future rent is known for certain. The downside is that the future rent usually ends up being either above market, in which case the tenant loses and the owner wins, or below market, in which case the tenant wins and the owner loses. The Consumer Price Index is commonly used to adjust future rent, but this method usually results in below market rates in normal or good markets. The problem is that there is no direct relationship between the Consumer Price Index and real estate rents for a certain area, so the results are just an approximation.

The surest and fairest way to adjust future rent is to base it on the then fair market rent, with the agreement stating that if the parties cannot agree on the rent, they agree to submit to binding arbitration following the rules of the American Arbitration Association or another arbitration process. If you provide for private arbitration (not using a service such as the American Arbitration Association), you should specify the qualification of the arbiters. Providing for future rent adjustments in this manner puts teeth in future rental adjustments because the parties have agreed in advance to abide by the arbiter's decision. Practically speaking, few of these cases actually go to arbitration because both parties know in advance that the arbiter's decision may not be favorable to them. Without arbitration the option is meaningless because it is difficult to enforce. The option should also provide that the tenant is to give advance written notice to exercise the option so, if the tenant doesn't renew, the owner has time to get a new tenant and limit the chances of a vacancy.

- The term of the lease is a function of many things. The tenant may want a long-term lease because he or she is putting considerable improvements into the property, or the landlord may want the security of a long-term lease. More often than not, however, the term is a function of what both parties think the rent will be in the future. If rents are rising fast, the tenant will want a long-term lease in order to fix a lower rate. The landlord, on the other hand, will want a shorter term lease, so he or she can adjust the rent to market rates. Leases can be very long term, ten years or more, with escalations built in using the methods described earlier.

- Most leases for multi-tenant properties will also include charges for maintenance of common areas (lobbies, public bathrooms, etc.). Obviously, landlords want to pass on all expenses for maintaining the common areas to the tenant, whereas the tenants, naturally, want to limit them. You should know how much the common area charges are estimated to be and what items are included. Many tenants try to limit the amount of common area "pass throughs," restrict what the landlord can charge for them, and obtain the right to audit the landlord's charges.

These matters, along with some new ones, will be discussed in more detail, in the following section on leases.

Leases

The lease itself is an agreement between a lessor (or landlord) and lessee (or tenant) for the use of property for a specified period of time for compensation, which is usually called, as we all know, rent. (A separate section on rent is included later in the chapter.) The lessee does not get free title to the property but rather the right to possess and use it. There are many different types of lease agreements — net leases, gross leases, full service leases, percentage leases, subleases, leasebacks, and so forth. Each area of specialty in commercial real estate tends to have lease types that have evolved over time to fit its needs. For example, full service leases, where the landlord pays most of the costs and then passes them on to the tenant in the form of rent, are common in office buildings where there are many tenants. Percentage leases, where the rent fluctuates based on a percentage of the tenant's sales, is common in retail. Triple net leases, where the tenant pays the real estate taxes, insurance premiums, and maintenance costs in addition to the rent are common in industrial leases.

Lease rates are typically quoted monthly or annually in industrial and retail leases and annually in office leases (although this varies from location to location and depends on many other factors as well). The terms of leases are all over the board. Many leases have three to five year terms, while some may be month to month, and others, 10 to 20 years.

Leasing is a big part of commercial real estate. It can easily account for 50 percent or more of your business. You should endeavor to understand all aspects of the lease agreements used in your area of specialty. There are literally thousands of different forms of leases. Some come from various associations of commercial Realtors®; some come from companies specializing in legal or real estate forms; some come from brokerage houses; and some come from attorneys. Many attorneys prefer to use forms they generate and revise by computer, rather than preprinted forms. Owners of multi-tenant projects typically have a single form lease so that all the leases in the project have consistent provisions for ease of administration.

In spite of the numerous variations of lease types and forms, there are some common aspects to all leases. Some of these are listed on the next page.

Standard Parts of a Lease

- The proper name of the lessee and lessor.

- The amount of rent and when it is to be paid. Leases will also provide for a security deposit and how it is to be handled.

- A complete and accurate description of the property, including exhibits, if necessary.

- The start date and the end date of the lease. Sometimes the occupancy date is not the same as the start date. There is usually some provision if the tenant holds over after the expiration of the term.

- Issues related to property and liability insurance, such as the amount of coverage, who is covered, and who is responsible for obtaining the policies and paying for them.

- What tenant improvements are to be made, who is to make them, who pays for them, and what happens to them at the end of the lease term. (For example, is the tenant required or permitted to remove any improvements?)

- What happens in the event of damage to the property or in the event of condemnation.

- What the premises are to be used for and prohibited activities.

- Who is responsible for repairs and maintenance and who pays the cost of repairs and maintenance.

- Who is responsible for compliance with laws either currently in effect or those enacted in the future. What rights does the tenant have outside of the premises (such as parking or shared loading dock usage).

- What security will be offered and what form will it take.

- The lessee's rights to assign the lease or sublet the premises and restrictions on those rights.

- What happens in the case of default or bankruptcy.

- In a multi-tenant project, what types of costs are passed through to tenants as additional rent, operating expenses, or common area maintenance charges and what types are excluded?

Common Points of Negotiation for Leases

There are many practical things well beyond the scope of this book that you should understand about leases. This knowledge will come with time. What follows is an introduction to a few key issues that may help you get started.

- The term of the lease can depend on many things. Most leases seem to be in the three- to five-year range; however, as mentioned earlier, many are done on a month-to-month basis and a few are long term (such as 10 to 20 years). Companies with short-term requirements may prefer a month-to-month tenancy or a long-term lease with an option to cancel. These companies are concerned that their space requirements will change. Multi-tenant office, retail, and industrial properties are often the best solutions for these prospects because they can often grow or shrink without moving. (One word to the wise on month-to-month leases: While many landlords and tenants prefer these because they leave their options open, keep in mind that they reduce security for both parties. A landlord may lose a tenant because a competing landlord offers a better deal, and a tenant may lose a location because another tenant offers the landlord more rent.)

  Some companies want long-term leases because of the high cost of moving or because they plan to spend a lot on tenant improvements or set up. Manufacturing companies are one example of this type of tenant. Owners often want long-term leases for the security of income, but some often prefer short-term leases if they plan to sell or redevelop the property, or do not want to pay a large leasing fee to the broker.

  Probably the single biggest factor that drives lease terms is rent. Generally speaking, rents increase over time. Tenants typically want long-term leases in order to lock in a long-term, fixed rate, while landlords want shorter-term leases so they can adjust the lease rate to market.

- Usually the lease start date is the occupancy date. Sometimes, however, a tenant will want early occupancy in order to set up or make tenant improvements. Some tenants will use this as a ploy to get free rent because the rent typically starts on the lease start date. In any case, if the landlord gives early occupancy, you should try to get the tenant to pay for the triple net or common area expenses for the early occupancy period. It also is important to have the terms of the lease cover the early occupancy period for liability and insurance purposes.

• The amount of rent is usually the major point of contention in negotiating leases. If you are quoting a market-based rent, it is easier to make a deal because it is supportable by comparable rents, which you should have available. This gets more difficult in rising and falling markets because you often are setting the market rent. Historic rates become obsolete when there is a surplus or paucity of space on the market. Landlords compete for tenants with reduced rates and free rent when they have vacant space and can command a premium from tenants when nothing else is available. Leases will usually have escalation provisions for rent in inflationary times. Sometimes this is just a fixed increase; sometimes it is based on some inflationary measuring index such as the Consumer Price Index; and sometimes it is pegged to comparable market rates with arbitration if the parties cannot agree. Arbitration will be discussed in more detail under the following section on "Options." Fixing arbitrary increases in the rent is a crapshoot because nobody knows the future. The tenant may end up paying above market or the landlord may end up getting below market rates. It is a way, however, to attempt to keep the rent at market without having to deal with the pitfalls of indexes and arbitration. Of all the indexes, the Consumer Price Index is probably the most widely used. It also is a crapshoot because there is no direct relationship between the index and market rents in commercial real estate. It does, however, tend to keep the rent within earshot of the market. If you want to ensure that the future rent is market rent, the best way, and perhaps fairest, is by renegotiation to market rates with arbitration. Generally, both parties will be assured that the rate is market. The downside is that if the landlord and tenant cannot agree on the future market rent and it goes to arbitration, the arbitrators may come up with a non-market figure, so one party ends up having to pay too much or the other ends up getting too little. Sometimes, depending on circumstances, it is better to keep the lease term short and just renegotiate the rent at the end of the lease. The landlord may be anxious to keep the tenant so he gives extra concessions, or the tenant may not be able to find a new location, so she pays a premium. This way, however, tends to work against the tenant because of the cost to move and the cost of new tenant improvements. Landlords, however, may be faced with new re-tenanting costs such as a real estate fee and new tenant improvements.

- Other matters concerning leases include how rent is quoted, the area rent is based on, and additional charges. The three basic ways to quote rent are triple net, gross, and full service. (A more detailed discussion of each is included in the section on "Rent" that follows.) Triple net leases are where the tenant pays real estate taxes, fire and extended coverage insurance, maintenance costs, and sometimes other costs of operation, in addition to the quoted rent. The landlord is looking for a net stream of income, so the tenant either pays the property expenses directly to the vendor, or reimburses the landlord for these expenses. There are a variety of opinions on what expenses are included and excluded in a triple net lease. For example, does the tenant pay the cost to put a new roof on the building, or a share of the cost based on the useful life of the roof in comparison to the length of the term of the lease, or no share at all?

In a gross lease, the landlord pays the taxes, insurance, and maintenance directly to the vendor, but then passes all of those costs, or some of them, on to the tenant in the form of additional rent. Full service leases are commonly used for office properties. In these, the landlord pays everything including taxes, insurance, maintenance, as well as common area charges such as utilities, cleaning, improvements and repair, landscaping, signage, and management, to name a few. These expenses are also passed on to the tenant in the base rent, rather than a reimbursement mechanism. For the same property, therefore, the net lease rate would be the lowest, followed by the gross, and then the full service. (This is why there is often a higher commission rate for net leases, because less money changes hands in the form of base rent). In order for the landlord to pass increases in costs on to the tenant, gross and full service leases will typically contain escalation, or pass through clauses. An example is an industrial warehouse gross lease where the tenant is to pay any increases in the property taxes or fire and extended coverage insurance over a base year. These additional charges are also often passed on to tenants through common area maintenance charges (CAM charges). These are assessed to tenants, in addition to the rent, and are usually found in multi-tenant buildings and parks.

- The area on which the rental rate is applied can vary. In office leases, it may include common areas such as hallways and bathrooms. In industrial leases, covered loading areas are sometimes included. You need to understand how the landlord arrived at the total area and what it includes. Rates are usually quoted monthly or annually. Office rates are typically quoted annually, such as $20.00 per sq. ft. per year. This means the rent for a 900 sq. ft. office is $20 per sq. ft. per year X 900 sq. ft.÷ 12 months = $1,500 per month. Retail and industrial rents are often quoted monthly (although in many areas they are quoted annually). For example, the rent for a 5,000 sq. ft. retail space at 90 ¢ per sq. ft would be .90 X 5,000 sq. ft. = $4,500.00 per month.

- Tenant improvements are often a major factor when negotiating office, retail, and industrial leases. The issues with tenant improvements include what they are, who is to do them, how much they cost, whether they are general or single purpose in nature, the terms of the amortization, and whether the tenant must remove the improvements at the end of the term. Generally speaking, landlords prefer to do general-purpose improvements that will add to the value and marketability of their property. They tend to avoid single purpose improvements that will be of no value to future tenants.

Commonly, the landlord will construct certain improvements for the tenant, at the landlord's expense, and then amortize the cost over the term of the lease and add it to the rent. For example, in industrial real estate, a typical quote for a warehouse is 30/65¢ per sq. ft. per month. This means the rent is 30¢ on the warehouse shell plus 65¢ for the office area, per month. Once the offices are fully amortized, as with older buildings, the quote will typically change to a blended rate. This means that the warehouse and office rates have been combined, or blended, in order to quote just one rate for the entire premises. In order to get the monthly cost of the tenant improvements down, landlords sometimes will amortize their cost over a term longer than the lease and then hope that they can pass them on to the next tenant. Alternatively, the landlord may require the tenant to pay for the unamortized cost of improvements if the tenant does not stay. In some respects, when landlords do improvements for tenants, the tenants are asking the landlords to act as a banker. This is because they are asking them to pay for improvements they need, which they then will repay over time. For this reason, the credit of the tenant is an important consideration of the landlord before doing any tenant improvements.

Tenant improvements are often a problem when subleasing property because sublessors do not want to put money into a property they do not own, and because they may have only a few months left on the lease. One way to resolve this issue, if the landlord is willing, is to cancel the lease and do a deal directly between the sublessee and the owner.

• There are many kinds of options in leases, such as the option to purchase the property, expand the premises, or extend the lease term (or renew the lease). A distinction is made between extending a lease and renewing a lease because a landlord may not want to give a tenant all the same terms in the original lease, such as a tenant improvement allowance. Options are generally in the tenant's interests and landlords usually give them only as a concession. Options to extend the lease term are common because tenants do not want to have to move and want to retain the flexibility to make a decision whether to move near the end of the term. Options to expand are less common. They allow a tenant to expand without having to move. Options to purchase are rare because landlords do not like to have their hands tied and because the landlords' lenders generally do not want the property encumbered by an option to purchase.

Typically, the central issue in options is establishing the future price or rental. Landlords do not want to fix a sales or rental price of property that is rising in value. Tenants like to fix the price. This puts them in the driver's seat because they have nothing to lose and everything to gain. If the option price is below market, they can exercise it, and if it is above the market, they can defer exercising the option and just negotiate. (Options will be discussed in more detail in a following section in this chapter.)

Other important factors to consider in negotiation are how long the options are and how much advance notice the optionee must give to exercise them. On the first point, options usually run the duration of the lease term. Sometimes, however, the tenant will only have a specified period of time — a "window of opportunity" — to exercise them. On the latter point, tenants should give a landlord ample advance notice, often six months or longer, to exercise an option to renew a lease. This gives the landlord time to find a new tenant and avoid vacancy.

• A first right of refusal to buy says, in general, that if the landlord receives an offer to purchase the property during the lease term, the landlord must first offer it to the tenant, who will then have a certain amount of time to exercise their "first right," and purchase the property, at the offered price and terms. Usually, if the tenant does not exercise it, the landlord is free to sell the property to a third party on any price and terms. Sometimes, however, the first right of refusal will provide that if the landlord negotiates a different price and terms with a third party, they must resubmit the offer to the tenant. From the landlord's perspective, first rights of refusal should be avoided at all costs because they make it almost impossible to sell the property to third parties. It is difficult to get an offer from a prospective buyer on a property when that buyer knows the tenant can match the buyer's best offer. It is tantamount to a free option. If the landlord must give a first right of refusal, a more palatable substitute for the landlord, is the first right to buy (sometimes called a "right of first offer"). This says that if the landlord should ever decide to sell the property, he or she will establish a price and terms and then first offer it to the tenant. If the tenant refuses to purchase the property on those price and terms, then the landlord is free to sell it to any third party buyer. It is also preferable, from the landlord's perspective, to provide that the landlord is not obligated to re-offer the property to the tenant if a different price and terms are negotiated with a third party. These subtle differences between a first right to buy and a first right of refusal give the landlord two significant advantages with a first right to buy. First, if it wants the property, the tenant is forced to pay the landlord's price out of fear of losing the property to a third party buyer. Second, if the tenant does not exercise the first right to buy, the landlord is then free to solicit offers on the property without having to go back to the tenant. Furthermore, a buyer will have an additional incentive to accept the landlord's price and terms or risk losing the purchase of property to the existing tenant.

- The entity that signs the lease is important for a number of reasons. People like to use corporations, limited liability companies (LLCs), and limited partnerships to limit their liability. Landlords, however, want security. If the tenant's credit is shaky, the landlord will often ask for an individual to sign the lease as tenant or to guarantee the lease, especially if the landlord is doing tenant improvements. This is often one of the most contentious and potentially deal-killing issues in leases. Some people adamantly refuse to guarantee a lease personally, and landlords generally are unwilling to risk dealing with an entity that may become insolvent and eventually bankrupt. For these reasons, it is important to carefully identify exactly who the tenant is.

(As mentioned previously, if the tenant is a corporation or other entity, the lease should specify what state it incorporated or was formed in. This subject will be discussed in more detail in the section on "Credit" in Chapter 11.)

- What stays and goes at the end of a lease should be carefully spelled out so there is no misunderstanding. In general, improvements to property become fixtures and remain with it. Trade fixtures can usually be removed by the tenant. However, this general rule varies considerably based on the particular state's common law and statutes and the provisions stated in the lease. For this reason, it is important for the tenant to specify things it wants the right to remove at the end of the lease, like trade fixtures, machinery, and equipment. Landlords like the right to determine what should stay and go at the end of the lease as well. Sometimes landlords want tenants to bear the cost of demolition and removal of special tenant improvements.

- Environmental matters are bigger issues in sales than leases. They also, for obvious reasons, tend to affect industrial property more than others. They can, however, be problems when leasing. Both landlords and tenants are concerned about liability from environmentally contaminated property. This is especially true of deep pocket, large, national corporations and wealthy individuals because both often become targets for any required remediation. Landlords, typically, want something in the lease that says the tenant will not contaminate the property, and the tenant wants something that says that it is not liable for any contamination it did not cause.

- The responsibility for repairs and maintenance to a property is often a contentious area when negotiating leases. The landlord wants the tenant to pay for repairs and maintenance, and the tenant does not want to get stuck with some huge expense, like replacing the roof. There are many permutations of solutions to this issue. A common one is for the tenant to take responsibility for routine maintenance, such as minor repairs, upkeep of HVAC (heating, ventilating, and air conditioning) systems, replacing broken windows, and sweeping the sidewalks, to name a few. The landlord could take responsibility for major repairs and replacement for things such as the roof, walls, foundation, and concealed plumbing. Other solutions are to assign a dollar limit to the tenant's responsibility, or spread the cost of major repair and replacement items over their life and have the tenant pay a prorated share. This issue can become quite sticky, especially when dealing with older buildings.

- Subleasing and assignment issues come up often in leasing. In a sublease, a lessee, who becomes the sublessor, leases all or part of the premises to another lessee, who becomes the sublessee. The sublessor is also called the sandwich lessor because they are sandwiched between the landlord and sublessee, like a slice of ham between two pieces of bread. Sublessors remain liable for the lease. Subleases tend to have special problems because the sublessor is not the owner, and the sublessee and landlord do not have direct contractual rights and remedies against the other. Questions arise such as can the sublessee make improvements to the premises? What happens if the sublessor goes bankrupt? And what if the sublessee wants to stay beyond the sublease term? You may need to get the lessor (landlord) involved, amend the lease, or cancel the first lease and sign a new one with the new tenant, in order to solve these problems. If the market rents are above the lease contract rent, the tenant will want to sublease and the landlord will want to cancel the lease and do a deal directly. Both want the higher rent. If the market rents are below the lease contract rent, then the tenant usually has no alternative but to sublease and take the loss. The landlord will not accept a lower rent when they have someone on the hook.

Sometimes the question of whether the tenant can assign the lease so that it is no longer liable becomes an issue. Generally, landlords resist this (and form leases prohibit this) unless the new lessee's credit is as good as or better than the existing tenant's. One additional issue you will encounter in subleasing and assignments regards the fee. Landlords will generally not pay a broker a fee on a new lease that replaces the existing lease, if they paid one on the first lease. They would end up paying two fees. The solution is to collect a fee from the existing lessee for the amount of rent that they are being relieved of paying, and then a fee from the owner on any extended term.

- Different specialty areas have numerous clauses for leases that are tailored for them. One example is the "go dark" clause in a retail lease, which says if a tenant vacates the premises in a shopping center, or the space "goes dark," then the landlord can cancel the lease or, in some cases, seek damages from the tenant. You should become familiar with the various clauses that pertain to your specialty.

Rent

As discussed earlier, there are many variations in the way rent is quoted. Both the nomenclature and practices of quoting rent vary from place to place. The Rent Quote Diagram shown in Figure 1 (see next page) is an effort to give a general idea of who pays what in the most common kinds of commercial leases. In general, rent is all about who pays what to whom, and how the landlord can capture future expense increases. Philosophically, the tenant pays everything, one way or another. They either pay it to the landlord and the landlord pays the vendor, or they pay the vendor directly, in addition to the rent. The most common methods of quoting commercial rents are triple net, gross, and full service. Triple net means the tenant pays the rent plus everything else including taxes, insurance, and maintenance (the triple refers to those three things). Gross means that the tenant pays for the utilities and the landlord pays for the taxes, insurance, and maintenance. Full-service generally means that the tenant pays rent to the landlord and the landlord pays all the vendors for taxes, insurance, maintenance, and all other costs. Tenants always pay for their own personal services like telephone. Office leases are often full service and industrial leases are usually triple net or sometimes gross. Retail leases are almost always triple net. Multi-tenant buildings often quote full service, while single-tenant properties often quote triple net. Multi-tenant parks will often quote triple net and then bill separately common area maintenance (CAM) charges. They quote a triple net lease, but collect the money and pay the vendors directly. Office leases

Rent Quote Diagram

This diagram is intended as a general example of how rents are quoted in commercial real estate. Practices vary considerably from place to place and the actual method of quoting rent in your area may be different.

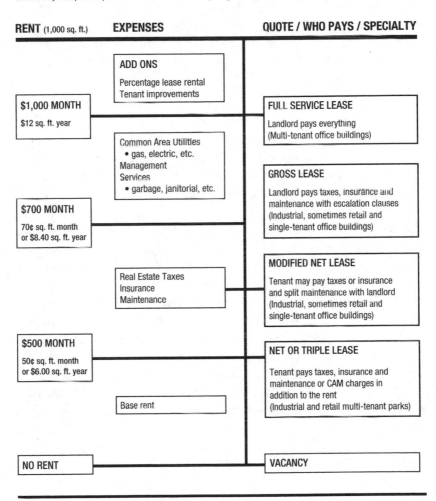

are commonly quoted on an annual basis and retail and industrial on a monthly or annual basis, depending on where you are. There are certain "add ons" that typically come in addition to the quoted rent. These include the amortization of tenant improvements and percentage lease rental in retail leases, to name a couple.

Triple Net and Modified Net Leases

Triple net or modified net leases allow for the tenant to automatically pay for any increases in expenses. In industrial real estate, a quote might be 30¢ per sq. ft. per month triple net ($500 per month in the Rent Quote Diagram). Because the tenant is paying the taxes directly to the government, they automatically pay any increases in the taxes. As mentioned earlier, triple net leases are most common in industrial tenants because the tenant's expenses can vary considerably. An example would be a manufacturer who uses a lot of electricity.

A downside to triple net leases is maintenance. For example, buildings occasionally need new roofs, and it is hard for a landlord to get a tenant to pay for a new $50,000 roof when the tenant is in the building for only five years. Tenants know this and resist signing purely triple net leases, especially on older buildings, to avoid big maintenance charges like these. The landlords, who have leased a building on a triple net basis, end up with an older building that needs a new roof, which a tenant will not pay for. Furthermore, the landlord cannot make a future tenant pay for it because it will not sign a triple net lease on an older building. Because the lease was triple net, the landlord did not collect rent for the roof, so it comes out of his or her pocket and, ultimately, reduces the return on investment. Modified net leases attempt to address this situation by allowing the landlord collect more rent, with the understanding that he or she will set aside a portion to pay for the roof when it is needed. In multi-tenant parks with triple net leases, this type of problem can be avoided by including in the common area maintenance charge a reserve for maintenance that the tenants pay into.

Gross Leases

In a gross lease, the landlord collects enough rent to pay for the taxes, insurance, and maintenance and then pays the vendors directly. A gross lease might quote 60¢ per sq. ft. per month or $7.20 per year gross ($700 per month in the Rent Quote Diagram). A gross lease has the advantage of assuring the landlord that the expenses have been paid and that enough rent has been collected to pay for maintenance. The downside of a gross lease is that, because the rent is fixed and the tenant is not paying the vendors directly, the landlord is faced with increasing expenses that cannot be passed onto the tenant. Because of this, gross leases usually include escalation clauses for taxes and insurance. This just means that the tenant reimburses the landlord for any increases in taxes and insurance over a base year. Such clauses are also called "pass throughs" because they pass the increased costs (or savings) directly to the tenant.

Full Service Leases

Full service leases are most common in multi-tenant office buildings. A full service lease might quote $25 per sq. ft. per year ($1,000 per month in the Rent Quote Diagram). Full service leases are used when it is difficult to segregate the expenses to each tenant in a multi-tenant building. The landlord just adds up all the expenses, prorates them among the tenants and then pays them directly to the vendors. These leases will also contain "pass throughs." It is becoming more and more common for multi-tenant office building leases to use net leases where tenants pay base rent and a proportionate share of operating costs based on their share of the building. These expenses are paid on an estimated basis. After the end of each calendar year, the landlord reconciles the difference between the actual expense and the amount the tenant has paid on an estimated basis. If the tenant paid too much, the excess is typically credited against rent. If the tenant paid too little, the deficiency is usually due and payable at that time. Because of the way landlords of multi-tenant office buildings handle the expense reimbursement issue (by a net lease, gross lease, or full service lease), it is very important to make sure you are comparing lease rates correctly when representing a tenant who is shopping for space.

Some Final Words on Rent

Triple net leases are popular because they make the landlord's job easy. Landlords just collect a 'net' stream of income from a property and let the tenant pay all the expenses. Properties leased on a triple net basis are called "no brainer" deals by investors because they require little brainpower to evaluate and manage. This is the lazy investor's way of doing business. Such landlords do not want to have to deal with the management issues of real estate, so they pass them on to the tenant. The reality is, though, that a landlord needs to take responsibility for the property to ensure that the expenses are paid and it is maintained. At a minimum, the landlord needs to monitor the payment of expenses and performance of maintenance. There have been cases, for example, where a tenant on a triple net lease goes out of business and the landlord is stuck paying past, unpaid real estate taxes. For this reason, full service leases, gross leases with escalation clauses, and triple net leases with CAM charges are, in the author's opinion, best. Purely triple net leases may look attractive, but they come with a price.

A few more pointers on rent and how it is quoted are listed below.

- When quoting free rent, try and collect the operating expenses for the period of no rent. Landlords will also want to "abate" the rent rather than call it free rent. That is, the lease will likely state that the rent is abated as long as the tenant performs its lease obligations. If the tenant defaults, the abated rent becomes due and payable.

- Be sure to explain the terms of how the rent is quoted to prospects. A triple net rate sounds lower than a gross rate, but the tenant may pay the same (or more) in the end.

- When comparing rents, such as for an opinion of value, be sure to compare apples with apples. You do not want to compare a triple net lease rate with a gross rate. Plus, you want to define exactly what expenses are passed through to the tenant in the lease document.

- Tenant improvements are usually added on top of the rent. If the office improvements in an industrial building, for example, cost 65¢ per sq. ft. per month to amortize over the term of the lease, then the quote would be 30/65¢ per sq. ft. per month. This means 30¢ per sq. ft. on the warehouse shell plus 65¢ on the office area. Note, however, that sometimes a tenant improvement allowance is included in the base rent. A problem with this method is that some tenants may demand that their base rent be reduced by the amount of the tenant improvement allowance they did not use. The lease should clarify whether this is permitted.

Please keep in mind that there is considerable variation and confusion, over the way rent is quoted. It is not uncommon, for example, to have five brokers with five different definitions of a triple net lease. You need to evaluate each situation to understand clearly who is paying what. The best way to do that is by reading the lease provision to determine exactly what expenses are the tenant's responsibilities.

Options

An option gives the right to purchase or lease, for a specified period of time, at either a fixed price or price that is to be determined, with some form of enforcement. Options can stand alone, but are more commonly part of a lease. A user or developer, for example, may purchase an option on property, rather than make an offer to purchase with contingencies, in order to evaluate a property. There is a certain psychological advantage to an offer with contingencies because the buyer has made the commitment to purchase, subject to satisfying themselves on certain things that are specifically stated in the agreement. An option makes no such commitment.

Options to Purchase

In an option to purchase, the optionee will, or should, pay for the right to hold the option. This is because options make it more difficult for the owner to sell or lease the property to anyone else during the option period, and because the owner will have ongoing expenses such as real estate taxes and insurance. The amount of consideration for an option is variable, but should at least cover the optionor's expenses. Beyond that, the amount of consideration usually boils down to however much it will take to get the optionor to take the property off the market. Options to purchase, typically, have a fixed price, but can also be based on the then fair market value with arbitration (similar to the previous discussion on leases).

The important thing to remember about options is that they

must be able to be enforced. If they cannot, they are not true options. An option to purchase, for example, that states that the purchase price is to be "agreed upon" by the parties, is meaningless. You cannot enforce an agreement to agree. If the parties do not agree on the price, they are at an impasse. There are no solutions in the option that resolve the impasse. Fixing the price in advance or setting a standard for determining the price, such as fair market value with an arbitration method to enforce determination of the fair market value, are solutions.

Many owners, especially those with a low tax basis, may want to provide for a Section 1031 Tax Deferred Exchange in the option, in order to defer payment of the capital gains tax. Because it is often difficult for sellers to find suitable exchange property, they sometimes will provide in an option to purchase, a clause providing that when the seller finds an exchange property, the seller can exercise the option and make the tenant buy the property at that time. In an option to purchase in a lease, the tenant usually has the right to exercise the option at the end of the lease, with or without an exchange.

Lease Options

Businesses will commonly have options to extend leases and sometimes options to purchase. Options to extend leases are important because tenants like to have the right to stay in the property, especially if they have made significant improvements. Some important issues involved in options are arbitration to determine the price or rent to be paid, rental floor or ceiling, advance notice time to exercise the option, and term. Many leases, for example, specify that the rental is to be the then fair market rental for similar properties and will provide for some form of arbitration, using the procedures of the American Arbitration Association or other arbitration method, if the parties cannot agree. In most private arbitrations (not using a service), each side picks an arbitrator, and they, in turn, pick a third arbitrator. The three arbitrators' final decision is then binding. As a practical matter, the decision often ends up being what the third arbitrator decides, so there may be some squabbling over the selection of the third arbitrator. For this reason, it is a good idea to provide in the option exactly what qualifications are required of the arbitrators.

It is interesting to note that disputes in options that provide for arbitration to set fair market value, tend to be rare. This is because both parties know that they cannot take advantage of the other side, so their expectations tend to be more realistic. They do not exercise the options unless they are prepared to take the consequences.

Sometimes, options will arbitrarily set a floor or ceiling to the renewal rental. Tenants want a ceiling because they want to limit future rental increases, and landlords want a floor because they want to keep future rental high. These floors and ceilings can be arbitrary or based on some formula, like the Consumer Price Index. Floors in renewal rentals are commonly established when a landlord specifies that the renewal rental is to be not less than the last month's contract rental. Generally, floors and ceilings in options to renew leases are rare due to their arbitrary nature.

Notice time is the deadline by which the option must be exercised. Some options allow notice at anytime during a lease, for example, and others may require advance notice. Advance notice is important in options to renew leases for a couple of reasons. First, it puts pressure on the tenant to decide early on if they are going to stay or not. Without this, some tenants just procrastinate until the last day of the lease. Second, it alerts the landlord well in advance if the tenant is not going to stay. This gives them plenty of time to find a new tenant and avoid any vacancy.

The term, or length of the option period, is variable. As mentioned, options in leases may run the full length of the lease or be limited to a specific time or timeframe. Options to purchase may be three to six months, or longer. The length of the option will usually reflect the party's motivations. It might be six months for a developer with an option to purchase who must obtain approval on a subdivision, or two years on some vacant land a company plans to expand onto.

A Few Words About Options

In very broad terms, options are in the best interest of the optionee and not the optionor. The optionee holds all the cards and can force the optionor to continue a lease or sell a property, whether the optionor wants to or not. Options to purchase also limit the marketability of the property, are disfavored by lenders who do not want the property encumbered by them, and prevent the owner from getting any monetary windfall that may come his or her way, if the option is at a fixed price. Any such windfall would go to the optionee, because all they have to do is exercise the option and then resell the property. Property can be sold or financed subject to an option to purchase, but this is hard to do. The buyer is reluctant to go through the trouble of buying something that someone else can buy from them sometime in the future. Further, if the option has a fixed price, the sales price will be limited by the option price because if a buyer paid over the option price, they would lose money if the optionee exercised the option. Options can also be assigned or sold. For these reasons, options are typically avoided in sales by owners and given away as a bargaining chip in exchange for something else, in leases. Sometimes rights to exercise options are not assignable and are personal to the original optionee.

Some things to provide for, and consider, in options, are listed below.

- They should include a full description of the property.

- Make sure the person signing the option is the owner of the property and has the right to bind the property to the option.

- They should specify what the commission is or how it is to be figured.

- If a survey is required, who pays for it?

- The price for the option should be specified as well as the purchase price for the property.

- The method of closing, how long to close, and the condition of title should be addressed.

- If there are any renewals to the option, specify how long they will be, how they will be exercised, how much advance notice is required, and how much to renew, if applicable.

- If payments are made for an option, specify if they apply to reduce the purchase price or not.

- Specify the terms of the purchase.

- Specify who pays for any studies and who gets them in the end. It is a good idea to provide that the owner get any studies if the optionee does not exercise the option.

- Make sure that all names in an option are proper.

- The same issues that are addressed in a purchase agreement for property should be addressed in an option.

Listings

The listing is an agreement between the owner and the broker covering the agreed upon terms of a sale or lease of property, along with both parties' obligations and duties to each other. The three main types of listings are discussed below.

- Non-exclusive listings, generally, allow the owner to deal with anyone without having to pay you a fee. The value of these listings is to confirm in writing with the owner the terms by which he or she is willing to sell or lease the property. Non-exclusive listings put you in competition with the world.

- Agency listings require the owner to pay you a fee if a deal is brought in by others, but not the owner. These provide some protection, but put you in competition with the owner. Any prospect could call the owner directly, and you are out.

- Exclusive listings generally require the owner to pay you a fee regardless of the source of the prospect. Your only competition in these listings is your own ability to move the property. As a general rule, you should only take exclusive listings, unless there is a very good reason to do otherwise. If you are going to spend your time and money on an owner's behalf marketing their property, you should be assured you will be paid if you make a deal. Prospects come from many sources and are often a direct or indirect consequence of your efforts. You could, for example, advertise a property under an agency listing, which causes a prospect or another broker to call the owner directly. In this case, even though your efforts brought the prospect, you would be out of luck if you did not have an exclusive listing. It is in both the owner's and broker's interests to use exclusive listings. The broker is given the incentive to work on the property by knowing he or she will earn a fee if it sells or leases, and the owner gets a broker who will work hard on the listing for the same reason.

The more important elements of exclusive listings for sale and exclusive listings for lease are discussed below. The two agreements are essentially the same — the only differences reflect whether the property is being offered for sale or for lease. There are also exclusive listings for both sale and lease. (These are not discussed here because they incorporate many of the same terms and issues.)

Listings for Sale

Listings for sale specify the terms and conditions by which an owner will sell a property. Listings for sale specify such things as the price, terms of sale, occupancy, and what stays and what goes.

A few of the most important elements and considerations for listings for sale follows.

- Term of listing. The lengths of listings are variable. Some listings are for 30 days and some for a year or longer. Many listings are for six months. The term of a listing is a function of how long you think it is going to take to sell the property and how long the owner is willing to wait for you to produce.

- Description and location of the property, including the legal description.

- Price.

- Terms of sale. This could be cash, contract, or exchange. If contract, the terms the seller is willing to accept should be clearly spelled out. For example, the seller may require 20% down with the balance amortized over 20 years at 9% annual interest, payable monthly, with a balloon payment at five years. The main problems with specifying the terms of a sale are 1) Often the seller does not know the terms he or she wants; and 2) If you specify terms, you cut yourself off from any better terms a buyer may be willing to offer, including cash. For these reasons, it is usually better to say that the owner wants "cash or other such terms the seller is willing to accept." If the buyer is willing to pay cash, then that is what you get. If not, the buyer can make the owner his or her best offer on terms, and then see what the owner says.

- Provide for an exchange if the owner requires it.

- Specify the occupancy date. Is it on closing or is the sale subject to an existing lease, which means that the buyer cannot get occupancy until the lease expires.

- Specify what stays and goes. Any items the seller is planning to remove should be carefully identified and itemized in the listing agreement, as well as in any promotional material for the property, and the final purchase and sale agreement. This is especially true of fixtures. Significant items that are to be included in the sale should also be identified and itemized in the listing agreement.

- Ask the seller for, and include, any information that the buyer should know, such as existing liens, assessments, existing assumable financing, and so forth.

- Listings generally require the broker to use his or her best efforts and diligently pursue buyers for the property.

- The listing will require the seller to pay you a fee if a sale is consummated and will contain the fee arrangements or refer to a schedule of fees (discussed later in this chapter).

- Listings usually have some provision for payment of a fee if a deal is completed after the listing expires with any prospect that came in during the listing period. The broker must provide a list of those prospects to the seller within 10 days of expiration of the listing. Often listings will provide that a fee is to be paid to the broker if a deal is made with those prospects up to 180 days after the listing expires. This requirement to list the prospects is often waived if the prospect made an offer during the term of the listing.

- Listings for sale will usually specify that the seller will pay the broker a fee if the property is leased or taken off the market.

- The listing will say that the owner agrees to cooperate with the broker on a sale and will refer any prospects to the broker.

- Owners will authorize the broker in the listing to accept deposits, advertise the property, and to put up a sign.

- Most states have specific requirements for real estate licensees' listing agreements. Make sure you comply with your states' specific requirements.

Listings for Lease

Listings to lease contain much of the same language and terms as the listing to sell, except that they specify the terms of a lease the owner is willing to accept. Some important terms not mentioned in the listing for sale, which relate to the lease, follow.

- The amount of the rental and the way it is quoted. Rent is usually quoted on a monthly basis, but could be daily or annually. It should discuss whether the rental is net, gross or full service, and what is meant by those terms. In short, the listing should specify who pays what when it comes to such things as taxes, insurance, maintenance, and utilities.

- The term of the lease. The length of the lease should be specified, whether it be 1, 5 or 10 years.

- An explanation of any options the owner is willing to give and their terms. These could be lease extension options or purchase options.

- When the premises may be occupied.

- What condition the property is to be in on delivery, whether the owner is willing to make any tenant improvements, and the terms of repayment for the improvements, if any.

- Listings for lease will often contain a provision that

the broker is to receive a fee if the property is sold or exchanged, whether to a third party or to the tenant. They also will provide that an owner will pay a fee on any lease extensions or expansions negotiated in the lease.

Common Concerns in Listings

You should be aware of a few practical matters concerning listings in general. Owners are often concerned that when they give an exclusive listing, they could find themselves having committed to a broker who does not work the listing. This is a real problem because some brokers do take listings and then do little or nothing to market the property. You need to assure the owner that you will use your best efforts to move the listing and then do it. Sometimes, with the right kind of owner, this concern can be overcome by including a provision in the listing that the owner has the right to cancel if the broker is doing nothing. If you think about it, this is the same basis on which attorneys and accountants work. If they are doing their job, they expect to continue their representation. If they are not doing their job, they should expect to be fired. Why is a broker any different? In many respects, this is a healthier and more honest relationship. As a broker, the advantage is that you can expect to keep the listing until it moves if you continue to do the work. The risk, of course, is that an unscrupulous owner may cancel the listing if he or she gets the opportunity to sell or lease the property to someone directly and thus avoid paying you a fee. You must use your best judgment of a client's character before offering this provision.

Another common concern of owners is that they are limiting themselves to one broker when they list exclusively. Many think that they will get more action if they deal with multiple brokers. The opposite is true. When they list with one broker exclusively, that broker will make the effort to ensure that all other brokers have the information. They will solicit the cooperation of all other brokers, thus increasing the number working on the listing. They will also have the incentive to spend the time and money to do everything else, including advertising, signs, calls, multiple listing, and so forth. The total marketing effort on behalf of the owner is actually expanded with exclusive listings, not constricted.

Many brokers dread having to renew listings. When you have to go to the owner to renew a listing that is expiring, the owner is alerted to the issue of renewal. Naturally, they will question whether it should be renewed. One way to handle this is to address it in advance, by providing in the listing that, upon expiration, the listing will continue on a month-to-month basis, cancelable by either party with 30 days written notice. This way the issue never comes up. The downside is that you may be canceled. Generally speaking, however, brokers who have worked a listing and have kept the owner informed of their efforts, have little difficulty in renewing listings. In general, owners want to see a broker who has worked hard on their behalf, compensated.

Owners requesting exceptions to listings are common. The owner may have a prospect or broker with a prospect that he or she wishes to exclude from the listing. Exceptions should be avoided. The prospect who is excepted may be the best prospect, and you may end up spending time and money to no end. It is better to tell the owner to try and make the deal with that prospect before listing the property. This accomplishes a couple of things. First, you don't waste your time. Second, these prospects are usually quickly qualified when they are told by the owner that they have only so much time in which to make a deal. The prospect will want to act quickly because he or she knows, once the property is listed and put on the market, there will be more competition. If this does not work, you could consider taking a listing where the prospect is excluded for only a short period of time, say 30 days. This way your investment is not so high if the excluded prospect makes a deal. One final idea is to have the owner reimburse you for your out of pocket expenses, or to pay you some agreed upon figure if the excluded prospect makes a deal. This method is better than nothing.

Counter Offers

Counter offers are simply responses to an offer or proposal. If the offer or proposal is acceptable, then there is no need for a counter offer. Usually they are not, so the principals receiving the offer make a counter offer, if they want to make a deal. Sometimes, if the offer is so far from their asking terms, the principals receiving the offer may ask the offeror to resubmit a better offer.

There are many counter offer forms, and different forms for different types of deals, such as a counter offer to lease or to purchase. These include preprinted forms, lawyers' forms, or a simple letter. There can be numerous counter offers to counter offers. It is not unusual to go back and forth four, five, or six times before agreement is reached, or the deal dies. Counter offers can cover many subjects such as price, terms, occupancy, fixtures, terms of contingencies, tenant improvements, and so forth. They can also add new terms to the deal. A counter offer to an offer to lease, for example, may add a contingency making the deal subject to the landlord's approval of the tenant's credit, which was not in the original offer. Whatever the case, the important function of counter offers is to methodically reduce the area of disagreement between the parties, in order to achieve a meeting of the minds on the terms of the deal.

A counter offer should carefully reference the offer. It should refer to the parties, to the original offer, the date, whether the offer was to purchase or lease, and provide a description of the property. Most importantly, the counter offer should say that the seller, or lessor, "accepts the terms of the original offer with the following changes" (and additions, if any) and then list the changes or additions. This is critical because it confirms that there is agreement on all the terms of the offer, except those listed. The party making the counter offer should then sign the counter and there should be a place for the other party to sign. If the other party accepts the counter, you have a meeting of the minds on all terms, and a deal. If the other party doesn't accept it, he or she can make a counter-offer to the counteroffer. This document will say that the party "accepts all the terms of the counteroffer" (which included agreement on the original offer), "with the following changes." This document should also be signed and a space for the other party's signature provided. If the one who made the counter accepts the counter to the counter, then you have a meeting of the minds and a deal. This can go on, back and forth, ad infinitum. The bottom line is that it is the best way to gradually and logically reduce the area of disagreement. It is a system of trade offs, where the parties give and take in order to reach agreement.

The most important thing to avoid in counter offers is negotiating on shifting sands. This means that the parties to a negotiation keep opening up and renegotiating things that have already been agreed to. This is a nightmarish way to do business because you never know if you have a deal. It's like trying to capture a puff of smoke with a fishing net. Some people prefer to deal on shifting sands because they want to be able to go back and try to better the deal. The problem with this is that when one does it, so does the other. What you end up with is endless, ongoing, and fruitless negotiations.

A Few Tips for Counter Offers

A few additional suggestions regarding counter offers follows.

- Always put counter offers in writing. People forget terms, and deals can get complex, so you need a written record. You want to carefully document where both parties agree and disagree.

- Have the party making the counter offer sign it and provide a place for it to be accepted. This will help avoid the shifting sands problem.

- It is better to have the one making the counter offer sign just the counter and not the original offer. If a seller, for example, adds to the original offer that a counter offer addendum has been added, and then signs the original offer and the counter offer, everyone gets confused. Even though the counter offer says that some terms of the offer have been modified by the counter, the seller has signed two documents, which conflict. Why do this? It is easier just to have the seller sign the counter offer, and not the original offer.

- Avoid rewriting the agreement in order to consolidate the original offer and any counter offers. Some like to "simplify" the documents by consolidating them into one document. All this does is open up the possibility for more negotiations if the final document does not exactly reproduce the meeting of the minds. There exists a meeting of the minds already with the offer and counter offers, so why try and make things more complex? The offer and the counters are the deal.

Fee Schedules

As you can imagine, fees are of real interest to owners and brokers. Fees are usually paid by sellers or lessors, except when negotiated otherwise. Owners, as a general rule, want them reduced, and brokers, as a universal rule, want them increased. Some owners understand the importance of giving the brokerage community the incentive to work on their property and, consequently, pay full fees and sometimes bonuses. Other owners, on the other hand, simply set their own fee schedules, which are often below the prevailing schedules. Whatever the case, commercial real estate fees vary considerably.

It is illegal to fix fee schedules today, so there are many fee schedules and considerable negotiation over what the fee is to be. Fees vary based on a number of factors, such as the type of property, difficulty in selling or leasing, and size of the deal. Raw land and exchanges tend to be more involved than leases and sales of improved buildings, so the fees for these are usually higher. Some commissions can become absurdly high, such as in long-term leases or very large deals. These fees are often negotiated. They may end up being a smaller percentage, a fixed fee, or, in the case of very long-term leases, treated as a sale.

The following paragraphs include a discussion of a typical commercial real estate schedule of fees. This is just a sampling because the methods and amounts described vary considerably between companies and locations. This is not intended to be a recommendation of a fee schedule, but rather an illustration of what one may look like.

Fees are typically paid when the property closes or the lease is executed. Occasionally, they may be paid over time, as in the case of a contract sale or lease when the owner does not have the money, or where the custom is to pay fees over time. If a fee is paid over time, there should be a written agreement specifying how it is to be paid. It is a good idea to try and get the owner to pay you interest and to provide some collateral, although these are often difficult to obtain. Lessors will sometimes complain that the broker, whose schedule provides that they be paid when a lease is executed, gets a full fee when they themselves get rent over time. They also sometimes express concern over paying a full fee up front with a marginal credit tenant who may go bankrupt, or default.

Paying a real estate fee is no different than paying a stockbroker a fee when a stock is sold. The broker does the work and gets paid up front, and the buyer takes the risk of the company going bankrupt. This is an owner's business decision that involves risk. To alleviate an owner's concerns, you should ensure that he or she has all the necessary financial information on the buyer or tenant to make an informed decision. You should also try to get enough money down on a sale or deposit on a lease, so the owner collects enough money to pay the fee. In worst-case scenarios, if a buyer or tenant does default, you can offer to remarket the property and give them some credit on a future fee. On a lease, this often is described as a credit for the unearned portion of the fee.

Lease Fees

In a gross lease, a fee may be 5% of the aggregate rental for the first five years of the lease and 2.5% thereafter. (Remember, a gross lease typically is one in which the landlord pays the real estate taxes, fire and extended coverage insurance, and maintenance.) The fee may be increased by 1% if the term is less than three years, because the aggregate rental is smaller. There may also be a minimum fee due equal to one month's rent. On a net lease (where the tenant pays the taxes, insurance, and maintenance), the fee may be one percent higher — or 6% of the aggregate rental for the first five years of the lease and 3.5% thereafter. This is because the same amount of work goes into making the deal, but less money changes hands. Again, in a net lease, if the lease is for less than three years, the fee may be 1% higher, and there may be a minimum of one month's rent. If a lease is month to month, the fee may be the average of one month's rent, with a dollar minimum stated amount.

Fees can be increased by 1 to 2% if the lease is a build to suit, a sublease, an assignment, or a transfer, because these typically require more work. When a lease contains an option to renew, the fee is typically figured on the option period's aggregate rental (as though the option period was an extension of the original term) and due when the option is exercised. Fees are also due (if an owner agrees) when a lease contains an option to purchase, which is based on the sales fee schedule. Any unearned lease fee previously paid will typically reduce this sales fee.

Special cases for fees involve leases with percentage rental and long-term leases, such as ground leases. In percentage rental, fees may be based on a tenant's gross receipts. In long-term leases, the transaction may be treated as a sale by capitalizing the average annual net income and applying the sales fee schedule, which will be discussed next. One special problem that occasionally arises in lease fees is whether or not a fee should be paid on tenant improvements. Often a landlord will pay for improvements to a space for the tenant and then amortize the cost over the term of the lease and add it to the rental. If the improvements are general in nature, such as offices built into a warehouse, better lighting for a retail tenant, or an office build out for an office tenant, they are usually considered additional rent and subject to the fee schedule. These improvements add to the value of the property and another tenant may use them. If they are special purpose in nature, like special wiring for a manufacturing tenant or a special storefront or layout for a retail or office tenant, they often are not subject to a fee. These improvements are typically of little value to future tenants, and may have to be torn out at the end of the lease. The owner is acting more as a lender in these cases, not a landlord. Be aware, however, that some landlords pay no fees on tenant improvements, and some brokers expect them with all tenant improvements.

Sales Fees

Fees on sales and exchanges are typically due when the transaction closes. The fee may be 6% of the first $5,000,000 of the sales price and 5% thereafter. This percentage is usually reduced or the amount negotiated as the size of the transaction increases. It is not unusual for fees to be 3, 2 or 1% of the sales price of larger deals, or to be fixed on very large ones. Brokers usually do not publish reduced fees on larger deals. They prefer to negotiate them on a deal by deal basis. Fees on raw land sales can be 8 to 10% or more because they often require more effort. Establishing and collecting fees on joint ventures in real estate can be difficult. Typically they are based on the percentage of the value of the property the joint venture covers, which is then subject to the schedule of fees for sales. Note also that it is difficult to collect fees on "inside transactions" such as transfers of property between ownership entities of the same person, transactions within a family, or between subsidiaries of the same corporation because these transactions typically do not provide for consideration on which to base the fee. This issue should be addressed directly in the fee schedule.

Net Listings

Net listings are one exception to listings for sale that provide that the broker is to be paid a percentage. With a net listing, the owner establishes the price he or she is willing to accept, without a fee. The broker is then expected to quote the buyer a higher price, one that includes the broker fee. If, for example, the owner listed the property for $100,000 net and the broker's fee is 8%, then the broker would quote a sales price of $108,000. These kinds of listings should be avoided. (See Chapter 10, "Things to Avoid" for a more complete discussion.)

Cooperating Brokers and Reduced Fees

Fee schedules sometimes do not cover all possibilities in commercial real estate deals. Occasionally, it is appropriate to negotiate larger fees for difficult, time consuming, and unusual transactions. It is also wise, sometimes, to offer incentives to cooperating brokers with an additional half or full fee. This means that the owner will pay one and a half or twice the normal fee schedule. Sometimes a listing broker will accept a reduced fee if there is no cooperative broker. This way the listing broker keeps the incentive to market the property because the commission is still larger than if the deal involved a cooperative broker. The cooperating broker keeps the incentive because he or she still earns the same amount, or half of a full fee. The owner gains if the listing broker sells or leases the property without a cooperative broker because the fee is reduced in that event.

One last comment on negotiating reduced fees. Everyone does it in order to get business and be competitive. Small, occasional reductions, especially for good clients, are not that significant. Wholesale, large reductions in fee schedules, however, often work against both the broker and the owner. The brokers make less money and lose the incentive to work on a listing. The owner loses by being penny wise but pound foolish. By forcing a reduced fee on the brokers, the owner takes away the broker's incentive to work on the listing. Wise owners understand that the fee is small in the overall picture and that it pays to see that hard work is rewarded. One or two months of lost rent or interest on a vacant or unsold property, will quickly eat up any advantages an owner gained in negotiating a reduced fee.

Finder's Fees

Finder's fees are fees paid to brokers who refer business to other brokers. They are fairly common. The amount of these fees varies considerably, depending on many factors including the degree of control the referring broker has or the difficulty of the transaction. Typical referral fees run between 10 to 15%. They can be higher if the referral warrants it or lower if the referring broker just passed on a name. Sometimes a bottle of Scotch is a sufficient referral fee.

CHAPTER 4
Technical Knowledge

To be successful in commercial real estate you must know your business. You need to gain a reputation as a knowledgeable and competent broker — an expert in your field. People should feel confident putting their real estate affairs in your hands. This is especially true because commercial real estate transactions often involve large amounts of money, which makes people want to deal with those who know what they are doing. Competence comes from many things, such as knowledge of the market and experience. It also comes from a broad technical knowledge of the business. Therefore, early on in your career, it is important to study and gain a through understanding of the mechanics of the business so you know what to do and how to do it. You need to understand many things including law, agency, title, leasing and sales, development, valuation, mathematics, environmental issues related to commercial real estate, construction, surveys, investment analysis, office management, exchanging, financing, and property management. You also need to be familiar with governmental issues such as taxation, zoning, and state licensing and brokerage requirements.

There is a tremendous amount of technical information in the commercial real estate business. There is always something to learn, and the most successful brokers keep on learning. They stay informed of the changes and trends. You are not expected to know everything about every area, but rather enough so you can properly handle real estate transactions and recognize situations where you need help. It is important to remember that if you do not know the answer to a question or what to do in a situation, you should admit it and then seek advice from those who do. Never make up an answer to a question. Always say, "I don't know the answer, but I will see if I can find someone who does."

A detailed explanation of all of the technical information needed in the business is beyond the scope of this book. However, you should know what to look for. This chapter is intended to give you a broad outline of some areas of knowledge you should endeavor to understand. It will also discuss some things that may be particularly helpful in avoiding problems that may hinder your success in the business. Also, note that although much of the technical knowledge in this chapter about the commercial real estate business applies geographically everywhere, much of it does not. Different areas often have different laws, practices, requirements, and nomenclature. Things vary from state to state, city-to-city, and even between areas within a city.

Agency

Although agency is part of law, it is mentioned separately here because it is so important. Commercial real estate brokers are agents, which brings certain responsibilities. You need to thoroughly understand the nature of agency and your duties. You should know the types of agencies and your obligations as an agent. It is important to always remember that you have a fiduciary relationship to the client. This is not just a legal requirement, but also a practical one. Keeping your client's highest and best interests in mind at all times engenders trust and repeat business.

Some of the duties of an agent to his or her principal are listed below.

- Agents must be loyal to their principals because they have been given a position of trust and confidence. Specifically, an agent may not do the following:

> » The agent cannot make a secret profit.
>
> » The agent cannot purchase property without making a disclosure.
>
> » The agent cannot purchase property through a middle-man (or "straw" man).

- An agent must account for all funds.

- An agent must not misrepresent facts.

- An agent must not represent both parties to a transaction.

- An agent must not be negligent.

- An agent must obey the instructions of the principal.

- An agent must obey the law.

Law

Much of real estate law is universal. It applies to most of the real estate industry. Commercial real estate, however, requires familiarity with a large body of specialized law and knowledge. Much of this law derives from the special needs of businesses and investors. Those that deal in commercial real estate are often concerned with matters like taxation, form of ownership, leasing, and liability. They tend to be more sophisticated individuals who are aware of many of the legal issues that may affect their dealings. Most will have an attorney who represents them. You do not need to be an attorney, but you need to know enough to be able to deal with attorneys, understand the issues, and be able to spot potential problems. Most important, you need to know what you do not know — that is, you need to know what not to attempt to handle yourself and when to get help.

A complete discussion of commercial real estate law is well beyond the scope of this book. However, for purposes of illustration, the following are examples and comments on some areas of law that affect commercial real estate in particular.

- Form of ownership. The form of ownership refers to the entity that holds the property, such as a corporation, limited liability company (LLC), partnership, or tenancy in common, to name a few. Taxation and liability issues drive many decisions around form of ownership.

- Title. The quality of title and title insurance are important. How good is the title and are there any defects to the title, like encroachments, liens, easements, or covenants, conditions, and restrictions that may prevent buyers from doing what they want? Standard title policies cover matters of the public record, forgery, contractual ability, and lack of authority. They do not cover many other risks such as unrecorded documents, rights of a person in possession other than the owner, water rights, location of improvements, acreage count, or the unlawful use of the property. Extended title insurance and ALTA title policies are sometimes issued, which require surveys. It is important to read any exception documents listed in a preliminary title report to see if there are any serious defects to the property's title.

- Leasing issues. What are the rights and limitations that affect the use of someone else's property?

- Taxation. Generally, issues here boil down to the question of how the taxes can be reduced.

- Liability. This is one of the driving issues in many areas of commercial real estate law. Everyone wants to limit his or her liability. This desire lurks behind many of the decisions that are made.

- Property description. Surveys, which can sometimes be quite complex, are often required.

- Financing issues. The form of debt may be contract, trust deed, or mortgage, with each affording different remedies.

- Agency. The obligations of agency, misrepresentation, and co-mingling of funds.

- Land use issues. Zoning and land use planning issues are often involved and can be political. In addition, issues like subdivision, partitioning, and development may also come into play.

- Contracts. This boils down to the need to produce unambiguous written documents that both parties accept, that meet the requirements of the law, and that address all the issues. Contracts include land sale contracts, leases, mortgages, trust deeds, and so forth, as well as estoppel certificates from tenants.

- Fixtures. What stays and goes when property changes hands.

- Deeds. The different types of deeds and the quality of the warranties.

- Leasing. Lease issues include subleasing and assignment.

- Recording and constructive notice.

- Closing and escrow issues. The fundamentals of closing, closing statements, and escrow.

- Insurance issues and their legal implications.

- Condemnation. Issues regarding immanent domain, and especially condemnation, in leases.

- Foreclosure and bankruptcy.

- Local and state building code laws. This is often a factor in tenant improvements.

- Regulatory issues. These include such things as asbestos disclosures and construction lien disclosures, regulations and laws imposing environmental liability, water well laws, and smoke detector requirements.

In addition, the law often requires special disclosures or warnings in documents such as Foreign Investments Real Property Tax Act (FIRPTA), zoning, fire, flood plain or environmental disclosures, or nondiscrimination provisions. Most of the preprinted forms have these clauses.

Development

Development is a broad term that, in commercial real estate, refers to the process of creating something new or developing something. Development includes things such as subdivisions, construction of new buildings, partitioning, assembly of property, or redevelopment of old buildings. Subdivisions typically involve the construction of infrastructure, such as streets and utilities, and the division of raw land into parcels for resale to end users. New building construction might include shopping centers, industrial parks, office buildings, and apartments or condominiums, to name a few. These could be multi-tenant or single-tenant buildings. New building development, in particular, might be on a speculative basis or might be a build to suit. A build to suit is just that — a developer builds a building to the exact specifications of a principal for either sale or lease. Multi-tenant buildings and parks often will have an anchor tenant. An anchor tenant is usually a large company that is the core of the development. Anchor tenants help in the marketing by taking in advance a large area. They also help in the project's feasibility (including getting financing) and, in retail, act as a magnet for customers. Partitioning involves the division of already platted and sometimes already improved property. A developer may, for example, buy a complex of buildings, divide it up, and sell them off individually. Assembly is when a developer pieces together a number of parcels for development, such as a downtown block for construction of an office building. Redevelopment involves the redevelopment and refurbishing of existing buildings. This commonly happens when there is a change of the property's highest and best use to a higher use. An example would be an older multi-level industrial building being converted to offices.

Development is highly susceptible to market forces. Supply and demand, financing, and construction costs play a critical role in the development process. Demand is the driving force for development, but the availability of product and the cost of construction play critical roles. Land use and code requirements have much to do with the supply. For these reasons, development often experiences cycles of boom and bust. There is a boom in the market due to prospects demanding product so developers rush out to develop it, which causes an oversupply, which causes less demand and a bust. Consequently, developers give considerable thought to timing. When is the best time to start a development so that the demand is high when the product becomes available?

Financing is also a big factor in development. The cost and availability of money for projects is often the determining factor in developers' plans. For this and other reasons (such as a lender's resistance to financing unimproved land), creative financing is common in development. Examples are contract purchases with lot release provisions or subordination when subdividing land. Lot release provisions are when the original seller of the land agrees to deed over a lot to the developer for resale to the end user. The original seller will want to insure that the value of the deeded lot is such that more than enough equity is left in the remaining parcels to secure the remaining indebtedness. Subordination is when the original seller subordinates, or takes a second position, to other financing the developer may obtain. This can be risky for the original owner because if the development fails, he or she may end up taking back a poorly conceived development along with the debt. If the owner decides not to take it, he or she loses the property. One solution to this problem is for the original seller to retain control over what the developer builds and the financing in order to provide the assurance that if the seller has to take back the property, at least he or she will be repossessing a viable development.

A typical development project would begin with a market analysis, pro forma, and meeting with the local governmental body. A pro forma is simply a future financial analysis of the development's feasibility. It considers the cost of the project, the income, and profit. A pro forma considers things such as who the prospects are, the demand for the project, trends, the time needed to market the project, tax consequences, the price that can be obtained, as well as the costs of the development, including construction and financing costs. Thus, the accuracy of the pro forma is the key to the success of any development project. Subsequent steps in a typical development project include finding and acquiring the property, obtaining financing, construction, and marketing. When purchasing a property, a developer will usually have contingencies for zoning, code and land use, environmental, engineering and design (including topographic, soils, and drainage). surveys, title, utility availability (including technology utilities), construction costs, and feasibility to name a few. Sometimes these are all lumped under one contingency called a feasibility study. One problem with sales to developers is that the transaction often requires a long period of time — perhaps six months or longer — to conduct these studies, during which time the owner's property is off the market. (Some suggestions for handling a situation like this are described in other areas of this book.) Once the property is acquired and governmental permits obtained, construction can begin along with the marketing. If the developer plans to keep the development, property management also becomes a consideration.

Developers are an interesting lot. They range from large national concerns like Trammell Crow to local one-man shops. Individuals, partnerships, corporations, or REITs (Real Estate Investment Trusts) can all be developers. Developers tend to be protean, creative, and risk taking by nature. They may build on a speculative basis, build to suit, or build for an anchor. They may build and then sell or lease to someone else or plan to retain ownership of the project themselves. Either way, they are truly investors because they do not use the property themselves. Occasionally, if there is a quick profit to be made, they can become out and out dealers or speculators by, for example, purchasing property for immediate resale (or double escrowing) or acquiring an option on a parcel in a rising market for future resale. Whatever the case, developers can be some of your best prospects and clients. A career can be built on a good relationship with one active developer. Developers need help in evaluating the market and properties, finding opportunities, locating suitable property, and marketing the product. In addition, you, as a broker, will often encounter situations where a prospect or a property lends itself to the services of a developer. As a versatile and successful broker, you want to be able to quickly bring one in when needed.

Title

The term "title" refers not only to the legal aspects of real property, but also to title insurance companies, title insurance policies, escrow, and the closing of transactions. The condition of title has already been discussed briefly in this chapter. Title issues in commercial real estate are often complex. Some of the issues that occur frequently that you should become familiar with include the following:

- The form of deed. There are four deed forms that are generally used in real estate transactions: warranty, special warranty, bargain and sale, and quit claim deeds. Principals in transactions may disagree on the form of deed to be used. Buyers, under the advice of their attorneys, want warranty deeds. Sellers prefer to limit their liability by giving only bargain and sale deeds. Since transfers using either deed form are insurable, an insured buyer can first turn to the title insurance policy for protection.

- Covenants, conditions, and restrictions (CC&Rs). The preliminary title report will disclose if the property is subject to CC&Rs placed by the previous owners. The buyer will then determine if they adversely affect the proposed use of the property.

- Mortgages, trust deeds, and lines of credit. These documents are recorded to put prospective purchasers and lenders on notice that the property is encumbered to secure an existing obligation. This is particularly important to investors who sometimes sell and resell commercial properties using creative financing methods, such as wrap-around mortgages.

- Easements and encroachments. Easements are common in real estate titles. The easement holder has a limited right to use the property of another. Easements can be for access and utilities, for example. Encroachments of an improvement onto the land or easement right of another may be disclosed by a survey. In some cases, the encroachment can be insured over by the title company instead of requiring removal of the encroaching improvement or adjustment of property lines.

- Leasehold interests. Recorded leases or memorandums are often disclosed in a preliminary title report. Generally, these must be removed or subordinated prior to closing a sale or loan on the property. Accomplishing this may be complicated if the lessee company is no longer in existence.

- Adverse possession and prescriptive easements. If a person uses the property of another without permission and satisfies certain necessary requirements, that person may be able to have a court decree that person to be the owner of the property or decree that the person has an easement across the property. Interests in the title or easements by prescription, only show on the preliminary title report and policy if they have been made a matter of the public record.

- Bankruptcy. Although most aspects of real property are a matter of state law, bankruptcy is in the jurisdiction of the federal courts. If the owner of real property petitions the bankruptcy court for protection from creditors, a prospective purchaser will need to work with the bankruptcy trustee and/or the judge in the bankruptcy court. Landlords face special problems when their tenants file a petition for bankruptcy. These include lost rent, the ability to re-let the premises, eviction, and FEDs (forced entry and detainer).

It is important in commercial real estate transactions to use the services of quality title and escrow companies. The company should have a strong financial position to enable it to pay any claim that may be tendered by the insured owner or lender. There are many very good title insurance companies. Reputable companies that have a track record in commercial transactions are the best to deal with. Their commercial divisions will usually be staffed with several experienced, professional title officers and commercial escrow closers. They should have the ability to handle multi-state transactions and tax-deferred exchanges.

It is a good idea to develop a good working relationship with commercial escrow closers and their support staff, escrow assistants, title officers, and customer service representatives. An experienced, efficient, knowledgeable, and business-like commercial escrow closer, who is oriented towards problem solving and getting transactions closed to all principals' satisfaction, is extremely valuable. These types of escrow agents tend to be in demand and busy. If they know that you recommend them and repeatedly bring them business, they will usually take special care of your closings. Also, buyers will often ask for the name of a good title company and commercial escrow closer, and you should have one ready.

In addition to title insurance and escrow closings, title companies are sources of property information. This information may include tax information, "trios" (copies of the taxes, last deed, and assessors plat), or matters of public record that affect the property.

Title insurance companies issue both standard and extended coverage policies insuring new owners, lenders, lessees, and in some cases, sellers. Standard coverage insures against what interests show as a matter of public record. Extended coverage goes beyond the public record to insure, for example, what an accurate survey would disclose or that there are no unrecorded easements on the property. Sellers generally pay the premium for a standard coverage policy insuring the buyer as the new owner. The buyer often pays to upgrade that policy to an extended coverage policy and also pays the premium for the loan policy insuring the lender who financed the acquisition. In most states, insurance companies issue ALTA (American Land Title Insurance) forms of policies for both the standard and extended coverage.

Escrow and closing are closely related to title because title insurance companies usually handle them. Escrow agents are licensed and bonded and, by definition, are to remain neutral third parties. Escrow is where the parties to a transaction deposit the funds and documents, along with written instructions to a third party (the escrow agent). This is done for a fee. The instructions will specify how the documents and funds are to be delivered. Escrow is analogous to the neutral individual to a bet, who holds the bettor's funds with instructions from the bettors to deliver them to the winner of the wager. Closing refers to the process of closing a sales transaction, usually by an escrow agent. In a closing, the escrow agent will do things like prepare escrow instructions, obtain title insurance, prorate items such as rent and taxes, obtain the funds from the buyer, pay any costs authorized by the parties, record documents, and disburse funds. A closing statement is the final accounting of all funds. It will show what money came in and where it went, for both the buyer and seller.

You should be aware of one potential problem with escrow agents concerning monetary deposits in sales. Sometimes a sales agreement will provide that the buyer will forfeit some, or all, of the deposit under certain circumstances. One example would be when the buyer agrees to forfeit part of the deposit in exchange for extending a contingency period, and if he or she does not close the transaction. Because escrow agents follow instructions regarding the disbursement of funds and because they are concerned about adhering to the legal requirements of escrow and liability, they may not give the seller the forfeited money if they cannot obtain the buyer's approval. Therefore, if there is a dispute between the principals, the seller may have to go to court to get the forfeited money. This is less of a problem if the real estate agent held the deposit and is generally no problem if it was paid directly to the seller.

Some commercial brokers have been known to handle the escrow and closing themselves. This is not recommended. It can be an involved and complicated process in commercial real estate, especially with trades. Some special issues that surround closing and escrow include the following:

- Special taxes like real estate transfer and excise taxes and who pays.

- Determining the amount and charging the appropriate party for escrow fees, recording charges, and title premiums.

- Paying off lien holders and acquiring the correct release documents.

- Determining and paying off any deferred taxes such as for farm deferral, forest land, or historic properties.

- Determining and prorating any special assessments such as water, sewer, and drainage.

- Prorating rent and advance deposits between the buyer and seller.

- Acquiring requisite estoppel certificates from the tenants.

- Establishing instructions for holding funds.

- Working closely with tax deferred exchange accommodators.

Appraisal

The appraisal of commercial real estate can be complex and involved. Appraisers spend considerable time learning the principles and methods of appraising in order to accurately and fairly establish value for a property. There are a variety of designations for appraisers, most notably MAI (Member Appraisal Institute) and ASA (American Society of Appraisers). Appraisals, which are supportable opinions of value for a certain property as of a specific date, are done for a variety of reasons. They are used for sale purposes, financing, trading, establishing equity value, insurance, estates, leasehold interests, condemnation, and taxation, to name a few. There are many kinds of values a property can be appraised for — for example, depreciated value, insurance value, present value, and market value. Commercial real estate brokers usually deal with appraisals that establish the market value of property. The market value is the amount a buyer will pay and a seller will accept (assuming both are ready, willing, and able; know the highest and best use; and are not acting under duress) as of a specific date. In laymen's terms, this is the highest price you can sell a commercial property for to a knowledgeable buyer, at any one time. Appraisals are usually made in compliance with USPAP (Uniform Standards of Professional Appraisal Practice). There are two types of appraisal assignments — complete and limited. A limited appraisal has fewer restrictions and may be similar to a broker's opinion of value.

The term highest and best use is important because different buyers have different ideas of what the same property may be worth. As a broker selling property, in order to get the highest price, you want to sell to the buyer who can put the property to the most profitable and likely use to which it could be devoted.

Commercial brokers will often provide opinions of value for the purpose of listing a property. These are not appraisals, but rather are the opinions of informed brokers, usually done for listing purposes. These opinions should use the approaches to value described below, but follow a format that establishes a range of value. (This concept is also discussed in Chapter 8 in the section titled "Range of Value.") Brokers should not do appraisals unless they are trained and licensed to do so. In some places it is illegal. It is best to leave the business of appraisal to the appraisers.

At the heart of appraisal and something that all commercial brokers should understand are the three methods appraisers use to arrive at a value — the sales comparison approach (or market data approach), the income approach, and the cost approach. A very brief summary of each of the three methods follows; however, keep in mind that each approach involves sophisticated methods, theories, and procedures — a complete discussion and description is beyond the scope of this book.

The sales comparison approach compares the subject property to other properties that have been sold. It involves locating comparable sales and rents, determining the circumstances surrounding the sale, comparing them with the subject property, and correlating these facts to arrive at a valuation. The income approach involves locating comparable rents and establishing a fair market rental for the subject and then reducing this rent by the subject property's expenses (which includes such things as taxes, insurance, maintenance as well as deductions for credit, vacancy, and management) in order to arrive at a net operating income (NOI). This net operating income is then capitalized with a market capitalization rate to establish a property's value. The cost approach first establishes the subject's cost, less the property's depreciation, and then adds the land value to achieve its market value.

Generally speaking, in commercial real estate, the sales comparison approach is probably the most reliable; however, it is only as good as the comparables it uses. The income approach is most useful when valuing income property and often arrives at a value less than the sales comparison approach. (The income approach is discussed in more detail later in this chapter under "Investment Analysis.") The cost approach is the least reliable and least frequently used method because of the difficulty in estimating deprecation for used properties. The cost approach is most useful with new property.

There are some additional terms, principles, and concepts related to appraisal that commercial brokers should understand and be familiar with. You will most likely encounter all of them at one time or another.

Terms

Depreciation	A charge against the reproduction cost of an asset for wear and obsolescence. Only improvements to land depreciate, never the land itself.
Goodwill	An intangible asset of businesses created by customer relations.
Utility	The ability of a property to fill a need.
Demand	The presence of a need as well as the monetary power to fill that need
Scarcity	The availability of product, which is influenced by supply, demand, and the alternate uses to which the product may be put.
Transferability	The ability to possess and control.
Obsolescence	The loss of value due to obsolete design or construction not in keeping with modern needs.
Cost	Generally, cost refers to the price to acquire something; however, there are various types of cost such as reproduction cost or replacement cost. Cost is not necessarily the value of an asset.
Economic Life	The remaining period in which real estate improvements generate more income than expenses.
Equity	The value an owner has in real estate over and above the liens against it.
Price, Cost, and Value	These are not necessarily the same thing. Price is the amount of money exchanged for something. Cost could refer to the price, or it could refer to a separate monetary value such as the replacement cost, while value is an opinion or estimate of worth.

Net and Gross Income	Net income is the amount remaining after all expenses have been met. (In appraisal, it also means the net operating income, which is discussed later in this chapter in the section titled, "Investment Analysis"). Gross income is the income from property before any expenses are deducted.
Net Return	A somewhat ambiguous term generally meaning the return to the investor.
Liquidity	The ease of converting assets to cash.

Principles and Concepts

Intrinsic Value	The inherent value of tangible property like silver or gold as opposed to intangible value, which is value that cannot be seen or touched.
Book Value	Generally, the amount of an asset as shown on a company's books. Book value may or may not be market value.
Contribution	When an investment is warranted because it adds enough income to cover the additional cost.
Physical, Functional, and Economic Depreciation	Physical depreciation is the loss of value due to age and the action of the elements. Functional depreciation is the loss of value due to causes within the property (like a poor floor plan) and is not due to physical deterioration. Economic depreciation is the loss of value from all causes outside the property such as lack of demand.
Regression	A mathematical technique used for economic models.

Risk and Return	Risk is the uncertainty or variability of a return. Return is the return on equity, which can be measured in different ways.
Substitution	The principle that market value is indicated by the value of another property with similar utility.
Value in Use	The worth of a property in a certain use, usually as it is currently being used. When marketing a property, a broker wants to find a prospect who sees the greatest value in use for the listing in order to get the highest price or rental.

Leasehold Interest

Leasehold interest is one particularly important concept that comes up often in commercial real estate leasing and valuation. A leasehold interest is the value of a lessee's interest in a property — in other words, the capitalized value of the difference between the contract lease rate and the market lease rate. For example, if the contract lease rate (what the lessee is paying) on a 10,000 sq. ft. warehouse is 20¢ per sq. ft. per month, triple net, and the market rate for the same warehouse is 30¢, then the lessee's leasehold interest is $120,000 with a 10% capitalization rate:

30¢ per sq. ft.- 20¢ per sq. ft. = 10¢

10¢ per sq. ft. X 10,000 sq. ft. = $1,000 (per month)

$1,000 X 12 months = $12,000

$12,000 ÷ .10 (capitalization rate of 10%) = $120,000

Thus, the owner's value is reduced by $120,000. If someone wanted to buy the tenant out, it would most likely cost $120,000. The above example is highly simplified because there are many factors that affect leasehold interests, such as the length of lease. Obviously, if the lease had only six months left, nobody would pay the full amount. Instead they would simply wait until the lease expired. Conversely, if the lease was for another eight years and they needed the property immediately, they might pay more. Leasehold interests come up often when leased investment property is sold and in condemnations

Some Final Comments on Appraisers and Appraisals

It's important for commercial real estate brokers to select and work with experienced appraisers who show a good bit of common sense. Some appraisers get so carried away with their theories that they lose touch with reality. Unrealistic appraisals can make it impossible to sell or finance properties. In some cases, a knowledgeable broker may be in a better position to establish the value of a property because he or she knows the market and trends. Appraisals are based on historic comparable data, which can lead to dated values. A prospect, for example, is more likely to make a deal on a lesser-priced comparable property that just came on the market, than one whose value was established by high historic comparables. Prospects typically will not pay more for something if they can get the same thing elsewhere for less. Conversely, many new prospects to the market may bid up the price of an existing listing. Much of value depends on supply and demand, which historic data has difficulty in anticipating. Also, appraisals are often only as good as their comparables, so if there are few good comparables available, the property's true value may only be known after it is put on the market. Brokers are fortunate in that they do not have to establish one value as of a specific date, like appraisers. Instead, they can recommend a range of value, and then see what the market says.

Appraisers are valuable sources of information who can help establish your reputation. In addition, appraisers often provide referrals to commercial brokers. For these reasons, it is a good idea to establish a working relationship with one or two of them. You also will occasionally be asked to recommend an appraiser, so you should have the names of a few good ones readily available.

Mathematics

Mathematics seems to be one of the areas of commercial real estate that scares people away. There really is no need for fear because most of the mathematical concepts used are simple and straightforward ones that deal with things like percentages rather than the more esoteric theories like calculus and algebra. In addition, as discussed in the following section, there are many tools available specifically designed for commercial real estate professionals that will help you come up with the proper calculation necessary for each occasion.

The following is a list of mathematically related concepts that are commonly used in commercial real estate. Most of these are discussed in more detail at other points in the book.

- Interest — Used when calculating things like financing, amortization, and tenant improvements. Brokers will need to understand the difference between simple and compound interest.

- Capitalization —Used primarily in appraisal to establish value via the income approach.

- Amortization — Used mostly when determining the repayment of debt when purchasing property or making tenant improvements.

- Area — Can include a linear, square, or cubic measurement. A general understanding of the methods of calculating size, as well as the units of measurement such as meters, yards, or feet, is important. It's a good idea to have a measuring tape and/or an electronic measuring device always available.

- Proration — Used in many areas including taxation, insurance, rent, interest charges, and closing. Closing statements will prorate items such as rent, taxes, insurance premiums, and utility bills between the buyer and seller.

- Commissions — Uusually a percentage of the sales price or aggregate rental. (Obviously, figuring your commission will be one of the most important mathematical applications you use.)

- Discount — Can refer to a lender's charge in a loan or can be used to reduce values for various reasons. Appraising and investment analysis commonly use the later primarily to offset the effects of inflation.

- Depreciation — Involves determining the decrease in the value of an asset due to deterioration or obsolescence. Depreciation is essentially used for tax purposes, although it is often used in appraisal in the cost approach to value.

- Taxation — Tax rate, tax ratio, millage rate, transfer tax, and sometimes the documentary stamp tax are commonly encountered in commercial real estate.

Calculators

There are many financial calculators used by commercial real estate professionals; however, one of the one most commonly used is the HP-12C (Hewlett Packard). This calculator is especially suited to solve problems and figure calculations related to specific commercial real estate situations. It is a good idea to have a financial calculator handy whenever you are talking to prospects or the public because it allows you to provide quick answers to a multitude of questions. It is important to know how to use this powerful calculator. You may never use some of the functions on your financial calculator, such as calculating the internal rate of return, but you should understand the concept and, preferably, know how to do it.

The following are some of the more important features you should consider when making a decision about a financial calculator.

- Addition, subtraction, multiplication, division, percentage calculations, and the storage of information. Their importance to commercial real estate is obvious.

- Calendar functions and the ability to figure future dates and the number of days between dates. This becomes important for many reasons, including prorating.

- Simple and compound interest calculations. These are mostly used for calculating repayment of debt or calculating future values.

- Present value calculations. Used often in investment real estate for a number of reasons, such as determining the purchase price.

- Amortization and balloon payment calculations. These functions are important for determining monthly payments and prepayment obligations.

- Investment and discounted cash flow calculations. You need to understand the calculator's cash flow methodology and how to determine net present value (NPV), internal rate of return (IRR), and yields. Additional investment programs can incorporate such things as depreciation, cash flow, and leasing analysis.

- Various lending calculations. These provide a way to incorporate things such as the lender's fee into calculations involving financing.

Other calculators include entry level ones, such as Texas Instrument's BA II Plus. These will compute the basic calculations required in commercial real estate such as the time value of money, mortgage loans, amortization, cash flow calculations, internal rate of return, and percent change. Of course, more advanced ones are also available, such as the HP-19B-11, which has more features, including property management equations, and is faster than the HP-12C.

Taxation

Taxation is probably one of the most cryptic and confusing areas in commercial real estate. If you want to be afraid of anything, taxation is a good choice. There are different taxes with different requirements from different governmental agencies that are constantly changing. Taxes are often the driving factor behind investors' motivations and the real estate decisions of businesses. For example, for many businesses, the decision of where to locate or relocate will often hinge on the local tax structure. Obviously, most people's objective is to avoid, defer, or reduce their taxes.

You do not need be an accountant, but you do need to familiarize yourself with the basic issues surrounding taxation. Two important areas to understand are taxes on property and taxes on persons. (In this book, taxes on businesses are included under personal taxes for purposes of simplicity). In addition to personal taxes, like the federal income tax, most of the taxes that deal with commercial real estate involve investments and businesses.

Property

Methods of taxing real property vary considerably. You should understand how your local government taxes property. You need to know how property is assessed, the tax rates, the tax year, how it is paid, and the requirements for appeal. Some areas base the taxes on the property's fair market value and others on an assessed value that is not fair market value. Some may include other things in the value unrelated to the property itself such as machinery and equipment. You should be familiar with exemptions and special tax deferral programs such as those related to historic properties. Keep in mind that there are some professionals (some appraisers and attorneys, for example) who specialize in appealing property tax and valuations.

Personal

Personal taxation is where things get complex. You should be familiar with important tax matters like personal and corporate income taxes, long- and short-term capital gain taxes, the purpose of and types of depreciation, treatment of installment sales and interest, the rules of exchange, and basis. You should also at least be aware of any special taxes your area may levy, such as an inventory tax. It is impossible to know everything about taxes, so this section will focus on three of the most important concepts related to personal taxes that affect commercial real estate. They are depreciation, basis, and capital gain.

Depreciation

Depreciation is a tax concept that says that some day the improvements to a piece of property will be worthless.

Consequently, the tax man allows some owners of property to take a deduction off their income to account for this phenomenon. (In taxes, a deduction reduces the taxpayer's income, while a credit reduces the tax itself.) The effect is to reduce the taxpayers' income and consequently their taxes. Prior to May of 1993, depreciation was the darling of commercial real estate investment because investors used to be able to not only accelerate the rate of depreciation, but also shelter other income. Because of this, depreciation was often the motivating factor for investors to purchase real estate. Depreciation methods included straight line and accelerated methods of 125%, 150%, 200% declining balance and the sum of the years digits method. (In short, straight line depreciation is when the amount depreciated remains constant over a set number of years, while the other methods allow you to take a greater depreciation early on.) The Tax Reform Act of 1986 changed all that. To make a long story short, starting in May of 1993, depreciation for nonresidential property held for trade or business must be taken on a straight-line basis over 39 years. Also, the ability to offset other income has been severely curtailed.

Basis

The basis of a property is generally what you paid for it with some adjustments. The basis is reduced by depreciation and real estate fees and increased by improvements to the property. The difference between a property's basis and the selling price, in general, is the gain. The higher the gain, the higher the tax, and vice versa. Consequently, those with a low basis are reluctant to sell property because they do not want to pay the high tax. People and businesses that have owned property for a long time usually have a low basis in their property. These are often the best candidates for exchanging property so they may defer any tax. Such exchanges are commonly called 1031 exchanges after a section of the federal tax code. These can be very involved and require expert help. Often the main problem in these exchanges is the problem of finding suitable property to exchange into. Keep in mind that the exchange does not reduce or eliminate taxes — it only defers them. You should also be aware of the role of accommodators for delayed or reverse exchanges.

Capital Gain

Everyone wants to convert income from ordinary income to capital gain because the tax rates are lower. Capital gains taxes apply to the gain one makes on the sale of an asset. Capital gain is important because it will often be the determining factor whether people sell property or not. The current federal capital gains tax for commercial property held for trade or business (which began in August of 1997) for example, depends on the taxpayer's tax bracket and the type of depreciation. Property must be held for 18 months to qualify for capital gain treatment. For properties with no depreciation, as in the case of raw land, all of the gain is taxed at the lower capital gain rate of 10%, if the taxpayer is in the 15% bracket, and 20% if the taxpayer is in the 28% bracket. For depreciable properties, as in the case of improved properties, any portion that is not excess depreciation (in other words, straight line depreciation) is taxed at 25%. Any accelerated depreciation (in other words, the amount over straight line depreciation) is taxed at ordinary tax rates of 15% or 28%. In general, straight-line depreciation is taxed at 25% and accelerated depreciation at ordinary rates. This is both good and bad for investors. It is worse because without the 25% provision, the straight line depreciation under the 1997 law would have been taxed at 10% if the taxpayer was in the 15% bracket. It is better for investors because, previously, depreciation was taxed at 28% if the taxpayer was in the 28% bracket. It is now 25%.

Zoning and Land Use

Zoning and land use issues primarily affect use, design, and development. Although they vary tremendously from area to area, zones are commonly specific to each area of commercial real estate. Jurisdictions will commonly have zones for office, including downtown and suburban, retail, industrial, and multi-family residential. There are many variations of these zones, such as mixed use zones, densities within zones, design, zones for open areas, parks, and overlay zones for such things as historic districts, buffering, height limits near airports, and noise restrictions. Zoning may also involve comprehensive plans and growth boundary lines. Some jurisdictions often have, in addition, district or specific plans that contain regulations unique to that area. The process usually requires fees and sometimes very expensive studies, such as transportation analysis. Much of zoning is not only to arrange land use in an orderly manner, but also to preserve some areas for specific uses, which is often difficult. Other zoning distinctions are intended to ensure that new development does not exceed the capacity of available public services such as roads, sewers, and water.

Zoning dictates not only what the property can be used for, but also what can be built and how an owner can modify buildings and property. Some existing uses may be nonconforming to newer zoning regulations, which will limit the owner's ability to remodel and sometimes may even limit the ability to sell or lease the property for its current use. Uses that exist in zones that no longer allow them are often "grandfathered." When grandfathered, owners will often find that their ability to alter the property is limited. Owners and tenants will sometimes apply for variances from the zoning code in order to do what they want to the property.

Because zoning and land use laws affect commercial real estate in so many areas you need to be familiar with the specific regulations in your area. This is especially true when establishing the price or rental for a listing because you need to know whom you can market the property to. For example, if an industrial building is grandfathered in a residential zone that will not allow the continuation of the industrial use when the property is sold, the improvements probably have no value. The actual property value may be the value of the land, as residential, less the cost of demolishing the improvements.

Zoning can have a particularly significant impact on real estate value. Although it varies depending on many factors, generally speaking, office zones (in particular, downtown office zones) tend to be the highest priced. Next is retail and multi-family (depending on the density). Typically, the least expensive commercial property is that found in industrial zones. Given the difference in value, there is often pressure by investors, speculators, and owners of less intensively zoned property to "upzone" to a zoning category that permits a higher use. Obviously, if a one-acre industrial parcel is worth $5.00 per sq. ft. as industrial and $25.00 as multi-family, there is an $870,000 profit to be made if the zone can be changed. This issue becomes acute when there is a growth boundary line or other limitation. A 10,000 sq. ft. lot zoned retail worth $50 per sq. ft. abutting agricultural bare land outside a growth boundary line worth $1.00 per sq. ft. translates to a difference of $490,000.

Another example of the impact zoning regulations can have on value is in the floor area ratios (FAR) and height restrictions in areas zoned for office use. (Floor area ratios may be called by different names in different parts of the country.) Generally speaking, an FAR determines the maximum floor area in relation to the land area that can be built. The height restriction is simply how high the building can be. If the FAR is 4:1, then a building with a floor area four times larger than the land area could be built on the site. A 40,000 sq. ft. building could be built on a 10,000 sq. ft. lot. However, if the height restriction limited the building to three floors, than that would be a limiting factor, because then the building size could be no more than 30,000 sq. ft. (10,000 sq. ft. per floor). Typically, the FAR is more restrictive than the height restriction. The point is that the size of the building, which is partly determined by zoning regulations, along with such things as rent, will determine how much a buyer can pay for the land. This is highly simplified, however, because there may be other factors, such as restrictive parking or design requirements, which also affect what may be built.

Developers are especially concerned with land use and zoning issues. They want to know if they can develop property for certain uses, how much the infrastructure will cost, and what density they can build. Land use issues are especially critical to developers in platting and subdivisions because they determine how many lots can be created. In addition, developers redeveloping property and contractors, as well as owners, will also be affected by building codes. Building codes are not the same as land use and zoning codes. Building codes are standards the state imposes, typically for construction and remodeling. These include such things as building codes themselves, seismic issues, ADA (Americans with Disabilities Act), fire codes, and OSHA (Occupational Safety and Health). In some cases, with state approval, a local government may have a few building code provisions that are unique to the jurisdiction.

Building codes are also a significant factor in the sale and lease of property. An owner who plans to remodel a building and applies for a building permit may be surprised to find that he or she will have to spend considerable additional money bringing the property up to code. If the listing will require significant code improvements before the buyer can get an occupancy permit or if it significantly reduces the investor's return, then the price may have to be reduced.

Additional areas often encountered that are affected by land use are partitions and lot line adjustments. Some properties lend themselves to dividing up or partitioning, which may increase their value or make them easier to sell. There are usually more buyers for small parcels than large ones. Land use regulations will govern how a parcel may be divided, if at all. Sometimes, in order to sell off one piece of a property, or to change the configuration of a lot, a simple lot line adjustment is all that is needed. If allowed, a lot line adjustment is usually a simpler and quicker process than a partition.

Zoning and land use ordinances can be administered by numerous governmental bodies such as cities, counties, and states. They often involve planning departments and planning commissions. The often subjective and political nature of zoning can be a problem for owners, lessees, and those who work in commercial real estate. Decisions about use are often a consequence of the community's goals, neighbors' concerns, and the planners' expectations. Thus, transactions that involve rezoning or some other form of governmental land use approval can be time consuming, risky, expensive, and frustrating.

Commercial real estate is affected by a seemingly infinite number of land use and zoning regulations. Some of the important ones to look for and pay attention to are listed below.

- What use is allowed?

- Is the existing use nonconforming and, if so, is it grandfathered?

- Are there limits on what improvements may be made to the property?

- Are there any regulations that affect the use of the property such as landscaping, set-back, environmental, drainage, height restrictions, parking, and public easements, to name a few?

- What is the public access to the property? This is especially important in retail.

- Are there design criteria for new construction? These may be subjective and might require a discretionary hearing with its incumbent uncertainty.

- Are there any building moratoriums?

- What are the fees? (Especially development fees such as systems development charges.)

- Does the jurisdiction have an urban growth boundary? If so, where is it?

Environmental Issues

Environmental contamination and the liability associated with it has become one of the most significant issues in the sale or lease of commercial property. It affects all types of property including office, retail, land, investments, and especially industrial. The federal government has passed laws such as CERCLA (Comprehensive Environmental Response, Compensation, and Liability Act of 1980) with the intention of cleaning up contaminated property and assessing liability. Environmental laws, however, emanate from all levels of government including federal, state, and city as well as special purpose entities such as sanitary sewer districts. The primary federal agency is the EPA (Environmental Protection Agency); however, you will most often be dealing with state agencies. In the state of Oregon, for example, the primary agency is the Department of Environmental Quality. State agencies must, at a minimum, enforce federal laws, but are often free to create even tougher guidelines.

Environmental contaminants can include things such as petroleum products, PCBs, and asbestos. The sources for environmental contamination include transformers, USTs (Underground Storage Tanks), and insulation. Significant liability concerns come when there has been groundwater contamination generated from either an onsite or offsite source. Offsite sources of contamination may be adjacent properties or properties a considerable distance away.

Property contamination problems are significant deal killers. Buyers, lenders and, to a certain extent, lessees, do not want the liability associated with contaminated property. Lenders worry that they may end up foreclosing on a property that is contaminated and will, by default, end up with clean up liability. In some cases, clean up costs for foreclosed, contaminated property may exceed the property's value. Sellers fear contamination because, generally speaking, the liability runs with the chain of title, unless the blame can be clearly pinned on one party. Buyers, of course, just do not want to buy property that is contaminated because they do not want the liability or anything else that will hinder their ability to resell the property. Tenants do not want to be blamed for any contamination on property they lease. As a consequence, almost all sales and some lease transactions involve some form of environmental investigation, if nothing has been done before. If contamination is found then it usually must be remedied before the deal can close. Usually the onus is on the owner to arrange and pay for the remediation and deliver the property free of contamination. There are many forms of remediation for soil and groundwater contamination. Contaminated soil can be removed or, depending on the situation, contained by encapsulation or capping. The determination of the lateral and vertical extent of groundwater contamination, as well as the follow-up monitoring and clean up, can be costly, time consuming, and stressful.

The environmental investigation process usually involves an environmental consultant and/or contractor and often an attorney. Environmental consultants come in all sizes, from large national firms to a guy with a backhoe. The most important thing is to be sure the consultant is qualified and that he or she appears on both the state's and lender's approved lists (if there are any). If the property has special environmental problems, sometimes an attorney who specializes in environmental law will be engaged. Most environmental investigations are broken down into two phases. The Phase One Environmental Site Assessment (ESA) usually involves a site inspection, historic research of the property, and review of regulatory and municipal records for the subject and adjacent properties. This phase is intended to determine if there is a possibility of contamination problems.

A Phase Two Environmental Site Assessment usually involves intrusive sampling to determine if the improvements, soil, or groundwater have actually been contaminated and if it warrants remediation. This report will also discuss how the property is to be remediated. If there is contamination that requires remediation, the final stages involve regulatory compliance and the actual clean up.

Practical Suggestions for Environmental Investigations

The list below includes a few suggestions to help recognize, avoid, and resolve some problems in the environmental evaluation and clean up process.

- Environmental consultants are usually reluctant to come out and say that a property is clean because they fear the liability if proven otherwise. They like to have conditions to reports specifying that the report is limited and that there could be contamination. This can be maddening because an otherwise clean property is left with a cloud over it that can turn off a buyer or lender. Try to pick consultants who do not speculate on what might be. Some are better than others in this respect.

- Often the cost of the Phase Two report is more than the Phase One report. This is because Phase Two reports are often open ended and tend to involve more work. An unscrupulous consultant doing the Phase One report may be influenced to say there could be environmental problems in hopes of getting the job to do the Phase Two report. To avoid this conflict of interest, you could specify that the Phase Two report will be done by another consultant.

- Do not hire a consultant who drives up in a car that costs more than you make in one year.

- Be wary of invoice padding as a result of "a review of the report" by another consultant or by some senior member of a large environmental consulting firm that charges astronomical rates.

- Be wary of charges for equipment, such as gas detectors or magnetometers, which most consultants routinely have.

- Some buyers and lenders will accept a private consultant's report that a property is clean and others may require some governmental certification that it is clean. Obtaining governmental confirmation that the property is clean can be a very expensive and time-consuming process. Try and get the buyer and lender to agree to accept the private consultant's opinion.

- Buyers sometimes use environmental issues to get a price reduction in the "after deal negotiations." It may be in the seller's interests to give it.

- It is a good idea to always have the seller handle all environmental issues. The property is theirs; they usually already have the liability; and they are going to have to clean it up before it will sell. They should control the process from beginning to end. They should do the reports and address any issues before putting the property on the market so the property's environmental status never becomes an issue with the buyer, lessee, or the government. If the buyer does the work, the seller loses control of the process and is helpless to influence the outcome.

- Avoid representing property owners who will not address their property's environmental issues. They are ostriches with their heads in the sand, and you will just waste your time.

Construction and Architecture

Commercial real estate brokers work with contractors and architects primarily on real estate deals involving new construction, property development, and tenant improvements. New construction includes all the areas of specialty — office, retail, industrial, and multifamily. Construction in development can include subdivisions, redevelopment, as well as modifications and improvements to structures. Tenant improvements tend to be specialized, depending on the use. Office design and construction may deal with layout, walls, carpets, painting, and specialized requirements like phone and computer lines. Retail projects may deal with storefronts, advertising signs, and lighting. Industrial projects can include electrical requirements, office build-out, dock or grade doors, and cranes. High-tech projects are a quasi-industrial/office area that has specialized tenant improvement requirements. Special computer lines, heavy duty power, high levels of lighting, and occasionally specialized requirements, like clean rooms, are some examples.

Architects deal primarily with design and contractors with construction, although there can be considerable overlap. Architects can oversee construction and some contractors can provide design services. The question is often asked whether an architect is necessary in the process. The answer is involved, but generally, if the project requires a city or county building permit, those permits will require drawings from architects or engineers, that detail the work to be done. Architects and interior designers are often used in space planning and designing tenant improvements. Some believe that architects increase the cost of a project. If the project is simple and straightforward and the contractor being used is experienced in that area and has a design team, then dealing directly with the contractor may be the way to go. Some think doing so will save the client money.

Commercial real estate brokers are often asked questions about construction and architecture. Which type of building to build, how much it will cost, how to get it done, and who to do it, are common questions. Brokers should have some familiarity with the costs of construction, the process, types of structures, methods of construction, and component names and materials. This is a complex subject in which too little knowledge can be dangerous. You should be sure to seek advice from a competent expert in the field.

A good broker should have fixed in their mind the general cost to build a structure in their area of specialty. They should be able to break down a project into its major components, such as off site costs, on site costs, the cost of the land, the cost of the site and building improvements, and soft costs. Improvements would include the cost of structures and any special improvements, such as offices in a warehouse. Soft costs include such things as brokers' fees, architectural and engineering costs, financing costs (including interest), permit fees, title costs, surveys and so forth.

The main reason for having a ballpark understanding of the cost of construction new is because, for valuation purposes, used property, in general, should not cost more than new construction. Why would anyone buy a used building when they could build just what they want new for less? For this reason, prices on existing properties must be considered in relation to the replacement cost of the structure. If the cost of a used property is close to the replacement cost, then the price may be too high, or the principal should consider building new, rather than buying used. You will not know the answers to these questions unless you have a working knowledge of the construction costs of a new building. There are cases where principals may be justified in paying close to, or more, than the replacement cost of a structure. One example is when a principal must have a certain location and nothing else is available.

Once a principal has located a site and made the decision to build, the first step in the process is to decide whether to approach a contractor directly and negotiate a contract, or hire an architect and/or engineer to design the project and then bid it competitively to the contractors. It is a good idea to pick a contractor and/or architect who has experience building what the principal wants. This can save a lot of time and money. Negotiating the contract, designing the project, and preparing the specifications are next. This is a critical step involving many considerations and decisions. The principal must consider what exactly their requirements are and how much they want to spend. Permitting and obtaining financing are next, although smart principals usually put feelers out early on in the process to determine the feasibility of financing the project. Permitting a project can be an arduous and time-consuming process, depending on the local government. Depending on project size, scope, location, and use, the permitting can take six weeks to one year. There are often fast-track permitting methods that can shorten the permitting time, sometimes to as little as a few weeks. Land use issues can further increase the time for permitting. If the project is controversial, the property's zone needs to be changed, or utilities extended, then permitting can sometimes take years. These kinds of problems are often found in new subdivisions of land. Financing typically involves two different loans — the construction loan, which pays the construction bills as the project is built, and the permanent, or "take-out" financing, when the project is completed. Some principals may use their main bank for financing, while others may solicit various lenders, often with the help of a mortgage broker.

The two main methods for the delivery of construction services are the negotiated contract and competitive bid. Negotiated contracts are when the client and contractor negotiate a contract for construction at cost plus a fee, and the general contractor bids out the project to subcontractors. This method saves time and is simpler. Competitive bidding is when the owner has the project designed in advance, and then bids it out to the general contractors. Usually, they then pick the least expensive bid.

There is a running debate over which method saves money. Negotiated contracts can establish a guaranteed price, but construction can be delayed until the drawings are complete and the bids received. The competitive bidding method is intended to get the lowest price by creating competition among the general contractors; however, many contractors will say that this method ultimately costs more because of any unforeseen contingencies or incomplete plans. In the end, if the project is straightforward and the contractors are not busy, then bidding may be the way to go. If the project is complicated or has some special features where the cost is difficult to determine, then negotiating may be the way to go. In general, the more complex the project, the better it is to go with a negotiated contract. "Open book" means that the contractor opens his books to the client so he or she can see exactly what everything costs.

The final step is construction, which can take anywhere from a few weeks for a simple tenant improvement to a year or longer. The time it takes to complete construction depends on many factors such as the style and complexity of the project, the weather, how busy the contractor and the subcontractors are, and the availability of materials. The completion time is an important consideration for many principals. They may have outgrown their existing facilities, have new business they want to capture, and need the new building right away. Other principals may need to time the completion date with the expiration of their lease.

Brokers should have some knowledge of the types of structures and methods of construction. Buildings may be concrete block, brick, precast or poured-in-place concrete, wood or steel frame, concrete or glass clad, to name a few. Concrete in warehouses or steel frame with siding in offices are common. It is helpful to have a general understanding of the relative merits of the different types of buildings. For example, in industrial real estate, metal frame and metal clad buildings may cost less than concrete, but they are often harder to finance, do not wear as well, and often have lower resale values. In construction, a warehouse may be built by the tilt wall method, a high-rise office building by steel frame erection and siding, and a retail shopping center with concrete block and mortar.

There are innumerable types of components and systems that go into commercial building construction. These could include the roof structure, HVAC system (heating, ventilating, and air-conditioning), electrical, plumbing and utilities (including telephone), security, and computer systems. Electrical could include different types of lighting such as incandescent, fluorescent, mercury, or sodium vapor. In offices, lighting may include specialty fixtures like parabolic lighting fixtures, and in retail neon. The number of different materials that go into construction is also endless — concrete, marble, steel, wood, plastic, paint, and so on. It helps, for example, to know the types of components and materials that pertain to your market specialty — for example, acoustical tile ceilings in offices, or types of neon signs in retail. Sprinkler systems are common to most improved buildings. In some specialties like industrial, older buildings may be wet (the water is always in the pipes), and in newer buildings, they may be dry (compressed air keeps the water out of the pipes). The list of specialty features and systems is also long and each area of specialty tends to have special requirements. You should familiarize yourself with the components and systems of your specialty area.

One last comment regarding contractors — they may become some of your best clients and best sources of business. Contractors will sometimes act as developers and require your services. They may subdivide land in order to get the construction business for new projects or develop property for their own account in order to keep their construction crews busy. These projects are often listed with brokers for leasing and sales. Make an effort to cultivate a good relationship with an active contractor in your area and help him or her get business.

Surveys

Surveys are fairly common in commercial real estate. Boundary surveys are used for a variety of reasons. Buyers and sellers often wish to establish a parcel's exact size or to establish the precise physical boundaries, especially when there is some question as to where a property line is located. ALTA/ACSM land title surveys are sometimes used to position an improvement or easement location on a site. Title insurance companies often will require surveys before issuing title insurance — especially for any insurance with extended coverage. Lenders will also sometimes require a survey before granting a loan. Title insurance companies and lenders are usually concerned with generating an exact legal description and knowing for certain what they are insuring or lending on, what the exact sizes are, and if there are any encroachments or other such problems. Subdivision or partition plat surveys are used when subdividing property into legal lots.

You should be familiar with the three basic types of legal descriptions commonly used in surveys. These are the metes and bounds; lot and block; and governmental survey. Metes and bounds is a description using a point of beginning to completely enclose a parcel with distances and bearings. These descriptions are smaller parcels described from larger unplatted parcels. The lot, block and parcel number method is for already platted property usually found within an incorporated jurisdiction. Subdivisions use lot and block numbers, and partition plats use parcel numbers. These are probably the most common for property descriptions in cities. The governmental survey is the original system of land division using townships and sections from which all other surveys are based.

You should also be familiar with the main terminology and methods of measuring land and buildings and the mathematics associated with establishing area and size. Commercial real estate is usually figured in feet, square feet, and sometimes cubic feet, and acres. You will be surprised how many people will ask you how many square feet there are in an acre (43,560 sq. ft.). You will sometimes even encounter measurements described in chains or rods. Sections, townships, and range lines are basic terminology for all surveys and descriptions. You should understand the concepts involved with their use.

Investment Analysis

Investment sales are a very big part of commercial real estate. All types and sizes of properties are sold as investments. Real estate investment product can include raw land or multi-tenant office buildings and deal sizes can range from $50,000 to $100,000,000. Depending on many factors such as the economy and investors' criteria, there usually is a strong demand for investment real estate and only a limited supply. There is almost always an investor ready to buy the right deal. Investors are ubiquitous. In commercial real estate, finding the investor is generally not the problem — finding the right deal is. This, of course, raises the question: What is the right deal? To answer this question, you first need to understand the fundamentals of real estate investing, including investment analysis, so you can talk with investors intelligently.

Different investors have different methods of investment analysis; however, most follow a standardized process. This process has many variations and permutations, but the basic analysis remains constant. In a nutshell, it involves establishing a property's gross rental income from which certain expenses are deducted to arrive at the magical figure called the net operating income (NOI). These deductions can include operating expenses such as taxes, insurance, maintenance, credit, vacancy loss, management fees, and so forth. The NOI is a before tax income stream similar to interest on a certificate of deposit and represents the income the investor will receive from the property. The NOI is then capitalized to arrive at a value, or purchase price, for the property. The capitalization rate can be seen simply as the reverse of interest. If a $10,000 investment is paying 10%, then the income is $1,000; so conversely, if the $1,000 income is capitalized at 10%, the investment is worth $10,000. Investors divide the NOI by this "cap" rate to arrive at the purchase price.

This, obviously, is highly simplified. There are innumerable factors and games that go into this analysis. What is to be considered income is one. Does income include just the current year's income or does it allow for future rent increases and expenses? Is it the below market contract rent or is it the market rent? Obviously, the higher the income is, the higher the purchase price will be. What deductions are allowed and the size of the deductions are common areas of dispute when figuring NOI. This is especially true of "soft" deductions like vacancy, credit, and management fees. The higher the deductions, the lower the NOI will be, and the lower the price. Furthermore, appraisers and investment analysis gurus have made a science out of determining capitalization rates. A higher cap rate will lower the purchase price, and, conversely, a lower cap rate will raise the price. In the broad scheme, the capitalization rate is supposed to anticipate risk. If the investment is risky (for example, a vacant building), then the investor wants a higher cap rate which means a lower price. If the investment is already leased to General Motors for ten years, it is a "no-brainer" deal, which means a low cap rate and a high price. There are many factors that affect cap rates such as comparable returns and the type of property. If no risk treasury bills are paying 7%, a riskier real estate investment will have to pay a much higher return to compete. The size of this spread varies based on things such as the prevailing rates for other investments, the supply of investment property, and buyer's demand, to name a few. As of this writing, the spread between treasury bills and investment real estate returns is anywhere between 200 to 500 basis points (a basis point is $1/100^{th}$ of a percent, so 200 basis points is 2%). If the property is single purpose and suitable for only a few types of tenants, the future income may be questionable and the return will be higher. Conversely, if it is multi-purpose and leasable to many different tenants, then the return will be lower. When the return becomes very high, the investor becomes a speculator.

Another important benchmark investors often use in evaluating property is the cash on cash return. This is simply the NOI, less the debt service, in relation to the equity. The equity is the value of the property less the indebtedness. If the NOI is $1,000 and the debt is $600, then the cash income is $400. If the equity is $10,000, then the cash on cash return is 4%. This measures the effect of financing, which is an important factor in investing. Generally speaking, the higher the debt, the higher the cash on cash return, and the lower the debt, the lower the cash on cash return. This will be affected by the terms of the financing such as interest rate and term of amortization. The higher the interest and the shorter the term, then the higher the monthly payments, which also means a lower cash flow and a lower cash on cash return). The lower the interest rate and the longer the term, the higher the cash income and the higher the cash on cash return.

Arranging the variables of down payment, interest rate, length of amortization period, or interest only and balloon payments, is creative financing.

More sophisticated investment analysis can involve spreadsheets, the internal rate of return (IRR), net present value (NPV) and financial management rate of return (FMRR). The method mentioned earlier, using the net operating income, measures only the first year of the investment. Spread sheets show the projected NOI of the property over time in relation to the purchase price. When the NOI is discounted, the result is a discounted rate of return called the internal rate of return or a discounted value of the property called the net present value. The purpose of these analytical methods is to evaluate your investment, in today's dollars, in light of other returns, risk, and inflation. These computations can be generated with the HP-12C (Hewlett Packard), a type of calculator discussed earlier in this chapter. One more analytical method, which was designed to overcome some of the deficiencies of the IRR (thus, confusing you even more), is the financial management rate of return (FMRR). This return is essentially the same as the IRR, except that it includes management of the cash flow, whether it be positive or negative, over time. Even more involved investment analysis can include the income a property generates after tax. This involves the tax savings to the investor when such things as interest and depreciation are accounted for. This is risky business because investor's tax situations and the tax code usually change.

Investment Risk

There are many criteria investors use to decide which property to purchase. These criteria can include level of risk, price, location, available terms, tax consequences, type of property, condition of the property, whether the property is leased, its leaseability in general, the market, and so forth. Of all the factors, the level of risk is often the driving concern, so you should be aware that certain types of property investments are more risky than others. The "Risk Comparison" chart gives one opinion of the relative risk of different types of properties. This is a very subjective list because there are innumerable factors that determine risk. A freestanding retail building, for example, in one geographic area may be less risky than a similar one in another. Additionally, the same industrial building leased to a national credit company for ten years will have less risk than an empty one. There are, however, some universal characteristics that influence the level of risk. These can include the level of demand for a particular type of property, the property's flexibility (such as its divisibility), and its all-purpose nature. Whatever the case, this chart is intended to give you a general idea of some of the possible relative risks of various types of properties.

Risk Comparison

LOWEST RISK	Small, well located apartment building
	Multi-tenant industrial building or park
	High-rise downtown multi-tenant office building
	Regional shopping center
MODERATE RISK	Large apartment complex
	Multi-tenant suburban office building
	Single tenant freestanding warehouse
	Local shopping center
	Motel
	Single tenant office building
RISKY	Big box retail building
	Single tenant commercial building
	High tech or flex buildings
	Manufacturing building
	Multi-story industrial building
HIGH RISK	Specialty buildings (lodges, restaurants, gas stations, churches, etc.)
	Raw land
	Free standing office in an industrial area

Sale and Leaseback

One form of investment deal you should be familiar with is the sale and leaseback. This is when the owner of property sells it to an investor and then leases it back. Owner/lessees motivations to do this are varied, but commonly it is because they can obtain a higher return on their assets in their own business or for tax reasons. If a company can make a 20% per year return in their business and their property is making a 10% per year return, they may be better off selling the property and leasing it back. Many large corporations have policies of leasing property only primarily for this reason. The sale and leaseback of property raises the distinction between real estate investment deals and financing deals. Some investors are willing to pay an inflated price for a property if the owner/lessee has quality credit and will lease it back for a long enough time at a high enough return. The owner gets more money for their property and the investor gets a long-term stream of guaranteed income and ends up owning a property, which has hopefully increased in value, at the end of the lease. These are financing deals and not investment deals because the price is not market. The danger in these leaseback deals is if the tenant defaults, the investor gets back a property worth less than what they paid.

Some additional terms and concepts commonly used in commercial investment real estate, which you should be familiar with, are listed below.

Estoppel Certificate	A document whereby a lender or lessor obtains certification from a borrower or lessee that the terms of a mortgage or lease are agreed to and correct.
Gross Rent Multiplier	The sales price divided by the rental income. If the sales price is $100,000 and the gross income is $10,000, then the GRM would be 10 ($100,000÷$10,000 =10).

Income and Expense Statement	A financial report that shows the amounts of revenue, expenses, and profit or loss.
Leverage	The use of borrowed funds to increase the purchasing power of an investment.
Pro-Forma	A financial statement showing what is expected to occur as opposed to the actual results. These are often used in investments and development projects.
REIT (Real Estate Investment Trust)	A real estate mutual fund that is allowed to avoid the corporate income tax.

Office Management

Office management is more important to those who plan to go into management or start their own company. However, even if you don't, you should be familiar with the operations of management because it will affect your chances of success in commercial real estate. Management's attitudes, policies, procedures, and level of support, all affect the environment in which you work and, ultimately, your company's ability to compete with other firms.

A company should have a policies and procedures manual that is the blueprint for its operations. It should be available to everyone, and you should make a point to read it. It should cover the policies and procedures for all operations of the firm. It should provide information on the commission splits between an agent and the company, between the company and other companies, and between brokers within the company. It should explain sales procedures, which is important when resolving disputes among brokers. It should discuss the management's policy on the rotation of prospects and transactions. It does not do a new agent any good if the office funnels all of the good leads to a few experienced brokers. It should provide information on company benefits, such as health insurance and vacations. It should explain whether you are an employee or an independent contractor, which is a very important distinction when it comes to taxes. Companies must withhold taxes and pay FICA taxes for employees. In addition, companies may direct the actions of their employees. With independent contractors, however, the company does not withhold taxes and does not have direct control of the independent contractor. Some companies prefer to name agents as an employee, pay the withholding, and control the agent's actions. Others prefer to save money and name you as an independent contractor.

Management is generally divided between office management and sales management. The goals of both are the same — namely to operate a viable business and make money — but their areas of responsibility differ. Office management runs the everyday operations of the company. They look after things such as the bills, support staff, hiring and firing, payroll, taxes, the client's trust account, insurance, and even the dress code. They often oversee the sales manager and sales as well. Sales management is important because it affects the individual agent the most. The sales manager will oversee all sales matters, such as establishing sales goals and objectives, meetings, advertising, and signs, as well as serving as the agent's immediate supervisor. Sales managers are interested in your production and usually have certain minimum production requirements in order to meet their desk costs. Desk cost is the expenses of the company divided by the number of salespeople. If you are not making the desk cost, then they are losing money on you.

The sales manager is an important person who often determines the success of the company and you. It is important to have an open, honest, experienced, imaginative, and "deal making" sales manager. He or she should support you with ideas and go with you on important calls, such as listing presentations. A sales manager should be available. He or she should be ethical and should believe in and enforce the Code of Ethics. In short, a sales manager should help you succeed.

Some of the things that make for good management include the following:

- Strong leadership. Commercial real estate firms are usually full of people with big egos, so it takes a strong leader to gain their respect and control them.

- Fiscal responsibility. You do not want to work for an insolvent company. You want to work for a company that invests in itself.

- Fairness. It is important that the salespeople know what management's position is, that it is fair, and that it is consistent. Agents should know they can always "get a fair shake" from management.

- An optimistic, forward-looking attitude. It is energizing to work in a "can do" atmosphere with confident and successful people. A management that has set goals and a positive direction is critical to establishing such an environment.

- Available and accessible. Management should be accessible and available (within reason) to talk with you when you need help.

There are some firms that offer the agent 100% of the commission, and all the agent pays is a fixed, monthly "desk fee." Variations of this program include splits where the agent may get 80% to 90% of the fee. These arrangements have had mixed results in commercial real estate. Generally, they tend not to attract solid, hard working, quality managers and owners. Because the financial incentive has been removed, these arrangements tend not to engender good management within a company. Good management is critical to the success of your firm, and you should be willing to pay for it with a split that rewards them as well. The 100% split is rare in very successful commercial real estate companies. Most splits start off in the vicinity of 50-50, with the agent earning a higher percentage or bonus, as he or she makes more money.

Exchanging

The motivation for exchanging property is to defer taxes. If you sell a commercial property and then buy another, you pay a tax on the gain of the property you sold and end up purchasing the new property with after tax dollars. If you exchange the properties you defer the gain and avoid paying the tax for now. This is tax avoidance, which is legal, not tax evasion, which is not. This is commonly referred to as a Section 1031 Tax Deferred Exchange or a 1031 exchange after the section in the Internal Revenue Code that governs federal tax policy on exchanging. The property must be of "like kind," and held for business or income producing purposes. Because it is difficult to arrange for a simultaneous exchange of property the law allows for a deferred exchange. This means that a seller can sell today and buy the new property at some future date. Once a property is sold the seller has 45 days to identify up to three replacement properties and six months to complete the exchange. The seller cannot take control of the sales proceeds to qualify for a 1031 exchange so arrangements must be made for some third party to hold the funds until the replacement property is found. These third parties are called accommodators because they accommodate the exchange by holding the sales proceeds until a new property is located.

There are additional reasons for exchanging and different kinds of exchanges. Some companies may wish to change locations and defer the tax, or investors may want to trade up to a bigger investment with more depreciation. There are innumerable tax reasons for exchanging into another property which makes exchanging of special interest to investors. Many exchanges involve investors and investments. There are also other kinds of exchanges, like a 1033 exchange. This is when an owner's property has been acquired by a governmental body. In this case, owners may accept the money and then have up to two years to find an exchange property.

Exchanges can be complicated. Multiple exchanges can involve three or four way property exchanges with multiple owners, or there may be a reverse exchange where an owner purchases the trade-in property before selling their property. The tax consequence of exchanging involves things such as boot (which is cash or other consideration from the exchange) and basis calculations. It is always a good idea to have an accountant's and tax attorney's guidance when exchanging.

For brokers, exchanging presents certain benefits and problems. Perhaps the greatest benefit to brokers is that they are presented with principals who have sold property, have the money, and are eager to find something to buy. Exchanging also increases brokers' business because sellers, especially those with a low basis who previously would not sell because of the tax, now have a way to do so and can defer the tax. Perhaps the biggest problem in exchanging is finding the property to exchange into. Good investment properties can be hard to find and it is not unusual to see investment sellers aggressively searching for investment property. This situation tends to work against these sellers because sophisticated brokers and sellers of property know that these 1031 exchange principals are under a time limit to complete the exchange. This disadvantage is offset somewhat by the fact that the seller of the first property can choose up to three properties, which puts the sellers of the property to be acquired in competition with other property owners. Documenting an exchange can also be difficult, especially with multiple exchanges. Documentation ranges from purchase and sale agreements providing that one party intends to complete a 1031 exchange, to actual exchange agreements.

It is common in exchanges to require that each party accommodate an exchange and to provide that any extra legal expense incurred due to the exchange will be paid by the one who benefits from the exchange. The splitting of commissions can also become a problem in exchanges. Should the listing broker of the trade-in property, for example, participate in the sales fee of the property sold? Fees in exchanges are occasionally pooled and split on some equitable basis.

Some terms you should be familiar with in exchanging are as follows.

Basis	Generally, the purchase price of a property adjusted for gains, losses, and depreciation.
Depreciation	A charge against the cost of an asset for its estimated wear and obsolescence.
Capital Gains Tax	The tax on the gain on the sale of an asset.

Boot	Unlike property included to balance the value of like properties exchanged, such as cash in a property exchange.
Gain	An increase in property value.
Recapture	When a property has been sold at a gain and the owner has used accelerated depreciation, they may be required to pay a tax at ordinary income rates on the excess accelerated depreciation. The accelerated depreciation is "recaptured" for tax reasons.

State Licensing and Brokerage Requirements

The commercial real estate industry does not typically involve interstate commerce, so those who practice it are licensed by individual states rather than the federal government. Because agents deal with other people's money and assets, and there is considerable opportunity for agents to take unfair advantage of an unsuspecting public, each state establishes entry requirements for those wishing to become real estate agents and regulates their activities as licensees to assure they comply with the laws. However, because state licensing and brokerage requirements vary so much from state to state, it is impossible to explain and summarize them in a complete and comprehensive manner.

Unscrupulous activity by real estate agents is generally less of a problem in commercial real estate because the principals tend to be more sophisticated and because highly qualified specialists, like attorneys and accountants, are usually involved in commercial real estate transactions. Nevertheless, commercial real estate brokers are subject to many state requirements that you need to know and understand. These involve setting qualifications for licensees, regulations relating to the handling of transaction documents and funds, and procedures for investigating and enforcing state laws and regulations. Because of the broad nature of state requirements, this section will not attempt to explain each area in detail, but rather summarize some of the more important ones.

To practice commercial real estate a license is required from the state. This is usually the same license for other areas of real estate, such as residential and property management. Most states have at least two tiers of licensing, an entry-level license and a license that entitles one to supervise other licensees. Requirements for these licenses include the following.

- Age, usually the age of majority in the state.

- Evidence of trustworthy character.

- Education. Some states require a certain level of formal education, such as a high school or college diploma. Almost all states require some specific real estate education.

- An examination. This is to assure that some of the education has been absorbed and retained.

The educational and testing standards are intended to assure that the licensee is knowledgeable and competent to perform real estate activity for others. Licenses are issued for a limited period, generally for a period of one to four years. Post license and/or continuing education courses are typically required for license renewal. The educational topics required are usually those that the state considers most vital to protect the public. These topics include some of the following:

- License law

- Anti-discrimination law

- Agency and agency disclosure law

- Contract law

- Real estate math

- Real property law

- Property descriptions

- Real estate documentation

- Financing

- Construction and architecture

- Commercial and investment real estate
- Appraisal concepts
- Property management
- Tax concepts

For licensees who wish to supervise other licensees, there are usually experience requirements, which include two to four years as a licensee, as well as additional educational requirements relating to office management, record keeping, handling of trust accounts, closing procedures, and supervision of licensees.

State regulation of commercial real estate involves laws pertaining to licensees and the general practice of real estate. License law regulates things such as place of business, educational standards, record keeping, creation and retention of documents, trust accounts, contracts, disclosure, as well as advertising, signs, and cooperation with out of state brokers. It also deals with criminal behavior such as forgery, embezzlement, unlicensed activity, private transactions, misrepresentation, and commingling and conversion of funds. Misrepresentation and commingling of funds are probably the two areas where brokers most often run afoul of the state.

Misrepresentation is when an agent gives wrong or false information, either intentionally or unintentionally. The state has little tolerance for caveat emptor (or "buyer beware"). It wants the agent to be professional and diligent in discovering and disclosing all pertinent information relating to the property to all parties in real estate transactions. Commingling of funds is when brokers mix client and broker funds. Brokers have been known to use other people's earnest money and lease deposits for personal gain. This is a big no-no. The state will occasionally audit brokers' clients trust accounts for just this reason. You need to take special care in these areas.

State regulations of real estate also cover areas directly and indirectly related to commercial real estate. Some areas such as taxation, code, and land use laws are not direct license or brokerage requirements, although running afoul of them may precipitate some penalty. Areas that are typically covered include the following:

- Discrimination

- Closing, escrow, and recording

- Management

- Condominiums

- Historic properties (special tax status encourages restoration and discourages demolition or alteration)

- Valuation (some states prohibit brokers from doing appraisals)

- Auctions

- Tenancy laws

- Securities

- Land use laws such as subdividing and partitioning

- Taxation

- Exchange

Finally, the state will engage in the investigation and enforcement of real estate law. Investigations can include audits or interviews. These are often precipitated by a complaint. Enforcement can include reprimands, fines, or in extreme cases, suspension or revocation of a license. They can also include some civil or criminal action that could result in damage awards or jail.

It should be mentioned that state licensing and brokerage requirements are the minimum requirements necessary to succeed in commercial real estate. They embody the basic knowledge needed to be competent and the minimum ethical standards for a good reputation. They deal with the most basic, common sense, ways of dealing with other people. They should be viewed as the beginning point from which you build a successful career. Special care should be taken to know all state requirements and to be sure that they are obeyed.

Financing

The four ways to purchase commercial real estate are cash, contract, mortgage/trust deed, or trade. Cash is cash and trading is trading, but contracts, mortgages, and trust deeds entail financing. When lenders lend money through mortgages and trust deeds, the seller gets cash. Mortgages and trust deeds allow buyers to pay cash for property when the seller does not want to give terms and usually involve lending institutions that have specific requirements for loans.

Contracts mean that the seller is extending credit to the buyer who will make payments over time to the seller. Contracts offer greater flexibility for creative financing, but they are more risky for the seller because the buyer may default.

Generally speaking, most sellers prefer cash. This is true especially if they are doing things like breaking up a partnership or settling an estate. Sometimes they prefer terms for tax reasons or because they can get a better interest rate on the contract than, say, a certificate of deposit. Some sellers actually prefer contracts because if the buyer defaults, they can get the property back. Many deals are just cash. You will be surprised how much money is floating around in commercial real estate. Sometimes wealthy individuals or companies will obtain the cash to purchase property out of pocket or from their own line of credit. Trades and exchanges were discussed earlier in this chapter.

Financing is a big issue and critical to the success of your deal. In general terms, trust deeds are preferable because a third party holds a deed in trust, which insures that a buyer will get the deed when they pay off the debt and because lenders can avoid a long redemption period and foreclose faster. The main variables in mortgages and trust deeds are the interest rate, term, amount of loan, and balloon payment. These variables are interrelated and dependent on many factors such as the following:

- Level of risk

- Borrower's credit

- Loan size

- Property type

- Property location

- Age of property

- The economy

There are two basic ways to determine the amount of the loan. They are the loan to value ratio (LTV) and debt coverage ratio (DCR). Lenders usually base the loan amount on the lesser of the LTV or DCR. The former is simply a percentage of the value of the property and the later a ratio of the annual net income from the real estate to the total annual debt. (At the time of writing this book, common DCRs for commercial real estate loans were 1.20 to 1.25.) If the LTV, for example, is 80% and the purchase price is $1,000,000, the lender will loan $800,000 (80% X $1,000,000 = $800,000) and the buyer must come up with $200,000. If the DCR is 1.1 and the net operating income is $150,000, then the amount the lender will allow for debt service is $136,363 ($150,000 ÷ 1.1 = $136,363). If the interest rate for the loan is 9% and the term is 20 years, then the lender would loan $1,263,004 on the property ($136,363÷12=$11,363.58 per month, which will amortize $1,263,004 over 20 years at 9%). If the property costs $1,500,000, then the buyer will have to come up with $236,996, or 16% of the purchase price. The loan to value in this example would be 84%. As a matter of interest, the constant in this example is 11 ($1,500,000÷$136,363=11). Many lenders think in terms of constants, which are simply the constant annual amortizing percentages. All you need are the annual interest rate and the term to derive the constant. The constant, for example, for a loan with a 9% annual interest rate over 10 years is 15.2, and for 15 years is 12.18. There are tables that give constants for different terms and interest rates.

The LTV gives the lender enough value cushion in the event the loan goes bad and the DCR measures the ability of the cash flow to service the payments. Generally speaking, lenders use the DCR when interest rates are high, and the LTV when they are low. The DCR is most common in investment property financing.

Lenders usually require credit reports, environmental reports, structural reports, appraisals, and sometimes surveys and charge various fees. For these reasons, dealing with lenders tends to be more expensive and time consuming than contract sales. Lenders come in all shapes and sizes including banks, insurance companies, pension funds, private investors, and the government. Small Business Administration (SBA) loans are sometimes used. Mortgage brokers are individuals who act as brokers in mortgages. They do not loan the money themselves, but act as intermediaries to locate the best loan and arrange the financing for a fee.

When people talk of creative financing in commercial real estate they generally are referring to contracts of sale. Contracts, as mentioned earlier, are when the seller extends credit to the buyer. The consequence is that the terms can be more creative. They can include below market interest rates, interest only payments, different balloon payment provisions, very high loan amounts, and long-term amortization schedules. It is possible, for example, for a seller to sell a property at an inflated price in exchange for very liberal financing terms, or to sell a property subject to a contract on previous sale (called a wrap-around contract) in order to collect a higher interest rate than they are paying. For reasons like these and because contracts often involve buyers with marginal credit, they tend to be more risky than conventional financing. One risk to borrowers in contract sales is the occasional difficulty of getting the deed from the seller when the loan is repaid. One solution to this problem is to have a seller execute a deed at closing, which is then deposited in an escrow account with instructions to deliver it to the buyer when the contract is paid off.

The general economy has a profound influence on financing. Interest rate levels, the federal reserve polices, supply and demand (including the government's borrowing demands), the level of economic activity in general, and competition are just a few of the things that affect the availability and terms of financing. It is not unusual for contract sales to become popular in times of tight money supply, high interest rates, and high inflation.

One other area of lending commonly encountered in commercial real estate is construction financing. This is the interim loan for construction that usually is retired by permanent financing when the project is done. The availability and terms of construction financing is of particular interest to developers, contractors, and those building something.

Some terms and concepts you need to be familiar with in financing are listed on the next page.

Amortization and amortization schedules	Amortization is a gradual paying off of a debt by periodic installments (for example $500,000 amortized over twenty years at 9% gives an equal monthly payment of $2,249.31). An amortization schedule is a table that shows the periodic payment for each period for a loan.
Subordination	Moving to a lower priority, such as allowing a mortgage to change from a first mortgage to a second mortgage.
Interest (simple, compound, and variable)	Interest is the cost of the use of money. Simple interest is interest paid only on principle; compound interest is interest paid on the original principle and the unpaid interest that has accumulated; and variable interest is an interest rate that is allowed to vary over the term of a loan.
Term of loan	The term of a loan to maturity. This may be one that is fully amortized or one with a balloon payment that is not fully amortized.
Balloon payment	The final payment on a loan, when that payment is greater than the preceding installment payments and pays the loan in full.
Points	Fees paid to mortgage lenders. Each point equals 1% of the loan principle.
Default and foreclosure proceedings	Default is the failure to fulfill an obligation or promise, and foreclosure is the termination of the right of an owner to redeem a property from a mortgagor that secures a loan.
Lot release and subordination	Lot release is when a parcel of land, or lot, is released as security for indebtedness and the buyer given title. Subordination is the moving to a lower priority, a technique often used by developers in order to obtain financing for improvements in a land sale contract.

Constants	In mortgages, the percentage ratio between the annual debt service and the loan principal (the formula is the annual debt service ÷ loan principal = mortgage constant).
Acceleration Clause	A loan provision giving the lender the right to declare the entire amount immediately due and payable upon violation of a specific loan provision.
Judgment	A court decree stating that one individual is indebted to another and fixing the amount of the indebtedness.
Liquidity	The ease of converting assets to cash.
Recourse and Nonrecourse Loans	A recourse loan gives the lender the ability to claim money from a borrower in default in addition to the property pledged as collateral. In a nonrecourse loan, the borrower has no personal liability, and the lender may take the property pledged as collateral to satisfy a debt, but has no recourse to assets of the borrower.

Property Management

Like office management, property management is not something that the average commercial broker deals with much. It is something that is better left to the property managers because it does require some special knowledge and, as a broker, your time is better spent making deals. It is important to know some basics, however, because some of your clients may ask you for advice on property management or for a recommendation of a good manager. It is also important to some commercial brokers as a source of business. Property managers often market the property they manage and sometimes list it with brokers. This can be a big source of listings business.

Property management is just that — the management of some-one's property for a fee. It is the effort to manage an asset to achieve its best possible performance for maximum profit. This is frequently done for investors by the gurus of property management, who are Certified Property Managers (CPM®) — a designation obtained from the Institute of Real Estate Management (IREM). Property managers handle all aspects of management including the day-to-day operations, personnel, collecting rent and paying the bills (including taxes), establishing and collecting CAM (common area maintenance) charges, insurance, financing, and keeping records. They oversee the maintenance of property, including contracting for repairs and routine maintenance matters. They market property, handle tenant improvements, leasing, sales and listing, when need-ed. They deal with the tenants on all matters such as complaints, seeing that lease terms are enforced, and also deal with legal matters, such as default and eviction. They also budget, provide accounting reports, and keep track of a property's cash flow and productivity by investment analysis.

Property managers handle all kinds of properties from single ten-ant buildings to multi-tenant parks. They deal with all kinds of prop-erties such as office, retail, industrial, or apartments, each of which has its own special management characteristics. One special challenge to managers is "turnaround" properties, which are properties that are experiencing some sort of difficulty like vacancy, obsolescence, or maintenance problems. These, along with the other day-to-day chal-lenges properties present, often make property management a thank-less and stressful job. They definitely earn their fees.

CHAPTER 5

Salesmanship

Salesmanship is undoubtedly the most overlooked aspect to success in a commercial real estate career but, unquestionably, the most important. To some, salesmanship is a bad word. It conjures up an image of the fast-talking salesman trying to get someone to buy something they do not want. Use of the word seems to immediately put most people on the defensive. However, true salesmanship has nothing to do with arm-twisting or high-pressure persuasion. Rather, it is very much an art. Those with fertile and creative minds seem to excel at it, like artists.

True salesmanship is, essentially, trying to help people get what they want and what they need. The problem is that most people are not sure of either. They may have some vague ideas or dreams and mixed, and often conflicting, desires and needs. Therefore, part of the process of selling, and one of its biggest challenges, is to help people determine what they desire and what they need, and then to help them get it. In commercial real estate, this all translates to presenting a product or service in such a way to a prospect, in order to show them how it fits with their needs. Consequently, part of the sales role is to help a buyer make a final decision. Those who never decide, never get what they want.

In addition to learning general rules of salesmanship, it is important to learn some commonly used sales points for prospects, clients, and the public, as well as points in response to other brokers' sales pitches. There are many situations, objections, and questions that come up repeatedly in commercial real estate that can either be an obstacle to success or can be addressed quickly and convincingly to the satisfaction of the buyer. Make note of what other successful brokers say, how they respond to these objections, and make them part of your repertoire.

Every successful person is a good salesman. Politicians, doctors, and lawyers all sell their services, and the most successful ones are the ones who sell themselves best. In commercial real estate, you often see two or three brokers who are constantly competing for business. They all are presentable, equally knowledgeable, and associated with good, reputable companies, yet only one consistently comes away with the business. Why? Because one is a better salesman. The point is, to be successful in commercial real estate, you must study and practice salesmanship (see the section below). It will probably be the most important thing you do. Other later sections in this chapter will deal with more specific issues such as the most common sales points and countering and neutralizing other brokers' sales points.

Basic Sales Strategies

A complete explanation of salesmanship is beyond the scope of this book. Many fine books have been written on the subject, a few of which are mentioned in Chapter 1. However, there are a number of broad suggestions that could help you succeed in this particular field. Some of the most important ones are listed below.

- Always be prepared. The spoils go to the one who has taken the time to prepare for the task at hand and know his or her business. This includes having the information available that the prospect needs and overwhelming them with your knowledge, abilities, and successes. It means knowing who they are, what they want, what is available, what the market can offer, and how you can help. If you are in competition with another broker, it is very helpful to build his or her presentation and sales points before yours.

This tells you what you need to say, as well as prepares you for questions and objections during the pitch. Success is where experience and preparation cross.

- Always keep the prospect's or client's interests in mind, not yours. Too often brokers confuse what they want with what the principal wants. Your benefits will naturally flow if you do the job right. Ask yourself what you can do, for example, to promote a client's property or solve a prospect's problem. Try and spend more time focusing on the property or how to solve the principal's problems, rather than yourself.

- Do not waste other people's time. Business people are busy people, so you want to be aware that they have only so much time to give you. People appreciate it when you value their time. Ask if someone has the time to talk with you. Start the conversation with "do you have a minute." You should get right to the point and stick to the important issues. You will lose the principal's attention if you drag out your points.

- Always keep a positive attitude and professional deportment. People appreciate and respect a businesslike attitude. A negative, defeatist, attitude will get you negativity and defeat.

- Be clear and understandable, but make prospects and clients keep up with you. People appreciate those who quickly grasp the need and who work to resolve the problem. People want to believe you and want to listen to someone who is knowledgeable. When people make important real estate decisions that involve lots of money, they want to listen to someone who knows the business and can give guidance.

- Be authoritative and display your knowledge. I once asked a motorcycle repair technician whether I needed a new tire and he asked, "Do you want to live?" I immediately bought a new tire because he was authoritative, believable, and decisive, and I wanted to live. His decisiveness made him believable. Display confidence and self-control. Exude competence and be straightforward.

- Never get mad or show anger. There is an old Arab saw that says "He who first gets angry, loses." You gain nothing from getting angry. Also, while we are on emotions, do not fake laughter or be glib. Be yourself. Keep your voice calm and relaxed, not nervous and high-pitched.

- Study the nature of a sales conversation and learn what works and what doesn't. When responding to questions or making a point, take your time, gather your thoughts and draw sound conclusions slowly and logically. Your comments should be so logical that they are overwhelmingly convincing to the principal. Some brokers talk as if they are afraid they will forget what they want to say. They have to get their comments out quickly, which usually results in a mass of forgettable comments that have no impact. You will get a bigger "kick" to your pitch with a few, well delivered, and convincing points, rather than a barrage of mediocre comments. It is also important to "hold for the end." You should ask questions in order to elicit certain information or to get a certain desired response, to which you should have a convincing answer. Let the conversation play out and make the convincing response at the end for maximum impact. Too many brokers cannot control themselves and dribble the same point out many times with minimal impact. Winston Churchill once said, "If you have an important point to make, don't try to be subtle or clever. Use a pile driver. Hit it once, then come back and hit it again." It is also true that principals often remember how you said something, more than what you said. To increase the impact of what you are saying, practice your delivery with gestures, dramatization, facial expressions, voice modulation, and pauses. One very powerful and often overlooked tool in a sales conversation is silence. People just cannot stand silence in a conversation. Stop talking with someone and watch what happens. They invariably will start talking. This can be a valuable tool when you want to know what a principal is thinking.

- Don't oversell. Once a prospect has decided he wants a property, you do not need to continue selling it. He is ready to do business, so ask for the order and proceed to finalizing the deal.

- When selling, try to "paint a picture" like an artist. Use broad strokes and weave an alluring image of what you want to communicate.

- Be a good listener. You should listen carefully to what prospects say for many reasons. First, you will learn what you need to know in order to sell properly. Second, you will gain their confidence because they will think you understand them. Third, they will appreciate your desire to understand their problem. Fourth, you will develop a true dialogue with the prospect rather than carrying on a one-way conversation or a lecture. It is the honest give and take of a conversation that eventually brings about decisions, which, in turn, ultimately lead to sales. At a minimum, if you are a good listener, it is hard to make a fool of yourself. Remember Shakespeare's admonition that it is better to keep silent and have others think you a fool than open your mouth and have them know you are one.

- Always be totally honest, open, and forthright. People naturally trust those who are honest. Most people have a sixth sense when someone is not honest with them. Your thoughts are revealed in many ways, such as facial expressions or body language, which others pick up. Many brokers shade the truth because they do not want to say anything that will diminish their chances of success. The opposite is usually the case. You will get much farther being totally honest because the principal will trust you. It also makes it easier to make a deal because the principal will have better information on which to make an informed decision. Use understatements and do not exaggerate. It is better to promise little now and look better later, than promise a lot now and not be able to deliver. If you are trying to get a listing for sale, for example, where the owner wants too much money, tell them the price is too high. If you are not the right broker for the job, say so, and recommend someone else. Honesty and straightforwardness are qualities that make others want to work with you. Do not fall into the trap of lowering your standards when competing with other brokers or principals who are using underhanded tactics. This is a constant temptation in both commercial real estate and life. Always take the high road. It pays professionally and personally.

• Don't procrastinate. Hustle. Do it now. Be the first one there.

• Develop a repertoire of persuasive and convincing points to commonly asked questions. A book could be written on this subject. You repertoire will vary depending on your circumstances. If you are with a big firm, you will make different points than if you are with a small one. There are, however, some commonly asked questions and objections such as "Why should I sign an exclusive listing?" Or, "You seem too inexperienced to handle my property." Lists of many of these points and counterpoints are outlined in the next section, "Common Sales Points."

• Always counter other brokers' sales points. Find out what your competition has said and then respond to those points. Many pitches have been lost because another broker made a point that stuck in the prospects' mind, which was not neutralized with a counter point. You should anticipate what your competition will say, and then have a response good enough to neutralize it. Always assume that you are in competition with someone else. Many potential listings have been lost because the broker assumed that she was the only one talking to the principal. People looking to buy, sell, or list property usually talk with a number of brokers, which they do not disclose to you. Always ask if there is competition. Again, the list of counters to other brokers' points is endless; however, there are some common remarks and standard responses. Some of these are discussed later in this chapter under "Countering Other Brokers Points."

• Always deal with the decision maker. This seems obvious, but is often overlooked. All your preparation goes out the window when you are dealing with an underling who does not make the decisions. This mistake is almost always fatal when you are dealing with an underling and another broker is talking to the decision maker. You don't have a chance. You are not in a position to persuade the one who makes the final decision, to learn what his or her real concerns are, or to grapple with the objections. Usually inexperienced brokers are fearful of approaching the decision maker and feel more conformable dealing with an underling. It is also harder to contact the decision maker, so the underling is more accessible. Get over your fear and always go to the top. It is better to spend your time trying to reach the decision maker, even if you are unsuccessful, than waste it trying to sell the wrong person. Many listing pitches have been decided simply because one broker was dealing with the right person and the other was not.

- Dress neatly and appropriate to the prospect. Someone who runs a machine shop and wears overalls sometimes resents a pinstriped suit. Conversely, a corporate president who wears a pinstriped suit, may be put off if you show up in jeans and a polo shirt. First appearances, however shallow, are important, and you should endeavor to dress accordingly. Look your best. Also, it helps to smile. Not a fake, plastic smile, but a real one. If you cannot conjure up a real smile, then you are working too hard (see "Vacations" in Chapter 10).

- Try to establish a rapport or relationship with the principal. Some people just seem naturally better at this than others. It is important to develop your social skills to the point where the conversation is easy and fluid. The idea is to put the principal at ease and reduce potential barriers. Believe it or not, a little small talk and humor can go a long way. It is better to be a relationship-based broker, than a transaction-based one. Relationships create long-term business in both good and bad economies. In time, you will find that you don't have to work as hard to obtain listings. Relationship-based firms focus on the relationship, and the deals naturally follow. Transaction-based firms are always frantically looking for the next listing, prospect, and deal. Their relationship ended when the deal ended.

- Be enthusiastic. Enthusiasm is contagious. It creates a kind of aura of success and excitement. It causes momentum, which principals get caught up in.

- Always sell in person and not over the phone. It is very hard to sell over the phone. You lose the personal touch and the ability to "read" the prospect. The phone should be used only to get an appointment.

- Promote yourself. Society discourages us from talking too much about our successes and ourselves. Commercial real estate is an exception. Get over the inhibition of extolling your virtues. Tell the prospect about your experience, past successful deals, and impressive clients. Display your knowledge. Drop names and mention people that you may know in common. Some of the most successful brokers are blatant self-promoters. Too much self-promotion, however, can backfire. Therefore, making yourself look good is an art. You should spend just enough time on it to establish credibility. This topic will be discussed in more detail in Chapter 7 under "Self-Marketing."

- Be confident. Confidence comes from parents, experience, and knowledge. We have little control over who our parents are, but we can control what we know and what we do. Know your business and, in time, with experience, confidence will follow. One way to build confidence is to build your public speaking skills. Joining a Toastmasters' Club is a good way to learn to speak more effectively and confidently. Also, if you are nervous, it is a good idea to admit it. Doing so often cuts the atmosphere and causes the principal to be sympathetic. Many started at the bottom themselves and have a soft spot for those just starting and striving.

- Always praise your competition. This will cause the principal to have more confidence in you. Central to sales and, ultimately, success in commercial real estate, is the ability to have people trust you. If you run your competition down, the only one who looks bad is you.

- Have promotional material available to hand out and leave behind. It is very handy to have available letters of recommendation, lists of past clients, lists of successful deals, as well as a resume. Flood the prospect with information. Be aware, however, that promotional material by itself will not get you the job. It should be viewed as backup material that bolsters your personal pitch. Promotional materials are also discussed in other parts of this book.

- Remember names. People like to hear their name spoken. They like to be remembered. Keep a list of the names of people you meet and endeavor to remember them.

- Stay in touch with prospects, past clients, and those who deal in commercial real estate. These include large property owners, large tenants, and managers of company real estate departments. Out of sight is out of mind. You should constantly remind people that you are successful and active and that you would like to handle their business. All too often, it is the last broker in the door that gets the business. Do not let clients or prospects forget you.

- Close the sale. Always ask for the business. Too many brokers make the error of not bringing the pitch to its logical conclusion, which is to get a commitment, preferably in writing. It helps, for example, to have a completed agreement prepared in advance to present for signature at the end of a pitch. It helps to summarize the salient points of your conversation, ask the prospect if she has any questions, and then present something to sign with a pen. Circumstances and psychology are on your side.

- Be persistent. Persistence always wins out over talent. This is perhaps the single most important element of sales. The world is full of unsuccessful, talented people and successful, untalented, persistent people. If you stay at it, you are bound to succeed. The toughest competitors are both talented and persistent. Never give up.

- Timing is everything in sex, comedy, and commercial real estate. Be aware that real estate deals have a certain timing or cadence. There is a natural give and take between the principals that you must allow to play out. Do not try and rush a deal or sales pitch. Don't try to pre-negotiate a deal. Many brokers make the mistake of trying to get a buyer, for example, to make an offer that they think will be accepted and end up never getting the offer. It is better to tell the buyer, in this case, to make the offer the way they want and let the seller respond. Let the principals make the deal and the negotiations do the work.

- In sales presentations, try not to make too many points. It is better to focus on a few important points than to do too much. Your presentation will be diluted and the prospect will remember nothing in particular. Also, try and determine when a prospect is receptive to what you have to say. Attempting to sell someone who is not listening is impossible.

- Make all of your contacts count. Treat prospects as if they are the most important people in the world. Focus on their problems and their solutions. Ask the right questions and keep a written record of what they say. Frame your questions in such a way that they elicit important information. The point is to discover what their needs are and then provide a way to solve them. Examples of some of these questions include

  » When does your lease expire?

  » Are you planning to do any real estate business in the future?

  » What do you own or lease?

  » Do you have an option to renew? When? How much advance notice must you give to exercise the option?

  » Are you interested in investing in property? What are your criteria for investing?

  » Is your building meeting your business's needs?

- Use the right language. This is more complicated than it sounds. Some experts think that using words like pitch, deal, and contract should be avoided. They say that when you say pitch, people go on the defensive; when you say deal, they think "fast buck"; and when you say contract, they worry about legal matters. Most people prefer softer words like agreement or paperwork instead of contract; investment instead of cost or price; approve or authorize instead of sign; executive or professional instead of broker; and handle or remit instead of pay. These same kind of people like gathered and passed away, for dead. Such euphemisms are not always necessary in commercial real estate. Most people who deal in commercial real estate are sophisticated business professionals and investors. They tend to be more interested in what the word means than being politically correct. They themselves use words like deal and pitch all the time. However, you should be aware that some people may be turned off by these terms and adjust your language accordingly.

- Use simple language. Some brokers try to sound like Einstein when they talk or write letters and contracts. You should speak and write in such a way that a 10-year old could understand you. Commercial real estate is not about impressing others with your vocabulary, but rather being clear and understandable.

- Get past the gatekeeper. Secretaries and receptionists act as gatekeepers for important decision makers in most companies. Often they will keep you from talking with those you need to contact. You must get past them if you are to be successful. Always be honest and tell them the purpose of your call, but endeavor to get around them. There are many ways to do this.

  » Develop a rapport with them and ask for their assistance. Many like to be helpful.

  » Always be courteous and respectful.

  » Tell them that their boss may be interested in what you have to offer. They should know that they will be responsible if they prevent the boss from getting information he or she may have wanted.

  » Get an introduction from someone the principal knows.

  » If you have a listing in the area, tell them that you are calling to give their boss information on a property nearby. People like to know what is going on in their area

  » Tell them your credentials. The fact that you work that area or have sold a property recently in their area, may be of interest to their boss.

» Go and meet them personally.

» Call the president's secretary and ask who handles real estate (even if you already know). The secretary will give you the name of the person you wanted to contact in the first place. However, now you have a referral "from the president's office."

» Call the decision maker after work hours when the gatekeeper is gone.

» Tell the gatekeeper you promise to be brief.

- Use voice mail. Many people do not like voice mail because it keeps them from the decision maker. On the contrary, if used properly, it can be of help. Rather than leaving a written message to return a call, voice mail gives you an opportunity to say, directly to the decision maker, sales points that may pique their interest. Avoid leaving too much information on voice mail. Give just enough to whet the prospect's interest so he or she will call you back. For example, you may leave a message that you sold the property next door, but don't give the price. Think about and practice a short voice mail message that will make the principal want to return your call. Remember, when making sales calls, the phone should only be used to get an appointment. Making an actual sales pitch over the phone is the last resort.

- Be aggressive. It is better to err on the side of being too aggressive, than not aggressive enough. It is better to be thrown out of someone's office than lose a deal because you did not push hard enough. If you are thrown out, you can always apologize for being too aggressive. Most business professionals accept it. The give and take involved in aggressively pursuing a prospect often leads to relationships, which lead to deals. Also, most principals recognize that the aggressive qualities you display are the same qualities they may want when looking for property, selling property, or negotiating deals. Remember Machiavelli's advice that fortune smiles on the bold. Always take the initiative. It is better that you rely on yourself to initiate activity, than depend on someone else. For example, it is better to say you will call someone back, rather than leave a message. Some brokers hang around waiting for calls to be returned. Never wait around for a call back, unless it is critical. Keep the initiative, move on, and take their call when you have time. As Jonathan Winters once said, "If your ship doesn't come in, swim out to it."

- Arouse fear. Fear is a powerful motivator. Nobody likes to talk about fear, but everyone experiences it and knows how important it is. Honest comments like "there is another offer," or "you are losing money because your property is vacant," seem small, but have a powerful influence on people's thinking.

- Use examples. Pictures, stories, articles, and charts may add to your ability to demonstrate a point.

- Follow up on sales calls. After a meeting with a prospect, reinforce your sale points with a follow up letter or e-mail.

- Practice what you want to say and how you want to say it. It is a good idea to role play with other brokers and practice what to say and your delivery.

- Practice your telephone skills. Much of your time is spent on the telephone, so you want to use it as effectively as possible. One telephone situation you will have to deal with is prospects calling on listings and not wanting to leave their name. The solution is to stop half way through providing information on the listing and ask for their name. They invariably tell you who they are because they want the rest of the information.

- Never be afraid to fail. Commercial real estate is full of rejection and failure. It just comes with the territory. Rejection and failure are the first steps to success. One of the real keys to success is to learn from your failures. Why did you not get that listing? Why did that prospect make an offer through another broker? The sooner you learn the reasons why, the sooner you will know how to avoid having that happen again. Smart people make a mistake only once; dumb ones repeat them over and over. Many sales manuals in real estate tell you that you will get acceptance on every tenth or so call. They tell you that you should rejoice in each rejection because you have to make nine calls, before the successful tenth one. This sounds good and it probably is true, but we are all human, and nine rejections are discouraging. It seems preferable to think of each call as a long-term contact, rather than a rejection. You may not do business with them now, but you are doing the things that will bring their business in the future. Failure means nothing if it eventually brings success. Besides that, it's just business. True rejection is when you get dumped.

Common Sales Points

The number of sales points that can be used are endless. It is impossible to list them all because there are so many and so many variables. The points you use will vary depending on whether you are experienced or not, your company size, the type of prospect, the type of property, whether you are pitching to list property or for tenant representation, etc.

However, there are many situations in commercial real estate that continually come up. Principals tend to ask the same questions and make the same objections. You should endeavor to identify these situations and be prepared to respond with a repertoire of persuasive sales points that you have drilled into your brain. It is not a good idea to memorize your sales points or pitch. They can become stale, and you may lose interest. Know the points in general and use them spontaneously. One of the best ways to learn how to make successful sales points is by observing what other successful brokers say. There is no arguing with success.

Probably the most important sales points you master are those that deal with listing property exclusively. The ability to list property exclusively is, undoubtedly, one of the most important things to be able to do in order to be successful in commercial real estate. The reasons for this, as well as more detailed sales points relating to listing property, will be discussed later in Chapter 10 under the section, "Focus on Listings."

The following are a few brief and commonly used sales points. This is a somewhat eclectic list intended to provide a sample of examples of sales points. Hopefully, this list will stimulate your imagination on the types of points to make when dealing with prospects. These points cover many common situations including getting the prospect's attention, selling yourself, motivating prospects, neutralizing objections, and stimulating a prospect's curiosity. Sales points used to counter other brokers' points will be discussed in the next section.

- I am experienced.

- I have prospects for your property.

- I have sold or leased similar property.

- I have similar listings now, which means that I will know all of the prospects for your property.

- I make a special effort to cooperate with other brokers because it is in your interest to have other brokers bring you deals. Some brokers, for example, prefer to try and keep a "pocket listing" (an unofficial listing where the broker, often, does not disclose the properties availability widely and can sell it themselves and collect the whole fee.) My philosophy is, "half a fee is better than no fee."

- We are a national company with national contacts, which other brokers do not have. (If you are with a small firm or independent, see the section in Chapter 13 on "Sales Points for Independents and Small Brokerages" for sales points that can be used against the large, national brokerage firms.)

- You are busy and I can save you time.

- I will do for you what you would do for yourself, if you had the time and knowledge.

- I'd rather do an excellent job for a few clients, than a mediocre job for a large number of clients.

- I specialize in your type of property.

- Your property is in my farm area.

- I will keep your property positioned in the market place at the top of the list of available properties.

- I just sold or leased another, similar property in the area (assuming you did) and therefore know all the prospects.

- To principals who think that listing exclusively restricts their market, explain that the opposite is true. Exclusive listings actually expand their market exposure because you will endeavor to market the property to all brokers, as well as all sources of prospects.

- To prospects who do not want to make an offer because they think the price is too high, you can explain that they have nothing to lose by making the offer they want. The worst that will happen is that it will be rejected. And there's a chance (however small) that it will be accepted or at least countered. Additionally, even if the offer is rejected, they will have found the owner's range.

- To an investor who says that he can make more money in the bank (assuming he can), than in real estate say, "True, but you will never own the bank."

- To the investor who objects to real estate because it is not liquid, explain that liquidity in real estate is just a matter of price. Any property can usually be sold within an hour, at the right price.

- When a prospect expresses concern about whether you will truly look out for her best interests because you have both ends of the deal, explain that you view your role as an accommodator or facilitator and that you will not disclose any confidential information to the other side.

- Drop names, mention deals done, and important clients represented.

- Suggest a range of value within which the property may sell. The high price may be a stretch, but at least nothing will be left on the table.

Countering Other Brokers' Sales Points

As mentioned earlier, when selling always assume you are in competition, because you usually are. More often than not, principals are in touch with a number of brokers. Furthermore, they usually do not tell you that there is competition until it is too late. You need to know if there is competition and what the competition is saying. Usually, just asking the principal will get you the information you need. You must counter other brokers' comments in order to neutralize their effect. Competing with other brokers is a little like war, without the deaths. It can be intense. Many opportunities have been lost because the other broker said one thing that stuck in the principal's mind as important, so they did not choose you. You lost the business because you never responded to the other broker's point.

As with common sales points, there is an endless number of counters to other brokers' comments. This, also, is an eclectic list of points that apply under differing circumstances. Hopefully, they will spark your imagination so that you can generate more that are specific to your particular circumstance.

- I may be inexperienced, but my company has plenty of experience to back me up.

- Another broker may have prospects for your property, but I have prospects for you too. So do other brokers. It is more important to have one broker who makes a point of dealing with all brokers, all of whom have prospects, than one broker who has a few prospects. You end up with more prospects.

- Another broker may have many listings, but that just means that he or she is too busy. After all, every "For Sale" sign is just a deal that is not done. Another response to this point would be to say ask, "How well do you think that broker will be able to represent you and to get the prospects for your listing when he has so many competing listings? He has a conflict of interest, which means he may take prospects to another listing. I do not have this conflict, so you will be assured that my efforts are not diluted."

- Conversely, in response to brokers who say that you have too many listings, say, "Yes, but they are just jealous. What else could they say? I have many listings because people know I move property. Also, because I have many listings, I know the prospects other brokers don't."

- In response to highballing (brokers listing property at too high a price in order to get the listing), point out that if you ask too much, you will scare away prospects, and the property will become shopworn and may not move.

- In response to other brokers who say they will not work with you, you can point out the following things: First, it is unethical, so that broker is unethical. Second, it is in the principal's best interest to have a broker who cooperates with other brokers because that is where most of the deals come from. Third, and once again, half a fee is better than no fee.

- In response to brokers who point out that you are not with a large company, you can say: "We are not a national company, but we cooperate with all of the national companies, all of which have prospects, local and national. We are better because if you list with one national company, you may lose out on another national company's prospects."

- In response to a broker who brings five brokers to the listing meeting ask, "Bringing five brokers to the listing pitch looks good, but who is in charge? When you list your property with five brokers, the fee gets split up so much that none have the incentive to really work the property." You can also say that it takes five of them to do what you can do alone.

A Few Final Points on Selling

If anyone ever asks you why you want their business, be honest. Tell them that you want it because you want to make money. Some brokers seem embarrassed to say this, even though it is the truth. Instead, they will say that they want to help their fellow man or that it fulfills them personally. These may sound lofty, but the prospect will see right through it. Everyone appreciates it when you tell the bald truth, and the truth is that you want their business because you want to earn a living. They appreciate it because they are usually doing the same thing. It just so happens that when you do a good job for others, you earn more money.

Finally, remember that when all is said and done, words are cheap and what really counts are results. People want to do business with brokers they know can move their property. Consequently, once you get the job, be sure to follow through and complete it successfully. Tips and strategies for marketing property are discussed in detail in Chapter 8.

CHAPTER 6

Organization

Some people just seem condemned to live their lives always behind the eight ball. These poor lost souls are the ones always behind, always late, always forgetting something, always overburdened, and usually confused. They seem to spend their lives drifting on an open sea like a sailing ship in the doldrums. They are the ones who complain about not having enough time, having too much to do, and not being able to get anything done. They live in a fog, which acts to screen the paths to success. Disorganization is fatal in commercial real estate. Without the ability to order the chaos of life and business, one is doomed.

Organizing is not that hard to do. It requires a little effort and some advance thought. The mere act of just sitting down and thinking through what you want to accomplish and how you are going to do it is the first step. When you organize your affairs, things simply come easier. You can accomplish more, focus on what is important, prepare yourself accordingly, and, ultimately, become more successful. What you want and how to get it suddenly become clearer. After some time, self-organization becomes a habit and second nature. Most successful commercial real estate brokers organize themselves automatically and unconsciously because they have done it for so long. This ability becomes exceedingly important as your career progresses because you will get busier, acquire more information that needs organization, and have more to remember.

This chapter will discuss some of the ways to organize yourself, as well as the attitudes and habits that help you organize. These topics include managing your time, the tickler file, the importance of setting goals, and some of the habits and attitudes that make organizing come more naturally.

Time Management

Most successful commercial real estate salespeople manage their time and prioritize what they want to accomplish. It is far better to be proactive than reactive. When you just react to what happens during the day, it is hard to accomplish your goals because you are letting others set your agenda. You end up just bouncing around like a pinball going from one place to another, with no direction. You see brokers like this all the time. They usually come into the office in the morning not sure what they are going to do that day. They always wonder why they can't seem to accomplish anything and why other brokers are doing all the deals. Salespeople who plan their schedules provide time to accomplish certain tasks, such as cold calls and listing presentations, as well as showings and paperwork. It is essential to plan your time. This will become even more important when you become successful and busier. A productive day would be when the sheet of paper is full and each job has been crossed off.

There are many techniques for planning schedules. Some are electronic and some just old-fashioned notebook calendars. Some like the palm pilots and others prefer the computer — there's an abundance of software available for both. One good method is to use a legal pad with each sheet representing one day. Write out the calendar for the next three to six months, and then use this as your worksheet from which all your activities are directed. Divide it into three sections. The top section is the daily schedule with appointments, calls to make, paperwork and so forth. In the middle, list people who have called who you need to call back. At the bottom, list the personal things you need to do during the day.

Put the most important things at the top, and least important at the bottom. In this way, if you do not get to them, you can shift them over to another day. Write down all the important things you must do over the next few months and add to it as they come up. It is usually best to make sales calls in the morning when you are fresh, and most business people are in. Also, if you have to leave a message, it gives an individual time to call you back during the day. The late morning and afternoon are good times to return calls, show property, and have meetings. It also is a good idea to plan your activities so that you kill many birds with one stone. Perhaps you can arrange two showings in the same area close together, and then plan to pick up a lease and deliver it afterwards.

It is a good idea to spend a little time at the end of each day planning the next day's work schedule. Calls, appointments, and showings, as well as paperwork should all be written down. This usually can be done in five or ten minutes, but as time goes by and you become more proficient at it, you will do it automatically during the day. You should put everything into the plan and make it part of your life. Doing so will bring many benefits. You will discover that when you write something down, it tends to become holy and you do it. This works especially well with things you don't want to do. There comes a sense of accomplishment and relief when a task is done and you can cross it off the list. It makes you think about what you want to accomplish, how to do it, and when. Prioritization of your work schedule makes unnecessary, repetitive, and nonproductive activities conspicuous. The consequence is that you will gradually focus on and do the things that really lead to success. Finally, once you write something down, you can forget about it because you know you will pick it up later. You no longer have to worry about remembering things. These time management suggestions will eliminate the confusion and ultimate frustration that comes with being a pinball.

Habits

In many ways, we are our habits. It stands to reason that if you endeavor to cultivate certain habits in commercial real estate they will become, in time, part of your make up. After awhile you will find yourself automatically doing the things that lead to and maintain success. If your habit is staying up until 1:00 a.m. every night partying, getting into the office at 11:00 a.m. with a hangover, talking with the secretaries at the water cooler until noon, and then spending the afternoon fumbling through your desk looking for something to do, the odds are you will fail.

What follows are a few good habits to get into in commercial real estate. Some of these have been mentioned elsewhere in this book, but they are repeated here for a couple of reasons. First, they relate to the fact that organized and successful people usually have good habits. Good habits help make you organized. Second, because some attitudes are a consequence of our habits, they warrant being repeated. Positive attitudes make successful people and good habits will help you have positive attitudes. Our beliefs often are a consequence of our actions. Ultimately, good habits will help you have good attitudes.

- Work regular hours. It may sound boring, but working eight to five is a good habit to get into.

- You may want to get into the habit of working Saturday mornings when you first start in the business.

- Get regular and sufficient sleep, get regular exercise, and eat right. Tired and fatigued people who skip breakfast are fighting an uphill battle. It is hard to be successful when you have no energy and feel lousy.

- Get into the habit of thinking about deals. Emerson said, "Thinking is the hardest thing in the world to do, that is why so few do it." Mulling over prospects' requirements, how to move a listing, or how to solve a problem in a negotiation leads to ideas and solutions. You should cultivate creative thinking.

- Organize your day in a logical and productive manner. As mentioned earlier, many brokers prefer to make the important sales calls first thing in the morning, when they are fresh. They plan meetings late morning, showings in the afternoon, and return calls at the end of the day. They always spend a few minutes at the end of each day planning the next one.

- Cultivate the habit of working 100 percent when you work. You will get more done in less time.

- Cultivate the habit of always taking the initiative. This may be more of an attitude than a habit, but if you do not have the attitude, cultivate it, and make it a habit. Do not wait for others to do something, do it yourself first. Do not wait for a prospect to call on a listing, or for a client to call you back, or for a buyer to get board of directors' approval before submitting the offer. Instead, go look for a prospect on that listing, call your client on his cell phone, and make the offer subject to the board's approval. Waiting for something to happen is an impediment to success.

- Go into the office a day early after a vacation and prepare for the next day and week. It is a waste of time plowing through mail and messages the morning of your return. Do this the day before, prioritize so that the important things get your attention first, and hit the ground running.

Work

In his book *Candide*, Voltaire writes that "Work keeps us from three great evils: vice, boredom and poverty." Work hard and smart. Learn to recognize what is productive time and what is wasted time, and minimize the wasted time. Meetings, broker consultations, discussions with the secretary, meetings with the management, busywork, paperwork, disputes with co-op brokers and encounter sessions, are time wasters. Talking to clients and prospects, getting listings, and negotiating deals, is time spent productively. As a comedian once said, "The only place success comes before work is in the dictionary."

Goals

Michel deMontaigne once said that "No wind works for the ship who has no port of destination." Analogously, the winds of fortune do not work for an individual with no goals. The simple truth is that without goals, you go nowhere. When you establish goals a number of things happen. First, you fix in your mind an objective, which, in turn, rallies your resources, including your imagination, to achieve. Second, when other people know what you want, they can help you. And third, when you have a goal, you spot opportunities. If, for example, you set a goal of having a swimming pool, you would notice the "pool for sale sign" on the road. If you had never set the goal you would probably have missed the sign and that opportunity.

Your goals should be proportional. If they are too low and easily obtainable, you will become bored. If they are too high and unattainable, you may become frustrated and feel defeated. They should be high, but not unrealistic. There is also something exciting and energizing about setting a goal and then achieving it. This enthusiasm translates to enthusiasm for the business and the desire to do better. Enthusiasm is infectious, and brokers who are enthusiastic get more clients and make more deals.

The bottom line is that when organizing yourself, you need to consciously set goals. You should, for example, set an annual income goal, monthly listing goals, and daily cold call goals. You should also review your goals on a regular basis to see how you are progressing. Doing so will help in a number of ways: For example, you may decide to change goals, figure out new ways to achieve difficult goals, or realize where you need to put your efforts.

Tickler File

In commercial real estate, you need to keep track of things that may happen two, five, or even ten years out. A sale you negotiated may contain an option to purchase additional property on which you are to be paid a fee. Leases often will include renewal options, options to expand, or options to purchase, on which you may also be paid a fee. You should keep a tickler file of all of these critical dates for the next ten years and review it at the beginning of every year. You should then make a note on your daily schedule when to follow up. Options typically require the optionee to give advance notice, so you need to figure out what the notification date is, and make the contact date well before it. If a lease has no option, then you should keep track of when that lease expires in order to be sure to contact the tenant well before the expiration date. This can be a big source of prospects and listings. If a tenant is not going to stay, you can find it something new and contact the owner to list the building or space the tenant is vacating.

A tickler file can also be used to keep track of deals you did not handle, but want to keep track of for future use. Significant tenant lease expiration dates, renewal option notification dates, or when an owner or lessee said they may want to start looking for property are things to keep track of. Tickler files keep you organized and ahead of your competition. Most brokers do not find out about prospects or property that may come available until the tenant or owner starts calling people. If you call first, you usually end up with the business.

CHAPTER 7

Getting Prospects

Many beginners in commercial real estate ask, "How do I get prospects?" Prospects are everywhere. All you have to do is drive through some commercial area and you will be surrounded by property owners and tenants who are prospects. The question is how to get in touch with them. Eventually, you will become more concerned with how to get in touch with the best prospects and how to convert them to clients.

There are many ways for the beginner to get in touch with prospects. Generally, the most productive and educational way is to directly contact the owners, existing tenants, and would be owners and tenants. Find out whom they are, pick up the phone or just walk into their office, and start asking questions. These cold calls seem to petrify beginners, but are probably the most productive way to start. There is no reason to be fearful. It's just business and most people treat it as such. You will often find people happy to talk with you.

The second way to contact prospects is through indirect contact. You contact the prospects through people who are in touch with them — attorneys, accountants, bankers, and so forth. Such contacts are useful, but not as productive in the long run. These sources may or may not recommend you, and you are not dealing with the decision makers. They can, however, lead to the best kind of prospect — one that calls you because you were recommended to them.

When getting started, you must do everything you can, directly and indirectly, to get in front of prospects and get the word out that you are looking for business. This chapter will first discuss the sources of prospects and how to find them and then move on to cultivating sources, networking and making other contacts, and marketing yourself. The last part of this chapter deals with the need to know your market and the necessity of keeping track of your prospects with a contact list.

Sources of Business

The prospects you want are the ones that deal in your area of specialty. The best way to meet them is to go to them directly and start talking. This sounds pretty obvious, but you would be surprised how many brokers don't do this. If you are in retail, start calling retail business and owners of retail properties. If you are in office, go to an office building and walk through the halls and knock on doors. If you are in industrial, go to an industrial area and walk down the street calling on all the business you see. If investment is your area, start researching whom the investors are and call them up. Do what you have to do to come face to face with those who deal in your area of specialty. You will soon find that the world is full of prospects.

As mentioned in Chapter 1, the first thing to do is pick a farm area. Most companies start agents off with a farm area. A farm area is simply a geographic area in which you specialize. If your specialty is office, your farm area might be downtown or in the suburbs; if it's industrial, it will obviously be in some industrial area. Many firms segregate farm areas by sections of the city and assign brokers to those areas. One or two brokers may have south east industrial, for example. Their farm area, in this case, would be all industrial areas in the south east part of the city. This is an excellent way to start. You simply go to your farm area and start working it. Your goal should be to call on every significant business and individual and to know every property in your farm area. In this example, you could start by just driving the streets looking for such things as empty buildings, cramped companies, different levels of activity, or too many or too few cars in the parking lot.

There are many other sources of prospects and business that you should be aware of, in addition to the ones that come from working your farm area. Some of the most common and important ones to cultivate and work are listed below.

- Cold calls. Make cold calls on anyone and everyone involved in your specialty area. The infamous cold call will dramatically improve your knowledge of what is going on in the market, who the prospects are, and property owners' plans. (Cold calls will be discussed in more detail in the next section.)

- Newspaper and television news stories. If you read that some business is growing or shrinking, call them.

- Advertising. Calls come in from listings, announcements, or general ads.

- Your list of contacts. Keep in touch with the people on your contact list. (The contact list is discussed in more detail at the end of this chapter.)

- Your tickler file. Your tickler file will remind you of lease expirations, option dates, or first rights of refusals that are coming up.

- Referrals from other brokers or your own company. Other brokers often refer prospects if the prospect is outside the referring broker's specialty area, the requirement is not their area, or they are just too busy. Companies often have regular repeat business that they spread around among the brokers. In addition, national brokerage companies get significant referrals from offices in other areas. Be sure you are on the management's list for referrals.

- Reputation. In time, your reputation will bring referrals.

- Past clients. Those whom you have successfully represented in the past can be one of your best sources of business.

- Listing calls. You should also keep track of all prospects who call on listings, which itself becomes a source of business. You can make a career on one listing. When you get a listing, call everyone. It is an excellent entrée to anyone who might have some interest in what you are offering, and you can learn about their plans in the process.

- Friends. Ask friends for referrals and information on prospects who may be looking. What are friends for?

- Property owners. Public records list all property owners for tax purposes. Get a list of all property owners in your farm area from a title company. Call on them and ask about their plans.

- Broker referrals from various associations. Broker associations such as the International Council of Shopping Centers (ICSC) and the Society of Industrial and Office Realtors® (SIOR) have significant referral systems between members. Brokers who make a point of being active in these associations and getting to know other members are usually the ones who get most of this referral business.

There are many other sources of business in commercial real estate that should be cultivated and worked. One very large source is people in allied businesses that overlap. Although these individuals are not prospects themselves, they regularly deal with people who own and lease commercial property. Such sources include attorneys (especially real estate attorneys), appraisers, lenders, contractors, engineers, environmental consultants, business consultants and "turn around" specialists, accountants, and state economic development departments, to name just a few. These sources often need someone to recommend in your specialty, and you may as well be the person. It is also a good idea to make up a list of influential people or those who have power and influence in your area of specialty. These often are major business or property owners within your farm area. Get to know them, let them know what you are doing, and ask for referrals.

Cold Calls

There is a reason why every sales manual in real estate emphasizes making cold calls on prospects. They do so because it is probably the surest and most reliable way to get prospects. Some people in business are used to people coming to them. Bankers are notorious for this. When someone needs a loan, they usually go to the bank and ask for the money. To be successful in commercial real estate, you must go to the people. You should make five calls on new prospects every day. These should be prospects that you have never contacted before — not repeat calls. Initially, they should include every property owner and tenant in your farm area. This will expand, in time, to other areas. You should ask questions that elicit the information you need in order to understand each prospects' real estate situation. You should keep a written summary of your call in your contact list, so you can refer to it whenever needed. Finding prospects to call on is not difficult. A few examples are listed below.

- Drive the streets in your farm area and list the companies.

- Get a list of property owners from a title company.

- Make a list of the largest companies in the area, the largest employers, the biggest developers, etc.

- Get a list of members of your local Chamber of Commerce.

- Make a list using the yellow pages of the telephone book.

- Scan newspaper articles and local business publications for contacts.

- Get a list of members from trade groups related to your area of specialty.

You will be surprised how much your business will increase by making just five calls per day. Eventually, you will find that you need to do this only when things slow down. Once you get some listings, a reputation, and develop some long-term clients, many prospects will come to you.

Making the calls should not be an end in themselves, but rather just part of your daily routine. For this reason, it's usually best to make only five calls per day, no more and no less. If you make too many calls, you may get burned out and eventually discouraged because such calls require courage and often involve rejection. However, if you do less than five you, are not covering enough territory. Just do five. In time, making just a few calls per day will become automatic, the rewards will add up, and you will have more business than you can handle.

Large Property Owners

One good way to get listings is to identify large property owners and simply treat them as your client. Most communities have individuals, corporations, partnerships, and developers, to name a few, that own and manage large holdings of commercial real estate. You should endeavor to identify them — especially those within your farm area. Get to know them and become familiar with their holdings. Stay in touch regularly and keep them informed of deals that have happened, market trends, and anything in particular that may affect their properties. Make it your business to know their plans and goals. It is particularly helpful to know their tenants and when their leases expire, so you are in a position to either relocate the tenant or list the property. Strong, long-term relationships are forged if you take the time and effort to research the answers to their questions or help them solve a problem for free. In time, they come to feel indebted to you. They usually, gradually, come to think of you as their agent and naturally call you when they have real estate needs.

Community and Professional Organizations

Becoming known and gaining a good reputation is one of the best ways to get referrals, prospects, and clients. In time, if you succeed in the business, a good reputation will follow, and you will find that you do not have to work so hard for business. Initially, however, you need to do all you can to let people know what you are doing and that you are looking for business. One very good way is to become active in community affairs. Call it what you like — networking, charity, community involvement, or volunteerism. In any case, it works, and it helps you establish that all-important good reputation that will lead to prospects.

The best community bodies to get involved with are those that are directly or indirectly related to the commercial real estate business. Those directly involved include professional organizations such as the National Association of Realtors®, its affiliates, and your state and local boards. The local board should be the commercial association, if there is one. Examples of commercial affiliates are the Society of Industrial and Office Realtors®, the Commercial Investment Real Estate Institute, and the REALTORS® Land Institute. Most have committees for a variety of things such as education, awards, events, ethics, and technology. Sometimes there are ad hoc associations of commercial real estate agents that you could join.

Organizations that are indirectly involved with commercial real estate include Chambers of Commerce and official, and quasi official, land use and planning groups. Chambers of Commerce involve many different professionals interested in all matters that affect business. They usually have committees that deal with a variety of subjects that affect business. Planning commissions and neighborhood planning committees may be time consuming, but they enable you to know whom the significant players are and what is going on in planning and zoning. It is particularly helpful to join the planning group in your farm area. They are a ready source of prospects who are interested and active in your farm area. You can quickly gain a reputation as the broker for that area among the local businesses. Less important, but also worthy, are charitable organizations such as the YMCA, Boy Scouts or Girl Scouts, Red Cross, as well as your local art museum and historical society. These may not lead directly to business, but they will raise your community profile.

This discussion of community activity should not be construed to mean that such activity is done only for your personal business gain. Everyone has an obligation to contribute to the social weal, and community activity is one way to do it. You should also work to improve your profession as a whole by joining your professional organization and donating your time. It just so happens, however, that in the process of doing so, you develop a reputation, learn what is going on, and get to know people who may help you succeed in the commercial real estate business.

Self-Marketing

Whales that surface get harpooned. This may be true for whales, but not for commercial real estate brokers. Some brokers feel squeamish about touting themselves. Our society frowns on those who show excessive pride and display their accomplishments. You must get over this disability if you really want to succeed. Self-marketing or self-promotion will give you a reputation that brings you prospects, leads, and referrals. You need to tell others that you are in business, that you want their business, and that you are succeeding. You must market yourself. All successful brokers do it to some extent, and those who do it the best are often the most successful.

Some of the ways you can market yourself are listed below. Some of these suggestions may be discouraged or flat-out banned by your firm, usually because such firms prefer the company to be marketed over individual brokers. There also may be some licensing and legal restrictions to what you can do. Whatever the case, you need to be creative and figure ways to get the word out.

- Include your name in all ads for listings.
- Join and be active in professional and business related organizations.
- Prepare a resume and distribute it to anyone who will take it.
- Prepare a list of deals done, especially those in your farm area, and distribute.
- Take digital photos of properties you have sold or leased or take traditional photos and scan them. Include copies of these properties in all listing packets or whenever you want to impress someone.
- Prepare a list of individuals and companies you have represented and distribute it.

- Advertise yourself on the radio. Supporting public broadcasting is one way to do this.

- Keep old brochures showing properties you have sold or leased and distribute them.

- Consolidate photos of properties you have sold or leased, as well as current listings, into one sales brochure and send it out via mass mailing.

- Develop a description of what you do in a pamphlet and distribute. This pamphlet should make you stand out and distinguish you from your competition. It might include a description of your area of specialty, your farm area, and your experience. It could also include testimonials from past clients or influential people. In addition, the pamphlet could communicate your philosophy of doing business, such as "being committed to excellence" or "preferring to do an outstanding job for a few clients, rather than a mediocre one for many."

- Send out an occasional newsletter.

- Tell everyone — especially clients and sources of clients — about yourself and your successes.

- Obtain letters of recommendation from influential people you know and distribute them.

- Ask influential friends and clients to call prospects you wish to cultivate.

- Take friends, clients, and prospects to lunch or breakfast and tell them what you are doing.

- Participate in seminars and conferences and tell other attendees what you are doing.

- Run announcement ads on significant deals that you have done.

- Cultivate media sources and keep them informed of any significant activity. This is an excellent way to promote yourself, your listings, and your transactions at no cost.

- Send out a news release on every deal that you have completed. It should include the names of the principals, the nature of the deal, a description of the property (including its location), and any unusual facts about the transaction. It should also mention, as a professional courtesy, all brokers involved and who they represented. On large, significant deals, you may want to call the paper directly and talk with a reporter.

- News releases can also be issued when you have listed a major property, or for general market observations and opinions. Many companies and individual brokers make a point of keeping track of market conditions, such as vacancy rates, prices, and rental rates and issuing the results on a regular basis. These releases are often widely quoted, and the brokers who issue them are often interviewed. These brokers become the reporter's source of information and regarded as experts in their field.

- Send property brochures not only to prospects, but also sources of prospects and influential people.

- Inform others of and display any designations you achieve.

Knowing Your Market

In the course of prospecting, it is important to make an impression on those that you come into contact with. You want them to remember you when they have some requirement in the future. Many brokers will call on them over time, and you want to stand out. One of the best ways to do this is to know your market. When you can talk fluently and knowledgeably about the market, prospects come to think of you as the expert and the one to call when they need advice or help.

This is especially true of your farm area. If you can discuss recent deals, rates, prices, or trends in your farm area, prospects in that area or those planning to do something in it will remember you. This will be magnified if you can give them any information on their property, such as a proposed rezoning or a change in their assessed value. They come to see you as their agent and primary source of real estate information. It is not unusual for these prospects to call you over time and ask various questions that pertain to their real estate matters. These questions can range from what the value of their property is for estate purposes to what a clause in a lease means. These are some of the best kinds of business contacts and prospects because they invariably convert into clients, listings, and deals. Some of these prospects may end up being lifelong clients and friends.

You should make it your business to know everything in your farm — who owns what, who leases what, the major buildings, streets, freeways, where the utilities are, what the zoning is, and so forth. You should know the market including rates, prices, vacancy, major deals, and trends. You should also be aware of any special issues or problems such as in parking, soil, environmental issues, or access. You should be aware of any trends in the local market such as whether prices are increasing or decreasing and whether landlords are giving free rent or other concessions such as increased tenant improvement allowances. You should know what major businesses are moving in or out, and why. You should also be sure to stay in touch with the largest businesses in the area to keep abreast of what they are doing.

Your knowledge of the market should not be limited to your farm area. You should also become familiar with what is happening in the real estate market regionally and nationally. Familiarity with the Consumer Price Index (and its effect on rents, vacancy rates, and absorption), construction activity, capitalization rate trends, as well as business activity in general, are examples of some larger issues. Nationally, it is wise to know the Fed's discount rate, the prime rate, leading indicators, and how the stock market is doing. These all affect business activity, and the more you know, the more you will impress prospects.

One last reminder when it comes to generating sources of business. Be sure to give every prospect your business card so they remember you. People forget names, but usually file cards away so that they can retrieve them when needed. The calls won't do you much good if the prospect can't remember who you are.

Creating and Maintaining a Contact List

As you develop your information, it is necessary to keep it in a well organized, centralized place where you can easily review and retrieve what you have learned. This is harder than it sounds. As you get more information your system can become overwhelming and confusing. Some brokers are helplessly lost in this endeavor. They have lists everywhere, files full of miscellaneous and eclectic information, computers with data that cannot be retrieved, and "mental notes" that have been forgotten. It is a good idea to keep a list of all contacts, prospects, prospective clients, calls from listings, calls from advertising, and information garnered from your effort to get business (such as cold calls, news items and observation) in one book or contact list. You should also keep track of information from other brokers on prospects, as well as general knowledge. This contact list can also include things such as lists of largest companies and/or employers, largest retailers, investors, and developers.

There are many ways to organize a contact list book. It can be done by prospect size, type, location, or simply alphabetically. You should record all the pertinent information on prospects, such as date of contact, names of real estate decision makers, addresses and telephone numbers, current building sizes, lease expiration dates, whether they own or lease, and any comments on their future plans and desires in real estate. Over time, this will become your bible of information and your primary source of leads, clients, and deals. It should be reviewed and updated regularly so you do not forget important information. When it alerts you to any upcoming lease expirations, you should call the owners and tenants well before the lease expires to relocate the tenant and get the listing. Whenever you get a listing or hear of a new property on the market, you should refer to your contact list for logical prospects for that property. This contact book is also very helpful in slow times or when your business is in a slump. All you need to do is start calling your list of contacts. You will be surprised how much this informs you of what is going on, how many leads it creates, and how it can invigorate your business.

One last comment on contact lists: They can be either electronic or physical. Some computer software, like Microsoft Outlook, is very suitable for this kind of record keeping. They have the added advantages of keeping track of, and sending, e-mail and faxes. Handwritten notebooks are nice, however, because they give you something to leaf through, you can take them wherever you go, and they still work if the power goes out. Many professionals are moving to hand-held personal digital assistants (PDAs). Not only are they affordable and portable, but your contact list is then automatically located in two places — your hand-held computer and your desktop computer — allowing for a ready back up if one system fails.

CHAPTER 8
Marketing

This book has emphasized the importance of salesmanship and listing property to success in commercial real estate. Salesmanship is important because it helps you get the listings, and the listings are important because you make money when they sell or lease. Neither of these, however, will be of much help if you cannot move the property. Some listings are easier to move than others. If the type of property listed is in demand or has the proverbial "location, location, location," it will probably sell itself. Sometimes you may just luck out and sell or lease a property before it even gets to the market. These, however, are the exceptions. The rule is that it requires a concerted effort on your part to move a listing.

There really is no secret to marketing property. The object, of course, is to get the information out so that prospects will find out about it, and one will eventually make a deal. It is also important, however, to present the property in its best possible light and in such a way that will cause a prospect to get interested in the first place. This chapter will discuss some of the most common ways property is marketed in commercial real estate, ways to make what you are marketing more appealing, alternative ways to market property, and some general things about marketing that you should know.

Know Your Listings

The first thing to do when you get a listing is to know as much as you can about what you are offering. Learn all you can about the property. It is not enough to gather some cursory information, take a picture, and then put it in the multiple listing service. One sure sign of true commercial real estate professionals is that they carefully study and research the details of what they are offering. In doing so, you will not only be providing your client with a service, but you will also become an expert in the process. Prospects will ask many questions about your listing, and you should have the answers. Being able to answer questions quickly and confidently will not only satisfy your client, but it will also inspire confidence and trust, which makes it easier to make a deal. Confirm sizes for improvements and land, be sure the addresses and legal descriptions are correct, have plats of the property, understand the environmental situation (if appropriate), get a preliminary title report, if you can, and a trio from the title company (a trio typically includes assessment information, copies of recorded documents like deeds, and a plat), check for surveys, get the assessed value and taxes, check the zone, know what financing is on the property and the terms, as well as the terms of your listing. Don't be lazy. Know your listing.

Marketing Property

Most of the techniques for marketing commercial property are the same as for other types of real estate, such as residential. Some methods of marketing, however, may be emphasized more and be more effective, for marketing commercial properties. For example, targeted marketing is used more than mass marketing in commercial real estate. Also, different methods of marketing may be emphasized more between the various specialties. Take investments, for example. Because good investment property is often difficult to find, it will often sell before getting to the market. This is especially true of large investment deals. Consequently, the buyer may be on a short list of obvious buyers. Because of this, brokers listing investment properties do not rely as much on signs, advertising, mailings, and open houses as brokers in other special-ties. However, they will usually publish an information packet containing financial information and analysis of the property, in addition to the physical property information. Office, retail, industrial and land will use most of the marketing techniques described in this chapter, but often in different ways.

In general, the most effective ways to market commercial property tend to be through signs, multiple listing services, key contacts, personal calls, and other brokers. Much of the marketing is intended to make other brokers aware of the listing. Brochure mailings to the brokerage community and to multiple listing services are examples of this approach. Perhaps the least effective way to market commercial property is through newspaper advertising. Those looking to buy or lease commercial property usually do not go to the newspaper. They usually get in their car and go drive around the areas they like or call a commercial broker. Auctions are rare and typically the last resort.

Brochures

A professional looking brochure should be prepared for every listing. Brochures provide information and create interest. They should present the property in its best possible light, highlighting its most desirable features, as well as provide the basic property information. You should give some thought to who are the most likely prospects for the property and target the brochure to them by emphasizing the features of the property that appeal to those prospects. This could include things such as a desirable location, visibility, any special improvements, and so forth. Many brokers include this information in the heading of the brochure to create interest. Even though the formats for well done brochures vary, all should include some basic property information. This includes a description of property (including a legal description if available), location, pertinent sizes, physical details, price or rental, terms of lease or sale, information on indebtedness, availability, tax infor-mation, zoning, and tenancies. An industrial property brochure, for example, may include physical details such as warehouse and office sizes, ceiling, sprinklers, number of dock-hi and grade level loading doors, lighting, posts and bay sizes, power, heat, restrooms, and the availability of rail service. A brochure should also contain a disclaimer that says something to the effect that the information in it was obtained from sources deemed reliable, but is not guaranteed by the broker and that the prospect should independently verify all information. It is also a good idea to say somewhere in the brochure that all sizes and dimensions are approximate, because they usually are.

There are two schools of thought regarding brochures and signs. One is that they should be specific and provide the information that the prospect is looking for. This school will typically say, for example, in both the brochure and sign, whether the property is for sale or lease. The other school prefers marketing tools such as brochures and signs to be vague (saying only perhaps that the property is "available"), so the prospect will call for more information. This way the broker can get more prospects because both qualified and unqualified prospects will call. In addition, if a prospect calls for information, a broker is able to present the property information personally and then be in a position to be able to respond to objections. Both methods have their merits. The author prefers the first method, because it just seems to be good business practice to disclose the details of what you are offering up front.

Brochures will often contain additional information that applies to the property type. Retail brochures may have demographic information, industrial brochures location or aerial photomaps, and investment deals investment analysis and financial information. Often, investment deals will provide a more comprehensive information packet with investment spreadsheets, income and expense data, financial and lease details, and pro-formas with projected income, as well as the basic property information. Brochures can also include title information, easements, plats or surveys, utility information, and sometimes a preliminary title report. Most brochures will have a picture of the property and often a location map, which could be just a street map or aerial photo with labels.

It is important to do a good job on the brochure. If done properly, brochures arouse interest. They are the property's calling card and the primary source of information. As such, they will be distributed widely. They are the first thing you hand a prospect when discussing or showing the property. They are what you give, mail, fax or e-mail to prospects when they inquire about the property. They are usually the source of other brokers' information on the property, as well as the information source for the multiple listing service. They typically are used in mass mailings, news releases, and open houses. They are also entrées when calling on a listing's neighbors, when making cold calls, and in listing packet presentations. The quality of your brochures often reflects your level of professionalism.

One last note regarding brochures. It is always a good idea to keep at least a few of your old brochures for future use. They come in handy in many situations.

Signs

Signs do many things for you. They advertise your listing, they advertise you, they bring in new prospects, they identify where your listing is located, and they make your clients feel like things are happening to market their property. And they do all of these things 24 hours a day. Such benefits from signs come when you focus on listing property. Brokers who represent tenants exclusively do not get these powerful advantages.

Signs are one of the most effective tools for marketing commercial property. You will notice, after awhile, that many of the deals you make came from a call on a sign. More often than not, prospects and brokers go to the area they are researching and just look around. Prospects, in particular, like to see an area and just look at properties. They often pride themselves in having found what they wanted on their own.

Signs should give a good impression and project a professional, business-like attitude. They come in different construction, shapes, and sizes. The most common sizes are 4' X 6' and 6' X 8', but they can be anything from small window signs to banners. They can be made from paper, metal, plastic, or wood. A sign should state whether the property is for sale, lease, or available and list your name and the company's name, as well as the telephone number. Some brokers like to put additional property information on a sign, such as size, 'tenant relocating', or 'price reduced.' It is a good idea to put up a sold or leased sticker when the deal is done because it shows you were successful in marketing the property.

Obviously, signs should be in the most conspicuous location and facing a busy road or freeway, if possible. Signs can be either on a building or in the ground, whichever gives the best exposure. Sometimes a "V" sign is best when a listing faces a busy road so it will be exposed to traffic coming in both directions. If your listing does not have exposure, it is a good idea to have a directional sign to the property.

Two comments regarding signs: Some brokers put signs on properties they do not have listed and some keep signs up long after the deal is done. These practices are not necessarily unethical, but they do tend to be frowned upon. Also, keep in mind that every sign up is a deal not done. Signs are nice, but they are no substitute for doing the deal.

Multiple Listing Services

Multiple listing services are one of the most effective ways to market property. Other brokers are talking daily with prospects looking for property. Consequently, they are one of the biggest sources of deals. Multiple listing services enhance and accelerate the sharing of information between brokers, primarily through the Internet. Their effectiveness is dependent upon broker cooperation and the willingness to share information. For this reason, it is important to keep all listing information current in the multiple listing service.

Multiple listing services are also used for other reasons, such as searching for property. They generally have search criteria where you can input requirements like size, location, type of property, and price or rental range. They then generate a list of properties that match your criteria. A downside to these services is that you usually are the last to know of a property's availability. Usually, the listing broker has already called all of the logical prospects. You may also waste a lot of time with unqualified prospects.

Commercial multiple listing services can be local or national, privately owned or operated by an association (like a local commercial association of Realtors®), and they can be fee based or free. There are numerous multiple listing services. Two main national services are LoopNet (loopnet.com) and Costar (costar.com). LoopNet is a free service and Costar is subscriber based and not available to the public at large. Often, the subscriber-based services are most effective because the service and its members work hard to keep the information current. More often than not, the local commercial multiple listing service is the most effective one.

In addition to sharing property information and allowing you to search for property, multiple listing services may offer other useful features as well. They can provide lender and mortgage information, market information, information on exchanges, broadcast e-mail and fax services (see following paragraph), and appraisal and property data, to name a few. Many multiple listing services will issue a monthly market report giving comprehensive information on your market. This information can include the volume of sales and leases, prices, vacancy, and absorption, all broken down by specialty area and location. These reports can be very helpful in keeping you abreast of what is going on in your market. They are also useful for listing presentations and providing general information to clients.

Broadcast e-mail and fax services can be particularly effective in marketing or looking for property. You can broadcast a prospect's requirements or information about a new listing. You usually input the information you wish to broadcast by category and select who to target. The information on an industrial property, for example, can then be e-mailed or faxed to every broker in your area that specializes in industrial real estate. It is not unusual to receive numerous calls from brokers with prospects within minutes of sending an email of this type.

As mentioned earlier, one problem with multiple listing services is that you will sometimes be flooded with calls from unqualified prospects. These include other brokers who are just fishing, owners who want information, or vendors who have some service to sell. This is especially true of open listing services that are free and do not require broker membership. Your time is valuable, so you need to limit the amount of time you spend with these kinds of inquiries.

Key Contacts

Key contacts are simply prospects you know who may be looking for what you have listed for sale or lease. These, along with the neighbors, should be among your first calls when trying to move a property. Often, these are some of the most productive calls you will make. The key contacts come from your contact list, which was discussed in Chapter 7. A quick review of your contact book should hopefully provide a list of prospects whose criteria are close to what you are offering.

Calling key contacts early on in the listing period is an obvious thing to do, but you would be surprised how many brokers don't do it. They list a property and then another broker brings in the most logical prospect at some later date. This is a sign that you are not on the ball. Calling the logical prospects not only increases your odds of making a deal on your listing quickly, it also means you will not have to split the fee with another broker. It is a Realtor's® professional obligation to always cooperate with other brokers, but there is no obligation to ensure that there is another broker. Getting to the prospect first is just good business and hustle. When you are there first, it means you are working effectively and doing a good job for your client. There is one other advantage to being the first one in the door. Prospects get excited about being the first one to look at the property and the opportunity to make a deal that beats others to the punch. Often, they have been looking for a long time and are discouraged at seeing the same old shopworn listings. They will tend to look at new listings with an attitude of wanting to make it work. They bring to the table an automatic sense of urgency to make things happen.

Personal Calls

Over the course of a listing, you should endeavor to call everyone who could be a prospect or a source of a prospect. This not only promotes your listing, but also you. Your contact list of prospects has already been mentioned and neighbors will be discussed in the following section. Other sources of prospects are those that may be in touch with, or know of, a prospect. Sources of prospects could be, for example, developers and investors — especially those who own or are offering similar property or listings in your area of specialty. In industrial real estate, for example, common sources of prospects are utilities, railroads, and to a lesser extent, banks. Sources of prospects are anyone prospects may tell of their need or ask for assistance.

Neighbors

One of the very first things you should do when you first get a user listing is call on all of the neighbors. They are often your best prospects. When they move, they tend to stay in the area. Consequently, they are always interested in what is going on in their market (like rents and prices) and what is available. Often, even if they have no needs, the listing will spark their interest and sometimes create a need. If nothing else, it is an excellent way to gain entrée to a prospect that may lead to future business. It is also a good idea to call on investors who own property in the area, if your listing is for sale. They tend to like to invest in areas they know and have had success.

Advertising

Of all the ways to market commercial real estate, advertising is probably the most overrated. Most prospects, whether they are in office, retail, industrial, land, or investments, do not go to the classified section of the local newspaper for help. They usually do not find what they want in display ads or on the radio. They tend to hear about a property from brokers or see a sign. Some brokers think marketing commercial real estate means putting an ad in the classifieds and then putting their feet up and aggressively waiting for the phone to ring. These are the ones who do all the cooperative deals.

There are different reasons to advertise and various mediums to use. The reasons to advertise are generally to promote property or to promote your company, and hopefully you. The variations on the ads that promote property are endless. How to advertise effectively is a specialty in itself. Generally, however, they should describe what is being offered in a way that creates interest and tell the reader where to call and who to ask for. Ads that promote you and your company can include such things as property ads, testimonials, announcement ads for completed deals, or general self-promoting ads that tell people why they should do business with you. (Self-promotional ads were discussed in "Self-Marketing" in Chapter 7.) Mediums for advertising include newspaper (including specialized newspapers such as a business journal or specialty area newsletter), radio, television, and the Internet. All advertising should be simple and professional.

Mailing

Mailings have become less important due to the Internet, e-mail, and broadcast fax. Nevertheless, they are one way to market property and/or yourself. There are different kinds of mailings used for different purposes. There are mailings to brokers, to prospects directly, to a target industry, or to an area. You should keep a current list of all brokers and their area of specialization (office, retail, industrial) and mail the appropriate ones a brochure when you list a property. Broadcast fax, e-mails with attachments, and multiple listing services are important, but the greatest impact will be made when a broker receives a well done, eye-catching brochure in the mail. They just remember it better and may be more likely to pick up the phone and call prospects they know for that property.

It sometimes helps to do mailings directly to prospects. These can be either targeted mailings or mass mailings. Some private companies, like infoUSA, can break down businesses by zip codes, SIC code (a government classification system for business type), number of employees, or sales volume so you can profile those prospects that might be most interested your listing. Mailings enable you to target, for example, your area's largest manufacturers, wholesalers, retailers, or a service group like lawyers or insurance agents. Often, title companies can provide lists from the public record of companies and/or property owners within certain zip codes, that are in the vicinity of your listing.

Mass mailings can be a good way to either promote one or many listings and, again, yourself. It is a good idea to occasionally combine all your listings within your farm area into one brochure and mail it to all businesses within your farm area. You should mark on the brochure which properties are available, which have a transaction pending, and which are sold or leased. Occasional mailings can also be made to real estate attorneys, accountants, major companies, largest employers, high-tech companies, investors, lenders, and other sources of prospects.

News Releases

By and large, the media is interested in commercial real estate activities. Send the local media news releases on every deal you do. (Be sure to take the time to find the name of the reporter or editor covering real estate or business and direct the release to her.) This tells everyone that you are active in the business and successful. In addition to releases on deals completed or general releases on market conditions (discussed in more detail in the section on Self-Marketing in Chapter 7), the media is often interested in what is available. You should send releases on any major listings along with a brochure. It is an excellent way to promote a property at no cost. E-mailing the release is often the most effective way to inform the media. You should also read the releases on deals other brokers have done in order to stay abreast of the market.

Other Brokers

One of the biggest and best sources of prospects is other brokers. Think about it. If there are 50 brokers who specialize in your area and each has two prospects, you immediately have 100 prospects when you give the information out to them. Usually, however, many brokers have the same prospect, which can cause problems. (Broker cooperation and registration is discussed in more detail in the section titled "Relations with Other Realtors®" in Chapter 11.) "Co-op" or cooperative deals can account for more than half of your business. Brokers spend all day looking for prospects; consequently, most prospects are in touch with a broker. For this reason, it is critical that the information on any new listing be disseminated to the brokerage community — especially those who work in the specialty area of the listing. If it is an office listing, then it should be marketed primarily to office brokers. It is especially effective to market to those brokers who work in both the specialty and the geographic area of the listing.

Many of the marketing techniques described in this chapter are primarily ways to get the information on listings in front of other brokers, capture their attention, and get them to call their prospects. There are brochure mailings to other brokers, calls on other brokers, multiple listing services, broadcast fax and e-mails to other brokers, and open houses for other brokers. It is important to get a reputation in the brokerage community as one who is trustworthy and willing to cooperate. You should be fair in your dealings with other brokers and see that they are paid promptly when the deal is done.

To increase broker cooperation, it is important to be sure that your client is paying a full fee. One of the first questions co-op brokers ask is the amount of the fee. If you have taken the listing at a cut rate, they are more likely to work on something else that pays a full fee. With cut fees, you lose because brokers are less likely to cooperate and you will earn less and your client loses because other brokers are less likely to work on the property. This is an important sales point when listing property. The owner should know that it is in their best interest to pay a full fee. A one or two percent difference in the fee is nothing compared to months of vacancy. The fee split arrangement is also important. There are many different fee split arrangements and customs in co-op deals. Some weigh the split to the listing broker because he or she has, ostensibly, done more work than the selling broker. Sometimes the listing broker will offer more to the selling broker as an incentive. Fee split arrangements vary from place to place; however, most splits in commercial real estate tend to be 50-50. It is hard to determine who did more work on a deal, and the amount of work varies from deal to deal. Generally speaking, it all seems to equal out in the end.

There are numerous techniques for increasing broker cooperation in commercial real estate. These can include offering brokers a full fee, prizes (such as trips or gift certificates), and bonuses. The truth of the matter is that other brokers will usually bring their prospect in, if they have one, regardless of the incentives. After all, they all want to earn a commission, and something is better than nothing. Besides that, if they don't, the odds are another broker will. The real value in incentives is to raise the level of awareness and interest in a listing. Be aware that real estate companies often demand a share of whatever gift you may receive.

Open Houses

Open houses are one way to raise the level of awareness for your listing within the brokerage community. The hope is that they will spark an idea in some broker's mind that may lead to a deal. In commercial real estate, open houses are rarely used for the public. One of the problems with open houses is getting the brokers to come. For this reason, they will often offer some incentive, such as a gift or money. Some brokers and owners may elaborate on the open house by requiring agents to visit multiple properties before they can collect a prize. A good idea is to have the open house during lunch time and offer lunch. Brokers can then kill many birds with one stone; get lunch, see a property, mingle with other brokers, and maybe win something. In general, however, open houses tend to be the last line of defense. They usually mean that the property has not moved for one reason or another, so they are having an open house to try and generate activity.

If you have an open house, the property should look good. You should be prepared to distribute brochures and give a little presentation regarding the major benefits of the listing. Open houses are a good time to announce any new incentives, such as reduced price or rent. It also is a good idea to have the owner present. You look good because they see you working on their property, and they can answer any questions. You should also make an effort to go to open houses. You can see a listing, meet an owner, find out what your competition is doing, have lunch, and possibly win a prize to boot.

Auctions

Auctions are rare in commercial real estate, and they tend to be the last resort to move a listing that has been on the market a long time. Most property is sold or leased through negotiation. For this reason, people tend to think of properties offered through auctions as bargains, and the prices often reflect that. This is especially true of properties that have been on the market for some time, before the auction. Nevertheless, auctions can be an effective way to move property. Most auctions are conducted by private companies that specialize in them. They go through the same hoops to prepare the property (such as a brochure, mailing and advertising), but then hold an auction.

The auction process is a specialty area in and of itself. There are different types of auctions, such as ones with a floor and ones with no floor. The floor, or reserve price, is the figure below which the owner can decide whether or not to sell. Often, in auctions with a floor or reserve price, the property will actually be sold in negotiations after the auction closes. That is, a prospect makes a bid on a property that is not accepted in the auction, usually because the bid is below the reserve price. After the auction, the owner counters the offer and a deal is negotiated. The value of the auction, in this case, is that it demonstrates to the owner that there are no buyers who will pay more than the one offering the lowest bid (which is below the floor), so the owner decides to negotiate. Auctions with no floor mean that there is no reserve price, so the highest bid gets the property — no matter how low it is. Perhaps the greatest virtue of auctions is that they reinvigorate the marketing of the property and create interest.

Usually, the auction company is your competitor. Some large brokerage companies have auction capabilities. You may end up losing your listing to them for auction. You can, however, negotiate different fees with auction companies if the property sells. Quite often, these are finders' fees. Of course, there is no reason you couldn't learn how to conduct an auction yourself, although it is unusual for brokers to do so.

Range of Value

Establishing the asking price or rental for property to be offered can be tricky business. If the price is too high, prospects get scared away, and if it is too low, money is left on the table. Fortunately, establishing a price or rental for listing purposes is unlike appraising, where one single fair market value must be arrived at. Instead, it is possible, and advisable, to establish a range of value for the property, within which it may sell or lease. The top of the range is the asking price, and the bottom is the upset price or the price below which the property should not be sold or leased. Generally speaking, you should use both the income and sales comparison approaches when establishing the range, and then, if your local assessor has one, compare it with the assessor's market value, as a guidepost. Assessors are often below market values due to various reasons, such as inflation, but they can act as a kind of benchmark for valuation purposes. If your range is significantly different than the assessor's value, there may be something wrong. Be sure that the assessor's market value is for the real estate only. They have been known to include additional property, such as machinery and equipment, in their values. Also, be sure that the assessor's value is a market value and not some arbitrary value or a percentage of the market value. You may use the cost approach if you like, but it has certain limitations which were discussed in the section on "Appraisal" in Chapter 4.

When using the income approach, use the comparative high and low rents and capitalization rates to establish the range. In the sales comparison approach, use the high and low range of comparable sales. When this is done, correlate the figures by considering things such as the relative merits of the subject to comparable properties or the strength of the market and then come up with a recommended range of value. The real trick is to try and establish a top price at which the best prospects will not be scared away.

Your final recommended range of value for a listing to sell may look something like this:

Range Of Value

	Low	High
Income Approach	$1,200,000	$1,500,000
Sales Comparison Approach	$1,300,000	$1,700,000
Assessors' Fair Market Value	$1,200,000	$1,200,000
Recommended Range of Value	$1,200,000	$1,700,000

In this example, you would recommend asking $1,700,000 for the property. However, the owner should be willing to negotiate on that price within the range to as low as $1,200,000, depending on the market. The property should not be sold for less than $1,200,000.

There are many advantages to setting the asking price up this way in a listing. First, the actual value of the property may be uncertain and difficult to establish. Different prospects have different requirements, and some may think it worth more than others. You may truly not know what it will sell or lease for until you put it on the market. Second, you are less likely to leave any money on the table because you are asking a top price, but you have left yourself open to negotiation if it is too high. Third, you have prepared the owner to negotiate on their price depending on the market, which will increase the odds of being able to move the property. Most owners think their property is worth more than it is, and this is a way to make them be realistic. Fourth, this method allows you to set the market. Comparables are old deals, and if the market has risen, your final sales price or rent may be the market's new high. This method enables you to establish an asking price over the market, and conceivably set it.

When listing property, owners are very susceptible to brokers who highball property in order to get the listing. Highballing is when a broker takes a listing at an unrealistically high price, in order to get the listing, with the hope that the owner will become realistic with time. They figure that if they can get it listed, they have a better shot at making a deal, than if they did not. Once they list the property, they immediately start trying to convince the owner to take a lower priced deal. Sometimes this works, but it usually backfires. When a property is listed too high, it often scares away prospects that may have otherwise made an offer. More often than not, the listing broker never knows who these prospects are because they never called or because their broker, who never discloses his or her name, told the prospect that the price was unrealistic. So the property sits on the market for a long time with no activity. Then, in order to stimulate activity, the owner lowers the price. The first thought that comes to every prospect's mind is, "how much lower will it go"? The owner usually ends up with more vacancy and less money, than if he or she had priced it right up front. To make matters worse, the listing broker gets known for highballing and a bad reputation. Do not highball; it is not in your or your client's interests.

When a broker lists property at a price over the market, the question naturally arises whether it is an attempt to establish a new market price or a highball. The answer is sometimes difficult to discern. It seems to depend on circumstances. With fast rising markets, strong demand, limited supply, or change of use, a high price seems warranted. If the economy is in a recession, there is little demand, and many competing buildings, it is probably highballing. These factors can be considered in your correlation, and accounted for, depending on the facts.

One final comment regarding the valuation of property: Be sure to keep a list of all prospects on the property, and what they say. If the owner does decide to lower the price, you want to be sure to go back to each of them and resubmit the property. In addition, feedback from prospects about the property can be critical information for both you and the owner when making intelligent price decisions on the listing. If prospects consistently tell you that the price is too high, then the price may be too high. If they say the roof leaks, then a deal may be made by reducing the price by the cost of fixing the roof. If they say that they can get a comparable property for less or build the same building for the same amount of money, you will want to quantify those numbers and adjust your pricing. If they say the location is bad, then you may have to completely reevaluate your pricing. The point is that both you and the owner need to know these objections in order to make intelligent decisions on pricing.

Rifle versus Shotgun

The two main ways to market commercial real estate is by rifle or shotgun. Both can be effective. Sometimes one works better than the other, depending on many factors such as the nature of the property or improvements. Rifling is when you identify a few of the most logical prospects and go after them. Shotgunning is when you spread the information far and wide, so everyone knows. Shotgunning is like a spider spinning its web. It spreads the web in order to catch any flies that may come near. If the spider did a good job on the web, it will get any fly that passes its way. Of course, if there are no flies in the area, then it does not matter how well the web was spun; it must look elsewhere for prey. Advertising, mass mailings, signs, and news releases are examples of shotgunning. Rifling, on the other hand, is like the spider hunting for prey. It first figures out where the flies are or are most likely to be and then goes after them. Brochures to neighbors or logical prospects, contacting brokers who work in the same specialty area, calls on logical prospects, and targeted mailings are examples of rifling.

If a listing has some special improvements that could be of use to a certain type of prospect, you should rifle those prospects. If the listing is a small, reasonably priced investment that hundreds of investors would want, you may want to shotgun in order to create competition. On the other hand, if the investment is priced at $50,000,000, you would have to rifle because there are likely only a few investors who could afford it. Most successful commercial brokers use both methods: They first shotgun a listing to the market and then follow up with the rifle method.

Types of Prospects: Users and Investors

When marketing property, you need to ask yourself who your prospects are. Who is going to buy or lease what you are offering? There are many types of prospects — companies, investors, developers, and speculators. All prospects, however, generally fall in two categories, user or investor. Users are those who plan to use the property, and investors are those who are looking for an investment. Each looks at property differently.

When purchasing or leasing property, users consider the things that make the property fit their use. Their criteria often include things such as location, visibility, employment, traffic counts, transportation, and prestige. A user's requirements tend to be more objective than, say, someone making a decision about residential real estate. Business professionals typically do not decide on which property to acquire based on how they feel about it. Instead, their requirements are usually driven by an objective analysis of current needs. In industrial real estate, for example, they will consider if a warehouse has dock-hi or grade level doors, if the ceiling is high enough, whether there is enough truck swing room, the proximity to their market, and, if applicable, if rail access is available.

In addition to the physical requirements of the real estate, there are numerous other motivating factors for user buyers or lessees in commercial real estate transactions. One obvious one is price or rate. A user who is purchasing may be interested in a property simply because it is a good price or the terms are attractive, and a user who is leasing might be able to obtain a low lease rate or better lease terms. It should be noted that price or rate driven types of deals are often the hardest to make. This is because one side to the transaction is motivated primarily by the price, so he or she tends to bargain harder. Other motivations for users can include things such as tax considerations or simple pride of ownership.

In general, users pay more for property than investors. This is because they evaluate it differently than investors. A user will usually consider comparable market prices and the replacement cost of a property. Invariably, the only way users can really get exactly what they want is to build it, which is the most expensive route. They will price out a new building, which establishes a very high value for the top of their price range. When they then look at used buildings, the prices look reasonable to them because they are comparing them with the replacement cost of a new building. They usually end up compromising when they buy or lease property to use. The point is that prospects intending to actually use a piece of real estate use methods of evaluation that tend to give higher values.

Investors look at things differently. They tend to be a cold-blooded group. They generally look exclusively at the income the property will generate. They typically will consider things such as the rent, the overall rate of return, their cash on cash return, and the internal rate of return, to name a few. The price they pay will be based on things such as the property's current income, the market rents, the return they require, the deductions they use to arrive at the net operating income, and the discount rate, if they are discounting the cash flow. Because rents typically lag behind sales prices and replacement costs, their method usually results in a lower price. In some types of real estate, such as apartments and leased investments, this is not a problem because they are only competing against other investors. But they have a hard time competing with users who are willing to pay a higher price. It is very common to hear investors complain that property is just too expensive.

The important thing to remember is that you should try to market listings to users, if at all possible, because they will pay your client more money. This means property should be marketed when it can be delivered to a user, such as when it is empty or near lease expiration. If your owner knows that, in the future, he or she will want to sell a property that is now leased, try and get a clause in the lease that allows for cancellation of the lease in the event of a sale.

Many wonder why users do not use the income approach to value. The answer is that they should! Even though they will be using the property, they are also investors, and should evaluate property as such.

Showing Property

Marketing property is just like selling a car; you want it to look as good as possible for the prospect. On all listings, you should evaluate the property to see how it looks and make any recommendations to the owner that might improve its appearance. Cosmetics such as painting, repairing any damage, carpeting, replacing light bulbs and cleaning are things that make a listing more attractive and marketable. Getting to your listing well before the showing and doing little things like turning the lights on, opening a door, or pulling up some blinds also helps. You should give some thought to how you want to direct the showing and what you want to say in advance. First impressions are important in relationships and showings, so you want the prospect to see the best first. You should make an effort to point out the listing's best features during the showing. It is very wise to try and learn in advance if the prospect has some special requirement, such as visibility, parking, or heavy electricity needs and point those out. You should also be prepared with brochures or other pertinent property information.

An old real estate saw says that when showing multiple properties, always show the worst first. This way, as the reasoning goes, the prospect is so delighted to finally see something they can actually use, they end up making a deal. There may be some truth in this but, by and large, commercial real estate decisions tend to be based more on the facts than emotional whim. Generally speaking, if a serious prospect has set the requirement standards, he or she will follow them. Meeting those requirements and the nature of the deal itself are usually more important than any relief experienced from finding a property that is better than the others. As mentioned previously, prospects for commercial property tend to be businesslike. They usually make decisions based on the facts and not subjective criteria, such as whether the colors are right or how it feels.

One last matter that comes up often in many situations — especially showings — is how to answer questions to which you do not know the answer. Prospects are always asking questions, especially at showings, and they expect you to have the answers. Many brokers know just enough to be dangerous. If you do not have the answer, say "I do not know the answer to your question, but I will get it," and then get it. Do not make up answers. It is amazing how much misinformation is disseminated in commercial real estate. Some brokers just seem compelled to provide answers to questions, whether they know the answers or not. Do not fall into this trap. You cannot know everything. Not only can you be sued for misrepresentation, but you are being unprofessional and misleading the prospect. Answers are usually readily found to most questions, and prospects appreciate your effort.

Reporting to Clients

In the acquisition of wealth, as the old saying goes, there are two problems. The first is getting the wealth, and the second is keeping it. The same is true of listings. Acquiring a listing does you no good if you lose it to another broker, who ends up making the deal. The best way to keep listings is to stay in regular touch with your clients and let them know what is going on. You should make a point of talking to them or leaving messages on their answering machines, at least weekly. You should also make comprehensive written reports monthly. Tell them everything, including what has been done to market the property, calls received, showings, and the market conditions in general. Owners are very interested in the status of their property and appreciate the reports.

If you have nothing to report, it is better to call your client and tell him or her that, rather than stay silent. Having nothing to report can mean many things. It can mean that that you are doing nothing to market the building, which should be a red flag to you. Brokers often do not report to clients for this reason. It could also mean that there simply are no prospects in the market. If this is the case, your client should know it because it may alter your marketing strategies (like lowering the rent or asking price, which could spur some activity.) It also gives your client the information he or she needs in order to make intelligent decisions about the property. If a client knows, for example, that comparable property has sold for less or that there have been no other deals on similar properties, he or she may take a lower price or rent and give better terms, when an offer does comes in.

This advice is especially important in slow times. It is common, in slow times, for a deal to be made by the second or third broker who has listed the property. Some shrewd brokers prefer to wait and be the second or third one on listings during these slowdowns. Don't give them the opportunity. Stay in touch with your client!

The Economy and Its Impact

The relationship between commercial real estate and the economy is complex. Commercial real estate affects, and is affected by, the general economy. In general, when economic times are good, commercial real estate is good, and when times are bad, commercial real estate is slow. Good business times are when the economy is growing and expanding. Bad times are when growth has slowed or is contracting, as in a recession. As businesses grow and shrink in response to demand, so does their real estate activity. When consumer demand for businesses goods and services approaches capacity, they expand, and when the demand is low, they contract. When the economy slows down, people make less, some lose jobs, the unemployment rate increases, consumers spend less, business activity slows, and so does commercial real estate. When the economy speeds up, people have jobs and more money, and they demand more of the goods and services provided by business. When times are good, businesses demand more space, and when it is slow, they give it up. The demand for commercial real estate is derived, therefore, from the demands of business. Things that affect the economy affect commercial real estate.

There evolves a kind of shadow business cycle in the development of commercial real estate that goes something like this. When demand is high, owners overbuild, which causes an over supply. In turn, vacancy increases and rents decrease, which leads to less construction of new product. As the supply goes down, vacancy decreases and rents increase, so developers start building again, which eventually leads to an oversupply. (Of course, this is a highly simplified model of events. There are other factors besides supply and demand that affect developers' thinking.)

Interest rates are one of the driving forces that determine activity. For most businesses, the key interest rate is the prime rate or the best rate they can get at a lending institution. If interest rates are high, then business borrowing is dampened, which decreases the demand for space. High interest rates for commercial loans on property will also dampen demand. Further, consumers will tend to borrow and spend less with high interest rates, which will dampen general economic activity. When rates are low, businesses borrow more and have more money to fund expansion. Low mortgage rates also make property more affordable and cause consumers to borrow and spend, which increases economic activity. The monetary policies of the Federal Reserves have a tremendous effect on interest rates, the availability of credit, and the level of economic activity.

The Federal government and governmental fiscal policies will also affect the economy and commercial real estate. If taxes are high, people have less to spend. If government borrowing is high, interest rates will increase due to the demand for money. If tax policies encourage business spending, business spending will increase. For example, tax credits for the purchase of machinery and equipment will stimulate businesses to make purchases. Eliminating certain tariffs, such as with NAFTA, will put businesses that cannot compete with foreign competitors, out of business.

There are a multitude of other economic factors that affect the level of commercial real estate activity. Inflation — when prices are rising and currency declines in value — causes investors to buy property because it is rising in value and also causes many businesses to lease because they cannot afford to purchase. Generally, prices go up every year. Deflation — when prices are declining and currency is increasing in value — may cause investors to sell real estate because it is going down in value. This has generally not been the case since the 1930s. However, a user may find property more affordable in deflationary times.

Some trends and innovations can change the face of real estate. For example, technology and the demand for information created the rapid expansion of the high-tech industry, which, in turn, spawned demand in commercial real estate for a new type of product. Consumer tastes and habits cause some industries to grow and others to shrink. Foreign competition and lower wage scales can put domestic industries out of business. Labor trends, politics, capital markets, consumer confidence and buying habits all affect the economy and commercial real estate.

When times are good, everyone is happy. There is demand, lots of deals, low vacancy, active developers, construction activity, and rising prices and rents. When things get hot, investors start speculating, flipping property, double escrowing, bidding up prices, and financing purchases with easy contract terms. When things get really hot, the greater fool theory usually kicks in. One investor buys a property at a price he or she knows is too high, but does so anyhow in the belief that that there is a greater fool out there who will pay even more. Eventually, there is a bust and the last one holding the property becomes the fool.

When times are bad in commercial real estate, most everyone groans and wishes for times to get better again. Demand slows, there are fewer deals, lots of listings on the market, vacancy rates go up, developers stop developing, contractors stop building, and prices and rents go down. Businesses downsize so more property comes on the market, often as sublease listings. Landlords start competing with each other for tenants by offering lower rents, free rent, and higher tenant improvement allowances. There are more proposals to other landlords' tenants in an effort to "buy" them away. Owners reduce the prices of properties that have sat on the market for a long time and give easy terms so buyers can afford them.

It is common to see a washout of brokers in commercial real estate in bad economic times. Good brokers usually make money in both good and bad times. They are the ones who learned the basics of the business in the beginning, so they know what to return to when things slow down. Brokers who did not learn the basics, or were "order takers" in the good times, get lost. They were used to easy deals, prospects they didn't have to work to get, and few problems. They were like a plow that just skimmed the surface that went around rocks in its way. Good brokers dug deep furrows and removed the rocks. In bad times, good brokers understand that the deals are still there, but that there is more competition, and they will have to work harder and smarter to make them.

There are opportunities in slow economic times. As already mentioned, there typically are more sublease listings available, investors looking for bargains, and distressed properties on the market. Further, experienced brokers know that it is often the second or third broker on a listing who makes the deal. They make a point of staying in touch with owners who have property on the market. They make more competitive and attractive proposals to their prospects. They make sure that their landlords make competitive deals because they know that just a few months of vacancy will destroy the return on any investment. It is usually better to lease a property today, at a reduced rate (with a future rental increase), than face extended vacancy.

A couple of final comments regarding the economy and commercial real estate. Investment real estate is often driven by factors in addition to those discussed here. Investors are often motivated by tax policy, returns, and price (like bargain deals in a recession). Some investors buy for reasons other than the general economy. The timing of commercial real estate deals is the result of a multitude of things, of which the economy is one. A business may move because its lease is expiring, an especially attractive property is available, there is a better deal, or it needs a branch location for a new franchise. The timing of the move can be a consequence of entirely different factors, such as when the slow season is or when the other property is available. Also, business activity in general slows during the holidays and summer months due to vacations. Investment activity can pick up at the end of the year due to year-end tax planning.

CHAPTER 9

The Deal

Up to now this book has focused on learning the commercial real estate business, learning how to sell and organize yourself, getting prospects, and marketing property once you get a listing. Now you are at the point where you have two parties who want to make a deal. Many brokers fumble the ball at this stage because they do not know how to facilitate and document the negotiations. Sometimes the principals are so motivated that the deal just makes itself. In this case, a good broker gets out of the way. These deals are more a matter of not bungling the negotiations, rather than handling them properly. More often than not, however, both parties are intent on getting the best terms possible, which involves hard bargaining and trade-offs. These kinds of negotiations require knowledgeable, savvy brokers who are adroit at helping people come to agreement. A little finesse and a lot of luck also helps. A third kind of deal involves one or more principals who are not motivated, or even interested, in making a deal. This is often the case with proposals to tenants in slow times. In these deals, the broker has to work to induce the principals, be creative, and generate interest. These are the hardest kind of deals to make.

Much of your success in commercial real estate will depend on how good a deal you negotiate for your clients. If, for example, you negotiated a lease for an owner with fixed rents that end up well below the market in the future, the owner will not be happy. Owners talk and you soon will find yourself with a reputation for negotiating bad deals. If, on the other hand, you had the foresight to include provisions for escalation, the same landlord will sing your praises, and other owners will seek you out. Your ability to negotiate good deals depends on many things, including your experience, knowledge of contracts, knowledge of the business, and salesmanship. This is the point where commercial real estate crosses from a business into an art. Creativity is required because the answers are not always clear, and you must conceive of the proper solutions on your own. Deal making and negotiation separate the good brokers from the mediocre ones. In a way, success in negotiations is where experience and preparation meet.

In all of the described cases, there are certain principles to follow and things to avoid as you facilitate the process. Most of these are presented in the section on "Negotiations," which follows. Negotiation is a process of give and take and not intimidation, as Robert Ringer describes in his book *Winning Through Intimidation*. (The title is a bit of a misnomer. The book is really about how to avoid letting yourself be intimidated by others.) Ringer is describing a broker who did not follow the fundamentals of commercial real estate brokerage, and therefore, must resort to intimidation. If you did everything the right way up front, intimidation is a moot point. Furthermore, intimidation rarely works with knowledgeable business professionals and often backfires.

The role of proposals, RFPs, and multiple offers in negotiations will be examined in this chapter as well. These are the tools by which commercial deals are initiated. The issue of credit is also addressed. In addition, the chapter addresses related topics such as credit, assembling property, and the importance of attention to detail in negotiations.

Negotiations

Once you have a buyer and seller or lessee and lessor together who want to make a deal, you still have to have them agree on all the terms before you can proceed. The goal of negotiations in commercial real estate is to arrive at a written record of the meeting of the minds. This is easier said than done.

The essence of deal making in commercial real estate is a give and take exchange between two principals who want something from the other. Core negotiations revolve around price (or rent) and terms. While price is pretty straightforward, terms can mean almost anything. Terms include financing, contingency periods, options, rights of refusal, closing date, time for acceptance, length of the lease, cancellation provisions in the lease, tenant improvements or tenant improvement allowance, personal property or fixtures to be included or excluded from the sale, and so on. A seller may give a lower price in exchange for cash and a short contingency period or demand a higher price in exchange for a contract with a low down payment, low interest rate, long amortization, and no balloon payment. Of course, the terms themselves can also become an important point for trade offs in negotiations. For example, the lessee may give the lessor a longer term in exchange for an earlier occupancy date, or a landlord may drop a security deposit requirement because the tenant offers good credit.

Negotiations should always be in writing and begin with an offer. Principals sometimes prefer to make a verbal offer, but this should be discouraged. If they are not willing to put the offer in writing, a red flag should go up in your mind. It usually means that they not a serious prospect. Further, verbal offers initiate negotiations on shifting sands because parties, intentionally or unintentionally, forget what they agreed to, so you end up having to go back and renegotiate points. When there is no firm commitment, nobody feels committed. This is the time to qualify the prospect. If he or she is a serious buyer or lessee, there should be no problem putting words in writing.

All counter offers should refer to the previous offer (or counter offer) and should state that the party agrees to all of the terms of the previous offer (or counter offer) with the following changes. Then itemize the changes. The idea is to gradually narrow the areas of disagreement to fewer and fewer issues until there is written record of a document that both agree to.

The question sometimes comes up regarding the best form of earnest money deposit that should accompany the offer. Should it be a note or cash? Notes are probably more common in commercial real estate. In general, cash is harder to obtain than notes. Some brokers prefer notes for just this reason. However, it is better to get cash if you can. Notes are just promises to pay, but cash makes the statement that the offer is serious. Notes are nice, but they are no substitute for cash. In principle, a broker should always endeavor to get a monetary deposit.

It is important for the broker to remember that negotiations are not like legal litigation or union/labor disputes. The emphasis in commercial real estate negotiations is to bring the parties together — not to emphasize the confrontational aspect of the process. Brokers will be less successful if they totally advocate one side of a deal, as in a legal dispute. There is no success in deals that fail. It is better to be positive, emphasize the aspects of the transaction that are in each side's interests, and work to bring about agreement. The best negotiations result in win-win deals for both parties. These deals are best achieved when the broker acts as an accommodator and not an advocate. Some feel that it is the broker's role to advocate one side of the deal; however, too much of this will often turn the other principal off and could kill the deal. Remember, it is also in your client's interest to make the deal.

The following negotiation techniques may facilitate both the transaction and your client's position.

- Set the parameters of what will be negotiated. For example, the seller may be flexible on the terms, but firm on the price.

- Go slow and resist making the first offer or being the first to concede a point.

- If you are making the offer, establish deadlines by which a proposal may be accepted in order to inject a sense of urgency. If you are receiving the offer, be aware that these deadlines are usually meaningless.

- Bring fear into the picture. Letting the buyer know that there are other buyers or letting the seller know that there are competing properties is a very motivating factor in negotiations.

- Make negotiations subject to some other entity's approval. An agent may fully negotiate a deal, but then have to get the approval of a board of directors, which may approve the deal with some changes.

- Keep your cards close to your vest. It pays to tell as little as possible and, at the same time, to learn as much as you can about the other side.

- Focus on the big issues and ignore the minor ones. Usually, if the big issues are resolved, the smaller ones will fall in place.

A couple of suggestions for brokers that may expedite negotiations are listed below.

- As a broker, think through each side of the deal and prepare your client for the response. If, for example, a buyer makes a low price offer that you know the seller will not accept, tell the buyer you do not think the seller will accept the offer. This mentally prepares the buyer for the inevitable counter offer. Likewise, if you know the owner might take something less than the listing price, tell the buyer. This way you get the buyer thinking about the counter offer and what higher price they may be willing to accept.

- Once the deal is negotiated and in escrow, if any routine problems or things that need to be done arise, it is a good idea to have the escrow agent handle them. If you call the principals, they often develop a "negotiations" mentality. They think they are still in negotiations and must counter the request. If the escrow agent calls them, they think it is just the paperwork required to close the deal. You have been the advocate, and the escrow agent is neutral. Most principals just comply with what the escrow agent requests.

Common Mistakes in Negotiation

Some of the most common mistakes in negotiations include the following.

- Not having agreement on all of the critical points. Many times brokers will skip over a point of contention hoping that it will resolve itself later. These are the brokers that are always trying to "close the deal in escrow," or the ones who had a "deal fall out of escrow." The deals failed because they did not get agreement on the points up front. Closing a deal is like zipping up a zipper — if you have taken care and connected each of the latches correctly, the zipper will close. If you missed one, it will not. In commercial real estate negotiations, if you have attained agreement on all of the points, the deal will close automatically, like a zipper.

- Lack of a sense of timing. Parties to a negotiation will give based on what they have given or taken. They may give on one point in order to obtain some other. It is during the heat of the negotiations that the principals are most accommodating to this give and take process, so this is where the issues should be resolved. Some brokers leave issues to be resolved to a later time or try and force agreement on some point outside of this period.

- Putting clients in touch with each other directly. Sometimes this works, but it is usually the last resort. When principals talk directly to each other, not only do you no longer know what is going on, but you lose control of the transaction and are no longer able to act as a buffer or mediator. Often egos and emotions get in the way when principals deal directly. You should only put the principals in direct contact when it looks like the deal will die. Sometimes the personal touch is just enough to get one side or the other to budge a little. Sometimes one principal will ask if he or she can talk with the other principal directly. More often than not, the reason is because that principal thinks he or she can get a better deal by dealing direct. You should resist this.

- Changing horses in the middle of the stream. This is perhaps the biggest deal killer of all. Many principals like to go back and renegotiate a point after it has been agreed on. Some are fond of saying that the deal is not done until they sign the last paper. This attitude makes negotiations very difficult because when one side opens up one issue, the other opens up another and your whole deal quickly unravels. This is one good reason to put everything in writing. You can remind the principals of what they had agreed to. You should endeavor to keep them at their word.

- Confusing your role (as broker) with that of the principals. Often brokers will put their interests ahead of the interests of the principals, which can cause a myriad of problems.

Some brokers filter information in order to achieve agreement. Parties to negotiations seem to have a sixth sense when they are not getting totally accurate information from the broker. Doing this can kill a deal and a reputation. Principals prefer to have all the bad news so they can make intelligent decisions. Sometimes brokers become too preoccupied about earning a fee. Remember, negotiations are about the principals, not you. The fee will automatically follow if you have handled matters properly.

- Trying to pre-negotiate the deal. Some brokers are in too much of a hurry and try to get agreement on the deal points all at once, or get the offeror to offer what they know the offeree will accept. This usually results in a convoluted mess and no offer. You must allow time for give and take between the principals, in order to resolve issues and arrive at agreement. It is a mistake to try and "ram a deal home." Remember, the principals are making the deal, not you.

- Not having a sense of urgency. Negotiations seem to go better when the principals feel a sense of urgency. They react quicker, resolve issues faster, and make the time available to finish up the deal. A sense of urgency will also give a deal momentum, which, once started, is hard to stop. Many transactions fail because a deal lost its momentum, time passed, and everyone lost interest (except, of course, the broker).

- Mishandling multiple offers on the same listing. You must be very careful when you are the listing broker and you receive multiple offers on the same property. You must be sure to treat all parties fairly. This is a volatile situation that often leads to angry buyers and lessees, and sometimes lawsuits. Usually, the problem is that the one who did not get the property blames the broker for some wrongdoing, like not submitting a counter offer or not providing accurate information. Beware of these situations. Treat everyone exceedingly fair and document everything in writing. On a positive note, multiple offers will drive the price up for your owner and make the deal. (Multiple offers will be discussed in more detail in the next section).

During negotiations, keep in mind that both sides want to feel like winners. Both sides want to feel as if they got the best deal or at least a fair deal. Also, keep in mind that some deals were just not meant to be made. It is kind of like fate; it just happens. If a deal does not happen, don't worry about it. However, keep the embers warm. Failed deals often heat up later and close.

Proposals, RFPs, and Multiple Offers

The custom in commercial real estate is for the buyer or lessee to make the owner an offer first. The owner then either accepts the offer or, more often, counters it. Sometimes, however, it goes the other way around. A proposal is when the owner makes the prospect an offer, or proposal, and an RFP, or request for proposal, is when a prospect requests the owner to make them a proposal. Multiple offers are when prospects make many, simultaneous, non-binding offers, to multiple owners. Proposals, RFPs, and multiple offers are discussed here together because, generally, they put owners at a disadvantage.

A proposal is similar to an offer to lease or purchase. It will usually contain all of the same terms and provide for a place for the parties to sign. The main difference is that proposals come from the owner, and, therefore, outline the terms that the owner is willing to accept rather than those the prospect will accept. The prospect may either accept the proposal, counter it, or do nothing. Proposals are generally not in the best interest of owners because once they have established the price and terms, they cannot better them. They cannot, for example, go up in price once they have committed themselves to one in the proposal. While prices are also set when listing property, the difference now is that the owner is negotiating "down" to one prospect's possible counter offer, and the prospect is no longer negotiating "up" to the owner's "top of the range" price. The listing price is intended to be the top price submitted to the market in the anticipation that there may be competition between numerous prospects, one of who will end up paying top dollar. A proposal, on the other hand, targets one prospect and removes this competitive element. For this reason, proposals are typically used when owners are aggressively trying to attract prospects, such as in slow times or when there are numerous, similar properties on the market. Proposals are often used to interest prospects who may not be actively looking, such as other owner's tenants. In cases like this, proposals may offer such things as lower rent, free rent, or other inducements.

Requests for proposals are proposals from prospects, usually to multiple owners, that request that they make them a proposal. (A request can also be to one owner.) Requests for proposals usually outline the prospect's requirements in detail. They may specify a certain area, type of property, size, improvements, and the terms of the deal. They are often made by governmental bodies or large corporations to ensure that they end up creating a competitive atmosphere between owners and end up with the best possible deal. Requests for proposals reverse the listing process because the prospect sets the terms and the owners compete to meet them. The prospect can accept, or counter the best proposal. Requests for proposals are not in the best interest of owners because they are put in competition with other owners and because prospects are under no obligation to accept the proposal. The owner ends up making his or her best offer, which the prospect may or may not accept. Also, as a broker, you may end up spending considerable time and effort responding to a request for proposal that may never result in a deal. Requests for proposals generate considerable work because they often ask for information that would normally be discovered by the prospect in the contingency period of an offer to lease or purchase. For example, a request may ask for information that shows there are no environmental problems with the property, which may require the owner to hire an environmental consultant to do a level one report. The owner may do the report, which shows no problems, but the prospect may never consider the property for other reasons. Further, the odds for acceptance are against you if there are numerous owner proposals. For these reasons many owners do no respond to requests for proposals.

Multiple offers, as discussed earlier, are when prospects make multiple, non-binding offers to lease or purchase to many owners. Like requests for proposals, they also are intended to create a competitive atmosphere between owners in order for the prospect to get the best deal. The owners are, in effect, competing among themselves to get the prospect, rather than the prospect competing to get the property. The prospect is not committed to the offer if the owner accepts it, or to accept any counter offer. The prospect can just pick the best offer that was accepted or the best counter offer. Conversely, the owner may accept the prospect's offer and still have no deal. Brokers must be wary of non-binding, multiple offers when the cooperating broker does not disclose the fact that this is what the prospect is doing. This is probably unethical and certainly bad practice because the owner and his or her broker are misled. The owner, under these circumstances, believes that the prospect is endeavoring to make a deal in good faith. The owner naturally assumes that if the right terms can be agreed upon, there will be a deal, when, in reality, the prospect is just fishing for the best deal on multiple properties.

Proposals, RFPs, and multiple offers do play a legitimate role in commercial real estate. Because they are in the interests of the tenants and buyers, they can be useful when you represent them. Entities that require competitive bidding, like governmental bodies, may have to use them. And in slow times, proposals can sometimes be quite effective in marketing property. It is important to remember, however, that all parties must be aware of the circumstances surrounding RFPs and multiple offers. Owners and their agents must be told if the RFP or offer is being made to other owners as well. You should also be aware that proposals and RFPs are low percentage deals for listing brokers. In proposals, you are trying to entice a prospect to make a deal, and in RFPs, you are competing with numerous other owners. Because a central theme of this book is the need to get listings, most of the advice is from the viewpoint of the listing broker. So, as a listing broker, you need to be alert to the pitfalls of these three methods of making commercial real estate deals.

Assembly

Sometimes commercial real estate brokers are given the job of assembling property for some purpose. This can be a downtown block for an office building, separate commercially zoned parcels at a strategic intersection for a shopping center, or a couple of contiguous parcels for a manufacturing plant. Assembling property presents some special problems including availability, timing, and price.

Sometimes one property owner just does not want to sell, which can subvert all plans. There are a number of creative ways to induce someone to sell. The first thing is to find out why he or she won't sell and then try and solve that problem. Price is the most common problem and raising it often solves it. Other methods may be to better the terms or to provide some inducement, like paying for moving costs. If taxation is the issue, then arranging for a trade may be the solution. Sometimes, however, nothing can induce a seller to sell.

Another problem is timing. The principals assembling the property usually wants it available for their plans as of a certain date. They may have a construction timetable or financing issues. It could also be, for example, that a developer is assembling for a user who needs the property by a certain time. Some properties may not be available due to leases or moving issues. Again, you need to be creative. Leases can be bought out, and companies can be persuaded to move.

Usually the biggest issue in assembling property is price. When the property owners learn that you are assembling property and their piece is part of it, the price almost always goes up. They all figure that the buyer *must have their* parcel in order to complete the assembly, so they raise the price. The easiest way to solve this problem is to avoid it. Assemble property in secrecy, and, if word does get out, make it appear that a particular piece of property is not necessary to the entire project. Assembling property in secrecy is possible, but exceedingly difficult. Once you start stirring around, the word usually gets out. A few hints for keeping an assemblage secret follow:

- Obviously, do not disclose that you are assembling property.

- Use options and not earnest money agreements. Earnest money agreements include a contingency that allow the buyer to cancel the deal if all of the property parcels cannot be assembled. This will tip your hand.

- Have the property purchased on behalf of an undisclosed buyer. In other words, use a dummy buyer.

- Use different brokers or entities, such as an attorney, to purchase the parcels separately.

- Make all offers at the same time and try to tie the properties up quickly. Alternately, assemble the properties over a long period of time, if the buyer can wait.

If word does get out, you want to be in a position to be able to say that a particular piece of property is not necessary to the entire project. This may be more of an engineering or construction issue. As a last resort, you could increase the option payment, increase the earnest money deposit, or make all, or a portion of them, non-refundable, as an incentive to the seller. If the property is necessary for your project and the seller knows it, your buyer may end up having to pay a high price and dear terms to get it.

Sometimes you may find yourself in competition when assembling property. This presents some special problems because now, not only do the owners know that you are assembling, but they can play you off against the other buyer. This is the worst of all worlds. A couple of suggestions to try and make this difficult state of affairs better are mentioned below.

- Always schedule your meeting with the owner after the owner meets with your competitor. If you must be the first to meet, have an understanding that the owner will do nothing until you meet again — after his or her meeting with your competitor. Sellers will often take the best, and last, deal. Meeting second will allow you to know what the best, last deal is. It will also give your client the opportunity to match, or better, the last offer.

- Absolutely never say this is your client's best offer, "take it or leave it." This is fatal. All it does is drive the sellers into the competitor's fold. All your competitor has to do is better your offer a little and, bingo, he gets the deal. You always want to keep the door open. Your buyer always has the right to say no to any counter offer, so keep his or her intentions to yourself.

Brokers are sometimes asked to acquire property on behalf of a buyer who prefers to remain anonymous. For example, an owner may want to buy the property next door, but is afraid that the price will go up if the seller knows it. It usually does. Sometimes, because the neighbor is in the same kind of business, he or she will not sell to a competitor. Whatever the case, purchasing on behalf of an undisclosed buyer is very similar to assembling property except that there need be no contingency for acquiring other parcels. For this reason it is often better to make an earnest money offer to the seller on behalf of an undisclosed buyer, rather than use an option. An offer carries more weight than an option because the buyer is committing to the purchase, subject to some specific things, whereas an option makes no such commitment. The downside with these kinds of offers is that the sellers become suspicious and sometimes more difficult to deal with.

Credit

Credit can be a major issue in leasing and contract sales because the lessor or seller is extending credit to the lessee or buyer. It simply is not good business to extend credit to someone who is going to default. Evicting a tenant or clearing the title to property is time consuming and expensive. They usually involve legal expenses and lost income. A little time spent up front carefully reviewing a buyer or tenant's credit is time well spent. Many owners are so anxious to lease or sell their property that they overlook, or accept, the risk of bad credit. The smart ones pass on these deals and wait for the next one. As a broker, it is your responsibility to remind the owner of this issue, provide a contingency in the deal for approval of credit, and arrange for the prospect to provide the necessary credit information to the owner. Credit information might include current financial statements (such as a balance sheet or income statement), references, recent tax returns, or a credit report from a firm such as Dunn and Bradstreet. A broker should not judge the prospect's credit status for the owner. Most are not qualified to do this, and it exposes you to liability if there is a default. Judging credit is largely a business decision that only owners can make, and it entails risk only the owner can assume. Your job is to see to it that the owner gets the information he or she needs to make an informed decision.

There are ways to deal with a tenant or buyer who has marginal credit. Common methods include asking for personal signatures, an additional security deposit (or down payment), or strict default provisions in the lease or contract. There is also lease guarantee insurance, although it is very expensive. There is quite a game that is sometimes played out in commercial real estate regarding liability and credit. The goal of the game is to limit liability. The owner wants security, and the prospect wants to limit his or her exposure. Tenants and buyers use things such as corporations, limited partnerships, and limited liability companies (LLCs) to limit their financial liability. If the prospect is General Motors, is rich, or has a track record of keeping his or her word, and the owner does not have to put much money into the deal, then credit will probably not become a problem. If the deal involves things such as high tenant improvements, shaky credit, start up companies, or interest only payments, there may be a problem. Many deals have been lost over credit and liability issues. This seems especially true when an owner asks for a personal signature.

In addition to credit, a broker should also know the reputation of the principals with whom they are dealing. There is no national regulating body like the Securities and Exchange Commission in commercial real estate. Other than a patchwork of laws and licensing requirements, it is largely an unregulated industry. Consequently, there are many characters in the business who use techniques that can lead to abuse. These include nothing down deals, subordination, and "walk away deals" (where a buyer pays an inflated price, obtains a second mortgage, and then "walks away" with the proceeds leaving the seller with more indebtedness). The business also has its share of forgery and fraud. It is important, therefore, to not only know the credit of whom you are dealing with, but also their reputation.

Attention to Detail

Paying attention to details is important for many reasons. You do a good job for your client, you get a good reputation for excellence, you gain the confidence and trust of others, you avoid legal and practical problems that could come up later, and you enhance the chances that the deal will succeed. It just is good business practice to be diligent and careful in all of your dealings. Many brokers gloss over the details because they are either lazy or thoughtless.

They allow misinformation to spread and misrepresentation to occur, both of which can result in failed deals, poor reputations, and lawsuits.

Some critical details to attend to include the following:

- Is the property information complete and accurate?

- Are all legal disclosures and requirements covered?

- Are the documents accurately, clearly, and properly written?

- Have all licensing law requirements, including handling of deposits, been properly discharged?

- Have you conducted a comprehensive marketing effort?

- Have you considered the many ancillary requirements that attend real estate deals including taxation, title, environmental, surveys, financing, and so forth?

- Have all legal requirements been met?

CHAPTER 10
Practical Knowledge

There are some things that are not discussed in books or taught in schools. They come only with experience. Most of us learn not from hearing, but rather seeing. The practical points for commercial brokers presented in this chapter pertain to this category of knowledge. In addition, because success in commercial real estate often depends on how we live, these points cover both our business and personal lives.

This is, by far, the most subjective chapter of this book. Everyone has his or her own way of doing things. It is often hard to say which way is the best because each has advantages and disadvantages. Some ways work better for some, and not for others. Usually, experience will tell us what works best given our own personalities. Some, no doubt, will disagree with portions of the advice offered here. It is helpful, however, to understand why some operate a certain way because it just may be better.

This chapter deals with common circumstances, personal beliefs, various practices, and technology, as well as some general, practical advice on how to succeed in commercial real estate. Circumstances include things such as office politics and vacations. Beliefs entail our attitudes, our views toward working at home, learning, and discretion. Various practices involving listings, site searches, and consulting, are presented for consideration.

Ubiquitous and ever changing, technology in commercial real estate is discussed, along with cell phones. Finally, some general advice is given for working smart, working on large deals and with rich people, and leasing versus sales. The final sections deal with some things that are best to avoid altogether and a few other helpful hints.

Office Politics

As Aristotle said, man is a social animal. It is very difficult to work in any office without having some office politics. It seems to be especially pervasive in commercial real estate offices due to the often intense competition. The office is a place to work and make money, and office politics is just a distraction. It does not contribute to your success in commercial real estate. The time, energy, and distraction it presents offer few rewards. Your energies are better spent focusing on matters outside the office, such as procuring listings or getting prospects.

Avoid office politics as much as possible. Remain neutral and protean. Acknowledge problems, but avoid taking sides. Do not speak ill of others, even if you do not like them. Forget small slights or injustices due to the behavior of others. Remember Albert Schweitzer's prescription for happiness — good health and a bad memory. What really matters is what you think about an issue, not the issue itself. Ultimately, you only control what you think and not the situation.

Sometimes office politics are hard to ignore. Unjust management, unethical brokers, and difficult people can make life miserable. Usually, untenable situations can be resolved by calm communication, frank and honest discussion of the problem, and patience. If they cannot, it may be best to find another company.

Attitude

Our success in commercial real estate and in life for that matter, often is the consequence of our beliefs and attitudes. Eliminate self-defeating attitudes and beliefs because they will only hurt you. "Can do," optimistic, and self-starter attitudes are the signs of a winner. It does not pay to go into a funk over the lost listing, lost deal, what others say about you, or rejections. Depression just slows you down. It pays to develop your will to the point that you become an inner directed individual. John D. Rockefeller, the founder of Standard Oil, and one of the wealthiest men in America, kept his own counsel. He did not require the approbation of others to gain success or feel good about himself. He had developed an internal set of standards that governed his actions and to which he was responsible. Attitudes, to a large extent, are a consequence of our beliefs, so it pays to hold positive, and ultimately productive, beliefs.

Perhaps the one key attitude that separates successful brokers from the pack is persistence. Persistence will always win over talent. Vince Lombardi once said that "the difference in men is in energy, in strong will, in the settled purpose and in invincible determination." If you stay at something long enough, you will prevail. Winners, truly, never quit, and quitters never win.

Vacations

In the final analysis, nothing really does matter and we all die. Nature bats last. The chess game is over and, as Tolstoy said, we are all stuffed back into that black sack together as equals. Don't take business too seriously; take many vacations. How much money do you really need in life? Money truly does make a good servant, but a poor master. Who wants to be the richest man in the grave? The truth is that living, and in particular relaxation, is an art. Contemporary American society does not provide for, or accommodate, relaxation. It is geared toward production and materialism. You must make the time to relax and enjoy life.

It is a mistake to work all of the time. Most brokers tell themselves that they cannot afford to take a vacation. They fear the loss of a deal, client, or listing. The opposite is true. You cannot afford not to take regular vacations and relax. Commercial real estate is a demanding business conducted in a pressure cooker environment.

The woods are scattered with the remains of brokers who simply burned out because they did not take time off. The integrity of your body and mind require that you get away and relax at regular intervals. You should take off at least one week per quarter. You should also take a one to three month sabbatical every five to ten years. You will be surprised how little you lose in the absence and how much you gain by the experience. Life truly is short. Enjoy it now. Do not fall into the traps of obligation and putting off what you want today for some questionable time in the future. Sophocles once said that it is a mistake to "...wait to the evening to see how splendid the day has been."

No Work at Home

It is best to leave the job at the office. When you go home, you should forget the day's work and focus on other matters, such as your family, if you have one. Commercial real estate does not engender many of the qualities needed for a successful marriage and taking the office home only exacerbates the situation. Competition may make good products, as Sarnoff (head of RCA) once said, but it makes for lousy human beings. You should try and keep a regular schedule, with normal business hours.

We are fortunate in commercial real estate because our hours are generally the same as other business professionals — eight to five during the weekdays. Rarely are we required to work at night or on the weekends. Certainly, sometimes a prospect will call at night or someone wants to see a property on the weekend, which rightly requires our attention. But an attitude that separates and balances the business and personal worlds, will bring much tranquility and peace to your life.

Cell Phones

There are advantages and disadvantages to cell phones. It seems that every commercial broker has one today. They seem to be an integral part of a commercial broker's repertoire. Many brokers believe that they are indispensable. They certainly are convenient when you are not in the office or need to reach someone and a pay phone is not readily available. They also allow you to cover more territory and talk with more people when you are not in the office. Unfortunately, you can also become a slave to the cell phone. They can be a distraction, and they can be expensive. Some brokers fear losing a deal or prospect, because they were not available the minute the person called. More often than not, the prospect or client that has just called is more than willing to wait until you return to the office. On a deeper level, a cell phone can make one feel "owned" by the business, rather than the other way around. Cell phones put you in high gear — you must always be on. More often than not, the deal will be made with or without the cell phone. The question you must ask yourself is, "Is it worth the aggravation and expense to have a cell phone so you do not miss that one deal?" If the answer is yes, then ignore this somewhat unconventional and eccentric advice and get one.

Health

When you lose your health, all you think about is returning to good health. All other worries fade away. Hence, good health enables us to worry. Commercial real estate is a high stress job, and that stress must be managed. You should attend to your physical, as well as mental, health. "Nature is easily satisfied" (Jonathan Swift, *Gulliver's Travels*), and you should endeavor to know what satisfies your health. You should get regular exercise and limit the alcohol. You should also get a good night's sleep. Burning the candle at both ends is a hard act to keep up when you have a demanding job. As Vince Lombardi once said, "Fatigue makes cowards of us all."

Focus on Listings

A central theme to this book on how to be successful in commercial real estate is the need to focus on getting exclusive listings for sale or lease. Different brokers have different methods of doing business. Some do tenant representation only, and others spend their time just tying to match buyers with sellers and lessees with lessors. The former has some merits and the latter few. Tenant representation has the advantage of working for someone. You have a client with a need, which is half the battle. It is, however, limited, and generates few of the benefits that are obtained when listing property. When you work to match prospects with owners, you are working on "one shot" deals, and you have no exclusive clients. You are, in effect, working for yourself. This method can be very frustrating, hit and miss, and full of failure. It generates virtually none of the benefits achieved when you list property. These brokers often find themselves feverishly competing with other brokers to "get there first." Because they represent nobody exclusively, they also often find themselves in disputes with other brokers — who said what, who got there first, who made the first offer, and so on. This is an excellent way to quickly burn yourself out. By far the best, and most productive, way to succeed in the business is to list property exclusively.

The Advantages of Exclusive Listings

When you focus on listing property, a number of things automatically begin to work in your favor that will help you become successful in the business. First, you get a listing that, when sold or leased, generates a commission. Second, you get to know all the prospects in the market. Brokers with prospects and prospects themselves will call on your listings. In short order, you will have a bird's eye view of who is doing what. Listing brokers usually know more about what is happening in their market than anyone else. You will find that when you have listings, everyone is coming to you. You become the cynosure of the commercial market. Third, you are in the position to control a property for a long period of time. Specifically, if you do a good job, that client will most likely list that property with you again. Careers are made by brokers who sell and lease the same properties over and over again. Tenant representation offers this to a certain extent because tenants will use you again when they move. However, "putting deals together" offers little long-term repeat business. Fourth, you promote yourself. When you market the property you are also marketing yourself. The sign, brochure, advertising, multiple listing service, broadcast e-mails, and news releases all contain your name, which markets you. Your reputation is enhanced because your name is associated with the marketing of properties and with making deals. This leads to more listings because people come to think of you as competent and successful. This is especially true of listings and prospects within your farm area because you gain a reputation as the broker to contact to handle property within your farm. Fifth, a listing can be used to make effective calls on prospects. When you have a listing in hand and call on a neighbor or some other prospect, they tend to be more interested in what you are saying or offering. Listings can be door openers.

Sixth, your odds of making the deal are greatly enhanced. Once the property is listed, the deal is half done. All you have to do is find the buyer or lessee. In tenant representation, the tenant may end up staying, and you may earn nothing (unless you made arrangements otherwise). When you are just "putting deals together," your odds of making a deal are dramatically reduced. This is because you are competing with everyone else for the deals; you represent nobody; and neither side has been qualified with a listing or tenant representation agreement. Seventh, by controlling the property, you are in a position to understand what the prospects are thinking because you hear what they are saying. This enables you to make better and more persuasive recommendations to the owner. This also enhances your ability to make a deal. Eighth, you come to understand the market better than other brokers. It stands to reason that if you are handling the listings and doing most of the deals, you will know things such as the prices and rents, trends, and demand better than anyone. Everyone seeks you out because you are an expert. This expertise will give you a special advantage when competing for listings in the future. If you are talking about important things with a prospective client that other brokers are not aware of, you gain instant credibility, which other brokers cannot overcome. Ninth, when you work on listings, you tend to focus your energy on the task at hand — "moving the listing" — which, in turn, leads to success. When you are "putting deals together," your energy and time tends to get dispersed.

These are the reasons that most commercial real estate companies, and almost all of the most successful commercial real estate brokers, focus on getting listings. They all know the benefits of listings, so they spend considerable time and effort getting them. This is also why the competition for listings is so intense. They all know that those who lose the listing battle are on the outside looking in. It is also this intense competition for listings that makes some brokers decide to focus on less productive methods. This is a mistake. You time is far better off endeavoring to get one good listing than chasing rainbow deals that have little chance of success. Of all the advice in this book, perhaps the most important point is the need to get, and keep, good exclusive listings. It is the most important thing you can do. If you are successful at this step, you cannot fail.

Getting the Listings

We've already discussed in detail the importance of focusing your business on exclusive listings. Of course, the next thing you need to know is what to do and what to say in order to actually get the listing. This section will discuss three important concepts in getting listings: the listing package, listing sales points, and advanced listing techniques.

The Listing Package

A listing pitch should be made face to face with the decision maker. More often than not — especially on high profile listings — you will find that you are one of many brokers pitching for the same listing. Everyone will have a listing packet — the folder of information that has the sales material for the listing. Some listing packets are just handouts with miscellaneous information given during the presentation and others are very slick and sophisticated. They are sometimes in binders with color charts and massive amounts of information. A listing packet should include the following:

- A description of the property. This could include title information, an aerial photo, plats, floor plans, as well as a map showing the property's location.

- A trio. This is the title company's information packet, which usually includes a plat, copies of documents, and tax information.

- A description of what the broker is going to do to market the property.

- An analysis of the market.

- A comparative summary of the property's strengths and weaknesses. It should also include the broker's analysis of what can be done to enhance the strengths and overcome the weaknesses.

- Recommendations on the asking price or rental and an explanation of how the value was arrived at. (This was discussed under "Range of Value" in Chapter 8.)

- Information on the broker. This is an area where you need to use your imagination and bring everything to bear that shows why you are better than your competition. This could include copies of current or previous listing brochures, photos of properties successfully handled, a list of references, a resume, a list of past clients, a list of deals done in the area of the listing, copies of announcement ads or news releases of similar properties you have handled, letters of reference, information on your company and its resources including local and/or national connections, a description of any professional societies you may be a member of, and letters of recommendation from influential people or past clients.

- Investment packets will often contain a rent roll and an investment analysis of the property, including a spreadsheet.

- Executive summary.

Sales Points for Listings

There are endless variations and points to be made in a sales pitch, many of which were discussed in Chapter 5, "Salesmanship." There do seem to be, however, a few tried and true points that are particularly helpful in a listing sales pitch. These points cover both why the owner should list with you, as well as why he or she should list at all. The following are some sales points to use with owners considering listing property with you.

- Tell them that you are experienced, and if you are not, tell them your company is. Owners want to list with those who have successfully marketed property like theirs in the past. They are often more concerned about the broker making a mistake, than getting the last dollar for the property. Experience engenders confidence.

- Tell them you have the horsepower to market the property locally and, if possible, nationally. Explain to them how you will market their property (see Chapter 8, "Marketing"). The marketing should include promoting their property to both public and private advocates. It should also include promotion through the Internet, via multiple listing services and a web page, if you have one. Owners want to know that their property will have the widest possible exposure.

- Tell them that they will save time and probably make more money by letting a professional like you handle the property. You know the market and you know how to get the top price for the property. Owners are usually busy people and do not want to deal with all the things that need to be done to market real estate. They also do not want to deal with showing property, unqualified prospects, and lots of different brokers.

- There will be more control and less confusion by quoting one, authorized price. With non-exclusive and agency listings, the owner could quote a different price than the one in your listing (they could also do this in an exclusive listing, but it is less likely). Brokers and prospects will often begin speculating over what the owner will accept and end up quoting different prices. This problem often gets worse with net listings, where the owner sets an acceptance price and the broker must add their commission on top. Some brokers get greedy and quote exorbitant prices, which means that the same prospect may be quoted different prices for the same property. This muddies the water and creates confusion for a listing, which is not in the owner's best interest.

- With an exclusive listing the owner will get more coverage because the broker can afford to spend the time and money to do the job.

- Remind them that your interests as a broker are in concert with the owners'. The more money they make, the more you make. Owners also like to know that you will be representing their interests. They should also know, however, that if you advocate their side too much, a prospect may be turned off. Their interests are often further advanced when you can help the prospect and act as a kind of accommodator.

- If an owner is going to pay a fee, he or she may as well have an agent handling the marketing and getting the best deal. It costs no more to have an agent if the property sells through a broker, because it is the same fee, which is then split with the cooperative broker.

- If they are worried that you may not work on the listing, tell them that they can fire you anytime if you are not doing the job. Or, you could suggest that they list the property for just 60 to 120 days, and then not renew the listing if you are not giving it 100 percent of your effort. If you have never had a client cancel a listing with you, be sure to mention that to the owner.

- Promise regular written reports on your marketing activities and a discussion of what the prospects are saying. Owners want to know what is going on.

- Tell the owner you have or know of prospects for the property, if you do.

- Tell them that the fee they pay is small in proportion to the services they get, and you often are able to negotiate a price or rental high enough to more than cover the fee.

- Point out that many of the sales points that you have mentioned are provided for in the listing agreement. Consequently, you are both morally and legally obligated to do what you say.

Advanced Listing Techniques

The listing pitch is limited only by your imagination. Some successful brokers and firms have unique methods and ways of getting listings. What follows are some examples of more advanced listing techniques.

- Prepare the property brochure in advance.

- Have the listing prepared and ask the owner to sign it at the end of the pitch.

- Make calls on logical prospects in advance of the presentation, so you can tell the owner that you have already started the marketing and have some prospects.

- Prepare a timeline of marketing activity and a list of prospects you plan to contact.

- Prepare a mass mailing list of prospects you plan to send the brochure.

- Bring a crowd to the listing presentation, including other brokers and your sales manager.

- Fly to meet an owner if he or she lives in another city.

- Provide extensive title and property information, including plats showing easements and utilities.

- Have clients, influential people, or anyone who knows both you and the owner, call the owner in advance and tell him or her how great you are. This can help set the stage for a listing presentation and give you a decided advantage.

- When in competition with other brokers, prepare their case first. Different brokers have different strengths and weaknesses. If you know these and prepare their pitch before yours, you will know what points to emphasize and what points to counter.

Be aware that different owners have different criteria for what they are looking for in a broker. A local investor may have entirely different needs than a large, multi-national corporation. James A. Sladack of General Electric's corporate real estate department once wrote an article titled "Secrets Revealed: Determining Good and Bad Brokers," in which he lists some of the qualities General Electric values in a broker. This will give you a taste of what a national corporation looks for when selecting a broker and what you need to know when pitching to one.

- A forward-looking approach to value, as compared to the appraiser's backward look, using historic comparables.

- Experience with rezoning.

- Good people skills.

- A fundamental understanding of corporate economics.

- Good administrative skills.

- Good legal and ethical sense.

- A professional appearance and manner.

- Experience and a good repertoire.

- The ability to be both aggressive and patient, as needed.

Some Final Words on Listings

Some final practical advice regarding listings is in order. There are many wood paths when listing commercial properties, which you will want to avoid. The main thing to keep in mind is that you want to take listings that will sell or lease. It does you no good whatsoever to take ones that never move. They are just a waste of your time. What follows are a few final dos and don'ts regarding listings.

- Focus on listings in your farm area. You will get more residual value from them.

- Do not take listings outside your community. If you take a listing in a city 50 miles away, not only do you have a big commute to show it, but the prospects you get are less valuable.

- Take exclusive listings only. This has been mentioned often in this book, but is repeated because it is so important.

- If you cannot agree on a price with the owner, bring in a neutral third party.

- When you have listed property exclusively, do not let other brokers call your client directly. It is unethical and undermines your relationship with the client.

- Do not take overpriced listings. They usually do not move, you end up wasting your time, and the owner loses because the property does not sell or lease. Let other brokers waste their time on these listings. You may be better off being the second broker to list the property because the owner has become more realistic about the price.

- Drop listings that cannot be sold or leased. You should occasionally cull your listings and drop those that are wasting your time.

- Stay in touch with the owner on a regular basis. Half the job is getting the listing and the other half is keeping it.

- Always counter other brokers' points. Most brokers, for example, will seduce owners by telling them that they have prospects. If they do, be sure to get some prospects of your own and tell the owner, in order to neutralize this point.

- When you have successfully marketed a listing, be sure to review the file and make a list of all of the important prospect calls for later use. This is a significant source of future business.

If you lose a listing pitch it is not the end of the world. Getting terminal cancer is the end of the world. There will be other opportunities. The important thing is to learn why you lost it and what you can do better the next time. Brokers that never learn from their mistakes are doomed to repeat them. Successful brokers learn from their mistakes. In fact, as mentioned earlier, sometimes it is better to be the second or third listing agent on a property. If the first broker listed it for too much money, then by the time it gets to you, the owner has become more realistic. This is especially true when the market is falling. In short, if you lose a listing pitch, be sure to stay in touch with the owner to see whether the property is moving.

As strange as it may sound, it is important to remember that the listing packet and presentation are not the things that really get you the listing. They are important because you must match what other brokers have done. However, they only put you on the same footing with your competition. There are many intangibles on top of the presentation and package that will truly determine your fate, such as your personality, the principal's personality, timing, reputation, how you say things, and how you respond to the principal's questions and objections. The listing packet and your presentation are important, but it is your ability to sell that gets results. After all, the owner is hiring *you*. The listing package and presentation are just tools to persuade the principal that you are capable of handling the listing. Once that is done, you must answer the next question: "Is this is the person I want handling my property?"

Leasing versus Sales

Generally speaking, leasing commercial real estate is easier than selling it. Certainly, there are some easy sales and hard leases. There are a number of significant issues and obstacles in sales, however, not generally found in leasing. Most leases do not require an environmental analysis and clean-up, if required. They typically do not deal with title issues such as exceptions to title like encroachment, easements, and conditions, covenants, and restrictions. Financing is rarely required in leasing, so the requirements of a lender (such as an appraisal) and the time it takes to finance are not an issue. Leases also rarely require surveys. Finally, lessors do not face the same tax consequences sellers do. This is not to say there are issues in leasing not found in selling; leasing just tends to be easier. Also, lease deals can be very large, and the fees are often paid upon execution of the lease. Many very successful commercial real estate agents focus primarily on leasing.

Tenant Representation

Some very successful brokers specialize in tenant representation only. It clearly is one way to succeed in commercial real estate, even though it does not bring all the benefits that listings do. If you just have a hard time getting listings or if the market is tight and there are not many available, then tenant representation is a good way to supplement your business.

The essence of tenant representation is to find a prospect looking for something, convert the prospect to an exclusive client, conduct a site search, and then handle the negotiations. Finding the prospects has already been discussed in Chapter 7. The real key to success in tenant representation is the ability to persuade the prospect to hire you as an exclusive agent to find what is needed. Many of the same sales points used in getting listings can be used in converting prospects to exclusive clients for site searches. Some sales points for tenant representation are as follows.

- Prospects will get professional representation. This means they will know what is available, what the market is, and how to make the best possible deal. You will also help them avoid any pitfalls.

- You will save the prospect time, which is better spent running his or her business.

- When the prospect just calls around indiscriminately looking for properties, generally, the brokers they call will spend little time looking over their listings. There is little reason for them to work on the prospect's requirement because they are not assured compensation. If a prospect hires a broker exclusively, he or she will get much better results. The broker can afford to put the time and effort in to do the job right, because he knows that he will be compensated in the end.

- The broker will be more likely than the prospect to uncover properties that are not on the market, but could be available.

- The broker will be able to recommend experts in other fields, such as attorneys, engineers, contractors, or environmental consultants who can help in the process.

- Only the most suitable properties will be submitted, thus saving the time the prospect would have spent looking at unsuitable ones.

- If the prospect personally contacts a listing broker, she is immediately at a disadvantage because that broker is working for the owner and negotiating in the owner's interests. You would be her broker negotiating in her interests.

- All of these services and benefits are at no direct cost, because the fee is normally paid by the lessor or seller. This is a touchy point because it is unethical to tell prospects that they can get your services for free. They will end up paying your fee, directly or indirectly, through the increased sales price or rental, and they should know it.

This last point raises a couple of interesting observations regarding agency and fees in commercial real estate. Brokers are required to represent one side to a transaction, yet they may be paid by the other. A broker, for example, who represents a buyer, will usually be paid by the seller. Furthermore, in reality, it does not matter who pays it, because in the end, it is a wash to both principals to the transaction (except that the one who pays the fee does get to deduct it). In a sale, for example, the seller gets the same net sales proceeds, after a fee is paid, as he would if the buyer paid the fee. Conversely, the buyer pays the same price, whether she pays a full price and the seller pays the fee or she pays a net price and the fee on top. In both cases, the seller gets the same net proceeds from the sale, and the buyer pays the same overall price. This highlights the difficulties of being in a profession where the practitioners make money as a percentage of the value of something that changes hands, as opposed to being paid "out of pocket" by the client, like other professions. This also reflects the reality that the role of a commercial broker is more of that of a facilitator than an advocate.

The Site Search

The tenant representation should begin with a written contract that specifies the nature of the relationship, the broker's job, and the prospect's requirements. Much of the job of tenant representation is helping clients figure out what they need. This could include size, location, price range, and special requirements such as tenant improvements. The search should uncover every available property in the market that meets, or comes close to, these requirements. The search typically begins with a search of the multiple listing service, but may also include reviewing the broker's brochure files, contacting other brokers and asking for their cooperation, sometimes advertising, and even driving the streets. Once the search is completed, the broker should give the client a written report on all the available properties, which includes all pertinent information. The broker will then set up a tour of the properties, help the client narrow the possibilities, and eventually make the offer and negotiate the deal.

A partial list of some of the criteria for an industrial client's site search is listed below for illustrative purposes. This list is not by any means comprehensive, but it does provide a general idea of what should be done to identify a client's requirements.

- Location
- Size of warehouse and offices (50,000 sq. ft. with 5,000 sq. ft. of offices)
- Land area (three acres minimum)
- Expansion requirements
- Truck maneuvering area (truck swing room, for example, may require up to 120')
- Truck and car parking (parking could be, for example, 2 cars per 1,000 sq. ft. of warehouse space)
- Ceiling height (may be 20' to 30')
- Sprinklers (wet or dry)
- Doors (number of dock-hi and drive-in), their sizes (dock door sizes may be 12'X12', grade doors 12'X16'), dock height (dock height may be 52 inches)
- Bay sizes (25'X50')
- Power requirements (240V, 1,000 Amps, 3 phase)
- Floor loading requirements (500 lbs. per sq. ft.)
- Lighting requirements (type and amount)
- Racking and storage handling
- Restrooms (men's and women's, and how many)

- Utilities such as telephone, gas, and any computer requirements

- Special requirements like landscaping, visibility, air-conditioning, etc.

- Lease or purchase, and budget

- Existing building, build, trade, or build for lease

- Term of lease, or terms of purchase

- Options

- Occupancy

- Financing issues

Comparing Rents

When representing a client to lease property, one of the main concerns is rent. Because the sizes of properties are usually different, the rate is usually more important than the total rent. When comparing rates, most brokers will compare the effective rents, not the contract rents, in order to account for any free rent. The contract rent is what the lessee pays each month. For example, in industrial properties where the quoted rent is $4,000 per month for a 10,000 sq. ft. warehouse, the contract rent is $4,000. The lessee is paying 40¢ per sq. ft. per month ($4,000 ÷ 10,000 sq. ft. = 40¢). However, if there were three months of free rent on a five year lease, the effective rate would be 38¢ per sq. ft. per month (40¢ X 10,000 sq. ft. = $4,000 per month X 57 months [60 months – 3 months free = 57 months] = $228,000 aggregate rental ÷ 60 months = $3,800 per month ÷ 10,000 sq. ft. = 38¢ per sq. ft. per month effective rent). This is a more accurate way to compare properties.

Effective rent analysis, however, does not take into consideration the time value of money. One more sophisticated analysis that does take this into consideration compares the discounted cash flow of different lease deals. There are a number of factors that can be considered when doing this analysis such as rent, term, and any advance payments. They could, for example, incorporate the effects of options to purchase, the cost of tenant improvements, as well as free rent. This analysis usually involves comparing the present values of a stream of lease payments for a specific period of time. There are some computer software programs that do this discounted lease rental comparison analysis.

The question of whether to lease or buy a property often comes up when companies relocate. The answer is complex because it depends on many factors, such as the cost of a new facility (or an existing one) versus the cost to lease and the principal's tax situation. One way is to compare the present value of a stream of lease payments with the cost (or present value if terms are involved) of a new facility, on an after tax basis. The cost of a purchase should include things such as principal build up as the loan is paid off, as well as the estimated increase in value due to inflation (if any). The after tax analysis should anticipate the effects of things such as depreciation, interest deductions, loss of interest on the down payment, and the taxpayer's tax bracket. It can get complicated.

Working Smart

It has been said that Custer's last words were, "Now we got 'em." Like Custer, many commercial real estate brokers live in serious denial and do not work smart. Working smart means doing the types of things that lead to making deals. Some brokers are just so happy to have something to do that they will work on anything. This is a mistake. You are far better off following proven methods of success, such as those described in this book, than laboring to no end. You need to do what makes you money, period. Anything else is a waste of time.

The following list outlines some of the most common mistakes and time wasters in commercial real estate. You should avoid these like the plague.

- Working on deals that have little chance of success. Hard deals are everywhere because the good brokers do not want to work on them, and because they are difficult to do. You must get it in your head that your time is better spent looking for a deal that can be made, rather than working on a deal that cannot.

- Dealing with the wrong people. This may sound callous, but in this business it is easier to do business with rich, smart, and ambitious people, than poor, dumb or indolent ones. Focus on working with the best people.

- Not dealing with the decision maker. If you are dealing with an underling and another broker is dealing with the decision maker, the other broker will make the deal. Your time is better spent getting to the decision maker than working with an underling.

- Not qualifying prospects. There are lots of lookers and dreamers in this world. Showing a prospect property that is too big or one that he cannot afford is a waste of time. Ask questions and qualify your prospects up front before you do any work.

- The inability to control prospects or clients. Prospects looking with ten other brokers or clients who compete with you in a nonexclusive listing are time wasters. Your time is better spent trying to convert the prospect looking for something to an exclusive client and changing the listing from nonexclusive to exclusive.

- Working on extremely complex deals. This is really not something to be necessarily avoided, because complex deals can be interesting and rewarding. However, the truth is that simple deals are easier to do. A four way exchange or a sale contingent on selling other property is harder to make and has less chance of happening. In general, sales tend to be more complex, take more time, and be more involved, than leases.

- Spending your time doing busy work. Some brokers delude themselves into thinking that they are being productive by spending time organizing, communicating with non-principals, and fiddling with the computer. Deals are made by talking to prospects and clients, listing property, and negotiating deals.

- Taking listings that will not move. Some brokers will take any listing because they need listings. Properties that are overpriced or have serious environmental problems are best avoided. Again, your time is better spent working to get a listing that is marketable than working on one that is not.

Large Deals and Rich People

It is probably good advice to be willing to work on all sizes of deals and for all types of people. However, the simple truth is that you make more money on large deals and with rich people. You can spend the same amount of time on a 5,000 sq. ft. month-to-month lease and a $5,000,000 investment deal, but make $750.00 on one and $100,000 on the other. It does not take a rocket scientist to figure out that the time you spent on the lease would have been better spent looking for that $5,000,000 investment deal. Further, the large investment deal is often easier to make because larger deals tend to attract professionals who know what they are doing and who do it more efficiently and quickly. It is a real pleasure to work with knowledgeable "deal making" commercial real estate attorneys, accountants, and escrow agents, to name a few. They usually take the transaction by the horns, ensure that it is on the right footing, and run with it. It is miserable to have to deal with unknowledgeable professionals who wrangle over the condemnation clause in a preprinted lease form on a month-to-month lease. Large transactions with wealthy people and knowledgeable advisors often just make themselves. They take on a life of their own, which cannot be stopped.

The truth is that rich people are often accustomed to making large deals, staying focused on a few important issues, and haggling less over insignificant details. Naturally, because they have money, they tend not to haggle over the price or rent as much. Those without money are some of the hardest to deal with because they have to haggle over the price, rent, or terms. They also tend to be some of the least knowledgeable principals, which causes them to be more cautious and tentative. Wealthy people tend to be more conservative because they want to preserve their wealth. This translates to realistic expectations and steady performance, which makes deals easier to do. Those without money usually have none for a reason. They often are dreamers or schemers with unrealistic ideas that never pan out. This is not intended to pass judgment on the relative merits of those with or without money, but rather to explain why, in real practice, it tends to be easier to do business with one than the other. The hard truth is that those who work with rich people and large properties tend to be more successful. Another hard truth is that most brokers know this, so there is more competition at that level.

Keep Learning

Commercial real estate is a dynamic business that is constantly changing. The most successful brokers are the ones who endeavor to keep up with what is going on and are informed of trends within the industry. It is vitally important to continue to learn and expand your knowledge. Some areas such as law, practices, forms, land use and zoning, and taxation change so rapidly that it is imperative to keep abreast of new developments. You should also keep on top of market trends like prices, rents, and vacancy rates. By continuing to learn, you become more competent, represent your clients better, become more competitive, and avoid liability.

Educational opportunities come from many sources. A few are listed below.

- Real estate books or cassettes

- Title company, attorney, and private educational seminars

- Real estate schools

- Realtor® associations, such as a commercial association of Realtors® seminar, meetings, breakfasts, and educational programs

- Various educational offerings of commercial Realtor® affiliates such as the SIOR or CIREI

- Real estate conventions

Silence is Golden

There exists in commercial real estate a natural conflict in how much to tell others about your prospects and deals. Many companies encourage you to be open and discuss what you know. There exists a certain conflict of interest and tension between management and brokers in these circumstances. Management wants you to open up and cooperate in the name of teamwork, and brokers want to keep what they know to themselves. Certainly, there are some advantages to opening up. Two heads can be better than one, and often someone else will have the information that, when coupled with what you know, can result in a deal. Also, sometimes others can help solve a problem that you have. Generally, however, it is better to keep what you know to yourself unless there is a good reason to do otherwise. You will often see other brokers who feel compelled to tell you everything. When they call on a listing, for example, they immediately tell you who they are working with. They discuss their deals, their prospects, and the listings they are pursuing. There is just no need to do this.

Discussing your prospects or deals in progress just opens the door to competitors. If you disclose your prospect to another broker, she may submit another property to your prospect. Or, if that broker had been dealing with your prospect on a listing, she may better her deal with your prospect, in order to beat you out. As time passes, brokers forget that you were the source of the prospect, and other brokers, who simply heard of the prospect through the grapevine (because you talked), will now go directly to the prospect because they did not know you were the source. And then there are always a few brokers who just do not want to cooperate because they want the full fee and will always go directly to the prospect (but only if they know who it is). The general Machiavellian practice in commercial real estate is always talk about the other broker's deals — never your own. Silence is golden. If you have a requirement, just give the requirement to the broker and not the prospect's name. Avoid discussing your deals until they are done.

Keeping information to yourself on deals and prospects does not mean that you should not cooperate with other parties, such as brokers and appraisers, when it comes to sharing information in general. There is an ethical, professional duty to share information about the market, property, and other general real estate matters. It is also wise to do this because it is a two way street. Others are more likely to share information with you, if you have helped them.

Technology

Technology is changing the world and commercial real estate. Many of the methods and techniques used just a few years ago are now obsolete due to the rapid changes and advancements in technology. Commercial real estate seems particularly susceptible to these changes and quick to embrace any new way to make it easier and quicker to make deals. Commercial brokers are an opportunistic, entrepreneurial, and competitive bunch with big appetites for new ways to do things better. They are driven by many things including the desire to be the best, to make money, to do a good job for their clients, and the fear of falling behind. Often they have no choice. To function properly in the business, they often must learn new things or adopt new ways of doing business, just to stay even with competitors. It is very helpful to be technologically savvy and stay abreast of changes, in order to succeed in the commercial real estate business. Be aware, however, that of all the information in this book, this section will become dated the quickest.

Computers, software and the Internet have made more of an impact on the commercial real estate business than anything else. The best advice is to get the most powerful computer you can afford. Additional speed and capacity are needed for increasingly demanding real estate applications, such as digital photos in brochures and spreadsheets and documents sent over the Internet. Before you purchase a computer, research the software and commercial real estate applications you are likely to use (or that other brokers are using) and then be sure the system you buy can support that and then some. Microsoft software is probably the most widely used form of software in the industry. Current Windows programs — Outlook, Excel, Office, and Publisher —are especially suited to commercial real estate needs. A good quality ink jet or laser color printer is necessary for printing. The ability to connect to the Internet is a necessity. A scanner and digital camera are very useful additions for creating brochures and transmitting copies of things such as plats.

The applications for computers are endless. Word processing is probably the most frequently used application you will have. Your word processing program will allow you to write letters, merge large mailings, create and manipulate forms and agreements such as leases and earnest money agreements, and forms. Microsoft Excel can be used to manipulate numbers for investment analysis, property management, financial analysis, or virtually anything that needs a spreadsheet. Microsoft Publisher can be used to create calendars, cards, brochures, or invitations. Microsoft Outlook can organize your time, keep track of meetings, and process your e-mail. There is specialized real estate software for things such as financing (including amortization) and investment analysis (including IRR and NPV calculations). You can even get voice recognition software in order to dictate letters rather than typing them.

Once you have arranged for a server and connected your computer to the Internet, the applications in commercial real estate expand exponentially. The Internet makes receiving and transmitting information easy and quick. E-mail allows you to keep in touch with clients, prospects, and other brokers. Documents, which were once mailed and then faxed, now are sent as attachments to e-mail. Property information, data, and forums for the exchange of information are all available over the Internet through multiple listing services. Brochures, which were also once mailed or faxed, are increasingly e-mailed. Broadcast e-mail allows one broker to instantly distribute information about a requirement or property's availability to hundreds of other brokers. Further, national multiple listing services allow a broker in one part of the country to learn of property or prospects in another. Local and national data services can quickly provide mountains of information, including comparables. It is critical that you know many of these applications in order to succeed in commercial real estate.

The technological future of commercial real estate may well be seen when most of the critical applications are consolidated into one device, such as the HP-540 Pocket PC or other similar handheld devices. This is like a desk computer, loaded with all the bells and whistles, reduced in size to fit in your hand. It contains all of the Microsoft applications such as Outlook, Word, Excel, and Internet Explorer, as well as e-mail. In addition, you can add memory, a modem, a digital camera, record voice messages, write on it, and load specialized programs for real estate. It seems that about the only thing it doesn't do is deals.

There are many other technologies and machines that commercial brokers deal with that you should endeavor to become familiar with. Some are new and some are old technologies still in use. Faxes are common and used for a variety of purposes such as transmitting documents and brochures. They are, however, rapidly becoming obsolete due to e-mail. Specialized real estate calculators, such as the HP-12C or 19B, are indispensable. Color copiers that collate and staple are the norm in most commercial real estate offices. Communications include cell phones, pagers, and voice mail. Even things like security systems and electronic measuring tapes are common. Of course, the old fashioned typewriter still has many uses.

The thing to keep in mind about technology and machines in particular is that they are tools and nothing else. They do not make deals. You make deals by talking to prospects, getting listings, and negotiating deals. Machines have a way of taking over and speeding up your life, often to no end other than anxiety. Some brokers get so carried away with machines and technology, they fail to do the basic things that one needs to do to become successful. Success in commercial real estate entails person-to-person contact, relationships, and trust, which machines cannot do. Make technology work for you — not vice versa.

Consulting and Appraising (Opinions of Value)

You will occasionally be asked to provide consultation or to appraise a property (if it is legally allowed in your area). Usually, you will be paid an hourly rate or some agreed-upon lump sum amount. It is wiser to leave the consulting and appraising to the consultants and appraisers. The reason is simple: You can make much more money selling and leasing and being paid a percentage of the deal, than you can working on an hourly basis. Further, every minute you spend on that consultation job is time you could have spent finding, or doing, that big deal. Consulting and appraising just distract you from your central goal, which is to list and sell or lease property.

If you must consult, it is better to do it on a limited basis for free in the hope of creating good will, so you can get the client's brokerage business in the future. People are very grateful, as they should be, if you take time to help them with a problem. They usually feel indebted and make a point of bringing you business when it arises. In these situations, it is a good idea to offer your services *gratis*, in exchange for their listing in the future. They usually oblige.

There are two issues with appraisals. First, appraisals are technical and follow very specific guidelines. Many brokers are just not qualified to do an appraisal (although many brokers know the real value of property better than a lot of appraisers). Further, appraisals are used for many financial and legal reasons such as financing, estates, and taxation. It is better to leave the business of appraisal to the appraisers. Second, when listing property, it is better to establish a range of value rather than one specific market figure. This is because different prospects will put different values on the same property, because they have different requirements. You want your pricing to remain flexible. Consequently, your value estimate should be in the form of an opinion of value that establishes a range of value for listing purposes. An opinion is less formal and looser. They are just that, your opinion of value, not the value. You should, however, be professional in your method of arriving at your opinion. You should have the necessary comparatives and use the appropriate methods of appraisal whether it is the income, comparative, or cost approach. This matter was discussed in more detail in the section titled, "Range of Value," in Chapter 8. Again, the idea is to provide information on an informal basis in hopes of obtaining the listing.

Things to Avoid

There are some things in commercial real estate that are not necessarily wrong, illegal, or unethical, but are irritating and counterproductive. These things are usually not written about in books or taught in seminars. Many are derived from poor upbringing, selfishness, personal problems, or just the nature of the business. Some are practices that many use, but that often cause problems and hard feelings. Becoming successful in commercial real estate is hard enough without compounding it with any of the following:

- Hype. Hype is distracting and irritating. Only the wrong kinds of people respond to hype. Keep a clear head, calm demeanor, and think carefully through your issues.

- Slang words. Some brokers think they sound better or smarter than they are when they use the latest slang word or phrase. They feel "in" or "in the know." It is better to use traditional, universally accepted, and widely understood words that have precise meanings. Clarity breeds confidence; confusion breeds distrust.

- Anger. Nothing productive comes from getting angry. People avoid angry people. Control your emotions, remain calm, and work through the things that make you angry. You will get much farther.

- Confused thinking. Confused thinking breeds confused and often litigious results. Try to think clearly and rationally.

- Two-timing. Two-timing is when a broker tells you one thing and does another. They usually have an agenda, like getting a full fee, so they tell you only enough to further their interests. An example of this is when you make an offer on property listed with another broker and that broker has an offer himself, without a cooperative broker, on the same property. Some brokers will try to hold you off in order to make their deal, so they can collect the whole fee. This is unethical, unfair, and exasperating to cooperative brokers. Do not become a perpetrator of this practice.

- Not returning phone calls. Some brokers chronically do not return phone calls. This makes it very hard for cooperative brokers to do business. It is discourteous and rude. Some of the most important people in the business world respond, in one way or another, to all inquiries. Be respectful of others and return their phone calls.

- Arrogance. Some are naturally arrogant and some learn it. Some companies preach it. Nobody likes arrogant, haughty people. Attenuate your pride, be humble when necessary, and, again, respect others.

- Disorganization. Some people are just so disorganized that they end up causing you problems. Their rush becomes your rush, their lack of preparedness causes you to be late, their mistake becomes your mistake. Organize yourself and avoid disorganized people.

- Not removing real estate signs when a deal is completed. Some brokers purposely leave their signs up to get prospects. This is misleading because the property is no longer available. Take your sign down promptly when the deal is done.

- Shopping offers. In order to get a better deal, listing brokers will sometimes take an offer you just made on their listing and call everyone who has expressed interest or made previous offers, saying "You better hurry up and make your best deal because we have an offer." This is unfair to both you and your client, and, depending on how it is done, probably unethical. These brokers get a bad reputation fast. Don't be one.

- Double escrowing. Double escrowing is when a buyer never takes title to property he or she has tied up, but instead "flips" it to another buyer in closing, making a quick profit. There is nothing inherently wrong with double escrowing. Some buyers in rising markets look for opportunities to do this. The problem is that, as a listing broker, your client should get that profit and not some intermediary speculator who has taken little risk. You look bad to your client. Double escrowing is hard to guard against, so you should be wary of investors' motivations, especially in rising markets.

- Multiple offers. In a multiple offer, a broker makes non-binding, simultaneous offers, on multiple properties, for one client. Like double escrowing, there is nothing inherently wrong with multiple offers. It is occasionally done. The goal is to find the best deal for the buyer or lessee. The problem for you, as the listing broker, is that your owner is put at a disadvantage. Your client is put in competition with other owners because his or her best counter offer may be shopped to other owners and bettered. The buyer/

lessee is saying, "Here is my offer that I may or may not do." It is especially important to be wary of brokers who make multiple offers and do not disclose this to the listing broker. The owner, in this case, makes a counter offer not knowing that he or she is being used. It is better to have one, binding, and good faith offer.

- Back-up offers. Back-up offers are simply when one buyer or lessee makes an offer on a property where a deal already exists. Again, like double escrowing and multiple offers, there is nothing inherently wrong with back-up offers. They "back up" the first offer. They are useful when a principal wants to be in a position to make a deal if the first one dies. The problem is that back-up offers tend to make the first deal. When the principal, who has the first deal, knows that someone is behind him, he tends to work harder to make the deal. After all, the one making the back up offer can make an offer anytime if the first deal dies. It is better to stay in close touch with the listing broker on the status of the first deal and wait until the first one dies before making the offer. Conversely, listing brokers love back-up offers because they help make the first deal, and they have a fallback deal if the first one dies.

- Non-binding offers. Some offers state that they are not binding, but rather subject to the execution of some subsequent agreement. The reason for this is because some brokers are concerned about liability if something goes wrong or because they are concerned that the agreement they drafted was done so improperly. These nonbinding offers are driven by legal concerns. They are really only letters of intent that say the parties agree to try and agree. The problem is that one side may have negotiated their best deal, while the other side is just trying to find the best deal, and after getting it and agreeing to the terms, may change their mind and back out. A seller or landlord could cancel a nonbinding agreement if a better offer came in, or a buyer or tenant could cancel it if a better deal on another property was found. As a broker, you want to be able to achieve a binding agreement on the business terms of a real estate deal. It is better to have an attorney review an offer before it is made or make the offer subject to legal counsel's approval of the final form of the document, rather than sign a meaningless, nonbinding agreement.

- Lack of punctuality. Some people are habitually late. Late for appointments, showings, or meetings. They are often disorganized or thoughtless. Whatever the reason, what they are saying is that your time is not important. They think that it is acceptable to keep you waiting for them, because their time is more important than yours. If you do not respect your own time, then nobody else will. You should wait for no more than 15 minutes and then leave. Let them struggle to reset a time that is convenient to you, if you are willing.

- Blackmailing landlords. Like some of the other unsavory practices mentioned earlier, there is nothing inherently wrong with a landlord paying a broker to negotiate a deal with an existing tenant. Some brokers who specialize in tenant representation, however, get into the habit of telling a landlord that they must pay them a fee if they want to keep their tenant. The implication is that the broker will move the tenant elsewhere if the landlord refuses. The broker should discuss this with the landlord before doing any work, and if the landlord refuses to pay a fee, the broker should try and collect it from the tenant. After all, it is the tenant who is hiring the broker. If the tenant says no and the broker still wishes to proceed, they do so at their own risk. There is nothing wrong with a broker trying to make a better deal for the tenant elsewhere. That is just business. But if they do proceed and are unsuccessful, they knew that going in. Do not fall into the bad and unethical habit of putting your interests ahead of your client's. You should give the tenant all pertinent information on available properties, including their own if applicable, with your recommendations, in a professional and impartial manner and then let them decide.

- Non-exclusive, agency, and net listings. The reasons for avoiding non-exclusive and agency listings were discussed earlier. Basically, they put the broker in competition with the owner or everyone else, including the owner. You may put forth a lot of time and effort and earn nothing. Net listings are when an owner lists a property at a "net" price, or a price that does not include the real estate fee. The owner expects the broker to add the fee on top and quote that price. The problems with these listings are many. First, some brokers get greedy and include very high fees. There would be nothing to prevent a broker from quoting $1,000,000 on a net listing of $600,000, thereby making a $400,000 fee. Second, the property gets muddied in the marketplace, and prospects get confused because many different prices may be quoted. One broker added a $30,000 fee, while another added $60,000. When a prospect for the property is quoted prices of $630,000 and $660,000 for the same property, they begin to wonder where the bottom is. This leads to the third problem with net listings. If that buyer makes a deal at $605,000, the broker makes only $5,000. If the eventual deal is done at $590,000, the broker makes nothing. Again, a lot of time and effort for nothing.

- Do not practice law. You should avoid preparing legal documents. You are not qualified to do so; it is unethical; you are not paid to do it; and you increase your liability exposure if something goes wrong. Any time there is a problem in a real estate contract, the first question the principals and attorneys ask is, "Who prepared this contract?" You can easily become the target. Having your client hire an attorney to prepare the contract is not only the right thing to do, but it also ensures that the contract is written properly, saves you time, limits your liability and usually, if it is a good attorney, makes the deal go smoother. You should limit yourself to the business terms of the deal and filling in the blanks on preprinted forms.

Helpful Hints and Things to Know

There are some things that may help you succeed in commercial real estate that do not fit neatly under other topics found this book. Some may be of direct benefit and others are just good things to know or do. This section is a catch all for these helpful hints.

- It is a good idea to keep lists of people that you can recommend. You will often be asked to suggest attorneys, contractors, engineers, appraisers, mortgage brokers, and those who specialize in appealing property valuations, to name a few. Keep a list of the best ones. It is also a good idea to mention to those people that you are the one who recommended them in order to build goodwill and land some possible future business.

- There are many ways to measure property. This is important because rent is usually based on the size. Area is often measured differently in each specialty area. If there were a general rule to measuring area of buildings, it would probably be from the center of the wall to the glass, but this is not always the case. In warehouses, for example, sometimes a covered loading dock or interior rail spur may be included in the total. In offices, the area may be usable area, which is from the glass to the inside of corridor walls and center of partition walls of the premises, or rentable area, which adds a load factor onto the usable area for such things as common restrooms, corridors, and lobbies. Load factors, which are a percentage of the usable area, may be a real percentage of those common areas, or a market number, like 10% to 15%. If the usable office area is 1,000 sq. ft., for example, and the load factor is 10%, then the rent will be based on 1,100 sq. ft. (1,000 sq. ft. X 10% = 100 sq. ft. + 1,000 sq. ft. = 1,100 sq. ft.). In retail they may measure to the "drip line." Other ways to quote area include store area and construction area. Standards for measuring areas are established by the Building Owners and Managers Association (BOMA).

- All agreements in commercial real estate should be in writing. Not only is this a legal requirement under the statute of frauds, but it is also a practical issue. People forget what they agreed to, or sometimes decide they don't want to do what they agreed to. Agreements need to be enforceable. Also, you want to have written evidence of your actions in order to protect yourself for liability reasons. You need to be able to show that the letter of the law has been followed. As a side note, if you ever find that you are getting into legal problems surrounding some situation, it is wise to spend a little time writing down the details of the circumstances, while they are fresh in your mind. Beyond this, it is just a good practice to write everything down. Brokers need to keep track of things to remember, as well as prospects and their activities.

- The importance of contingencies in offers. Contingencies are a sales tool that enables a deal to proceed subject to certain things. They allow you to take the initiative and create momentum to a deal. Buyers can sign an offer, for example, when they are ready to buy or lease, even though they need to satisfy themselves on certain items before they actually commit to the purchase. A deal can proceed with the principals working on what they need to accomplish simultaneously. Sometimes, creative contingencies, such as making a deal subject to a board of directors' approval or the completion of a pro forma, are just enough to get a deal started.

- The "after deal," second round, or contingency negotiations. When a purchase agreement has a contingency for things such as an environmental analysis or engineering inspection, which indicates that there are some problems with the property, a second set of negotiations is often precipitated. These "after deal" negotiations usually involve price. For example, if the building needed a new roof that costs $50,000, then the seller might split the cost 50-50, and reduce the price by $25,000 to offset the buyer's cost of replacing it. These are entirely legitimate negotiations because the seller will be faced with the same cost whether he sells it or not. He also, most likely, will have to face the same issue with a future buyer. "After deal" negotiations are often necessary to keep a deal from dying. Sometimes sophisticated buyers use these negotiations by fabricating some problem with the property, in order to get the price down.

- Sometimes commercial brokers are used by lessees or buyers who are trying to improve another deal. A common example is when a tenant is renegotiating its lease with a landlord, so it makes an offer on your listing in order to get another deal at a lower rent that it can use as leverage against the landlord. This is pretty hard to prevent. As you gain experience, you will be able to spot these kinds of dead end deals and, if possible, avoid them. Another solution, of course, is to make the deal on your listing so attractive that the tenant ends up moving.

- This may sound a little silly, but you should know where north, east, south, and west are. You will be surprised how often the need to identify directions comes up. You are often asked to give directions, locate something, follow directions, and write descriptions of a property's location, all of which require this knowledge. Besides that, you will look pretty stupid if you can't point to north for a prospect looking at one of your listings.

- Most of the decision makers in commercial real estate matters are in their late 40s, 50s and 60s. Brokers in that age bracket have an advantage over others because they are contemporaries, and they often know them.

- Dropping the lease rate, or price, in order to create interest in a listing that is not moving is a two-edged sword. On one hand, it may stimulate some prospect to make an offer, but, on the other, it may cause the offer to be very low. Generally speaking, the first thing a prospect thinks when you drop the rate or price is "How low will it go?" If the principal dropped it once, buyers often think it may be a sign of desperation and he or she will drop it again. It is best to establish a realistic rate up front, or offer free rent or better terms, rather than cutting the rate or dropping the price. It is the last ditch effort when marketing property.

- Confidentiality agreements. It is often necessary to share sensitive information in commercial real estate. This could include financial statements, rent rolls, or ownership. Also, sometimes owners wish to market property on a confidential basis because they don't want to upset the tenants or have people (such as employees) know they are selling. Sometimes brokers wish to submit listings to prospective buyers on a confidential basis because the owner requested it or because they are conducting a limited marketing program. These often occur in large investment properties or in businesses where there are many employees. Confidentiality agreements are often used in these cases. A confidentiality agreement usually provides that the person receiving the information cannot discuss, copy, or pass on the information to anyone else. In other words, the information is confidential.

- Tenant improvements. Landlords will sometimes try to get subsequent tenants to pay for the cost of earlier tenant improvements, which were amortized over a period longer than the lease. A tenant should pay no more than market unless there is a good reason to do otherwise. One good reason could be that the new tenant can use the previous tenant's improvements. Generally, however, you should be sure that the rent rates are market. Also, when renegotiating market rents in leases where the tenant has paid for the tenant improvements, landlords will sometimes try and base the new market rent on those improvements. The lease should specify that they are to be excluded.

- Be creative. The ability to think of ways to do deals that others don't is a key difference between very successful and mediocre brokers. Seeing different uses for a property, different ways to finance a deal, different ways to make a deal, or unusual ways to market a property, are a few examples of creative thinking in commercial real estate.

- Pick your battles carefully. You cannot win every listing pitch or bring justice to the world. Some battles are lost before they are started. Pick the battles that you have a chance to win, and then win them.

- Some brokers' motivation to enter the field of commercial real estate is to acquire commercial property for their own account. This is a two-edged sword. On one hand, it is helpful to know what is available and to have the knowledge of what to acquire. On the other hand, being a broker tends to put you at a disadvantage with sellers because they think you know more than they do and, consequently, become more careful. It is a requirement in some states to disclose to a seller that you are a licensed broker. Also, if you are a broker with a reputation for buying good income property and are listing a client's investment property, buyers will sometimes wonder why you did not buy the property you are offering. This tends to put your seller/client at a disadvantage. If you are a serious investor in commercial property, it may be in your own interest to be unlicensed.

CHAPTER 11

Professionalism

Some question whether real estate is a true profession like law or medicine. It is true that some aspects of the industry do not fit the traditional mold of a profession. Chief among these are the need to advertise and the emphasis on salesmanship. Many think of real estate brokers as sales people. It is true that sales is an integral part of the business; however, other professions also sell, and there are more similarities with other professions than not. The similarities include an educational process in order to become a practitioner, a base of technical knowledge, a specialized language, a code of ethics, and a fiduciary relationship with clients. To conduct the business of commercial real estate properly, one must master certain knowledge and, hopefully, become an expert. It is not for amateurs. For these reasons, there seems to no question that it is a profession.

As a profession, commercial real estate carries certain responsibilities in terms of how you conduct yourself and how you relate to others. The important thing to remember is to never mix your personal feelings with your professional obligations. Personal prejudices, dislikes, problems, attitudes, resentments, and emotions should be checked at the door of your office. You may dislike another broker, or feel unfairly treated by a prospect or client, but you cannot let issues such as these interfere with your good judgment. Attention to your client's needs and a sense of fair play are essential.

The four main spheres of professional relations involve the relationships with the public, relationships with clients, relationships with other Realtors®, and relationships with other professionals such as attorneys, accountants, and appraisers.

Relations with the Public

Commercial brokers get calls from all sorts of people. Some are prospects, some are looking for information, some have something to sell, some are looking for leads, and some are asking for advice. It is your professional obligation and in your best interest, to always treat the public fairly, courteously, and honestly. Your professional image is important and people talk. People's opinions have a way of congregating together to form facts. What the public says about you and the image that emerges is important.

If you have listings, you will get calls from many prospects. It is important to maintain professional relations with all prospects. Some are not qualified and some are, but you will not know this until you talk with them. Even unqualified callers can be a good source of information and leads. It is important to give all prospects prompt, courteous, and accurate information on any listing. Wise brokers treat everyone as potential clients or as a future source for clients, because they may be one. You just never know where business can come from.

In addition to the obligation to be civil, it is also good business to be involved with community activities. It will add to your reputation and your visibility, which will enhance your chance of success. Business organizations such as local chambers of commerce, governmental boards such as planning committees, and volunteer organizations such as the local historical society or charity are good places to contribute your time and effort.

Relations with Clients

The relationships you keep with your clients are the most important. How you relate to them will largely determine whether you succeed or fail. The ultimate goal, obviously, is to handle their properties. But you also want to gain their respect and admiration for your abilities in order to keep their business and to get it again.

You must remember that you have a fiduciary relationship with your clients. You must look out for their interests. This is sometimes easier said than done. You will find yourself in many circumstances where their interests are, ostensibly, not the same as yours. Trying to get them to lower the price just so you can make a deal and collect a commission is a common area of conflict. Promising something you know may not happen in order, again, to collect a commission is not in your client's interests, nor is persuading a client to buy property for development when you know the market for that product is thin. These are not necessarily illegal or unethical acts, but rather subtleties that may help you and not the client. You should always make your best good faith effort to represent your client's best interests. Do not confuse your interests with your clients.

You also owe it to your clients to be competent and to use your best efforts. Obviously, some brokers are better than others, but there is a line in the sand where inexperience crosses into incompetence. If you do not know the answer to a question or how to handle a certain situation, admit it and get help. If you feel that you are not capable of handling a certain requirement, recommend someone who is. If you are too busy to work a listing, don't take it. If you have a listing that you are no longer working on, either return it to the owner or redouble your efforts to move it. It is a real disservice to a client to have a listing that is going nowhere because you are not working it.

There are a few practical things to keep in mind that will help you get and keep clients. Always make a special effort to keep clients informed of what is going on, even if the information makes you look bad. Clients are keenly interested in all activities on their property and really appreciate information. Keeping them informed accomplishes a number of things. First, you get appreciative clients. Second, it makes you aware of any problems. If there is no activity on a listing, for example, you know it. Third, it can spur you to activity. If your report is that nothing is going on, then ask yourself what you can do to create interest and activity. And fourth, it gives the client the necessary information that helps make deals. Perhaps they need to spend some money on advertising or lower the price. Or, if a lower priced offer comes in, they may take it based on the reports you have provided.

Do not shade the facts. Some commercial brokers get into the bad habit of telling clients only what they want them to hear in order to further their own interests. The broker is playing a chess game, and they view the client as a pawn. They have an agenda, so they tell the client only enough to advance it. Inducing a prospect to list property that the broker knows is overpriced, with the idea that, once the property is listed, the client can be worked on to get the price down in order to make a deal, is one example. The broker figures he or she has a better chance of making a deal with an overpriced listing than none at all. Do not fall into this habit. Always endeavor to be totally honest and straightforward with your clients.

In the end, it is as much in your interests to follow these suggestions, as the clients. People appreciate honesty and integrity. They trust those who exhibit these qualities. They will speak highly of you and use you for future business. Everyone speaks of the need for client control in the commercial real estate business. This is true, but the term is a misnomer. Brokers don't "control" clients; rather, clients stay loyal to good brokers. "Control" is just another word for the loyalty that comes when a commercial broker does the job right.

You should keep in mind that, in spite of all this high-minded talk about responsibilities to clients, the bottom line is results. Prospects list property with brokers who perform. There are many highly ethical brokers who do little business. Hopefully, the advice in this book will help you avoid that fate.

Relations with Other Realtors®

Real estate is one of the few professions where agents are required to compete and cooperate at the same time. It makes for some very odd situations and schizophrenic brokers. Brokers compete for listings and prospects like cats and dogs and then turn around and work hand in hand with the same brokers to make a deal. One minute you are explaining to a prospect why you are better than the other guy, and the next minute, you are working cooperatively with that same person to make a deal. In the long run, it pays to get along with other brokers. You will find yourself in positions where you need other brokers for information, to make deals, or for advice. They also are sometimes sources of referrals. If you cut them off, you cut off your ability to make deals. You only hurt yourself. Also, you have an obligation to clients to cooperate with other brokers in order to ensure that their properties or requirements are fully exposed to the market. In this respect, you have a professional obligation to remain on good terms and cooperate with your peers. When it comes to cooperating on real estate fees, remember that half a fee is always better than no fee.

There are many situations and circumstances that can cause friction between brokers. These can be dramatically reduced if brokers would just follow the Code of Ethics, the golden rule, and use common sense. Unfortunately, many do not, so there is often disagreement found in the profession. The following are a few of the more common problems found between brokers, along with some suggestions on how to avoid them.

- Fee splits. The biggest source of conflict between brokers involves commission disputes. These can be between firms or brokers, and they can be dicey. Fifty-fifty splits are probably the norm between cooperating brokers, but this not always the case. Ideally, a broker should be paid in accordance with his or her contribution to the deal. Unfortunately, it is often hard to determine exactly what that contribution is, and brokers usually have inflated ideas of what they did contribute. Fair splits and advance agreement as to what the spit shall be, are the best solutions.

- Instigating cause. Instigating cause refers to the broker who instigated a prospect's interest, which caused a deal to happen. One broker, for example, may have told a prospect about a building, which caused the prospect to go look at it and get interested. Unfortunately, the prospect then makes an offer through another broker. The first broker was the instigating cause of the deal even though the second broker brought in the deal. Some brokerage firms do not like to consider instigating cause when splitting fees because it can be so subjective. To simplify matters, they prefer to recognize only the broker who brings in the offer. There may be some benefits to this hard philosophy, but it may result in an injustice. It seems only fair for brokers to make an effort to try and determine the instigating cause of a deal and then include that broker in the deal on some basis. The public, by and large, does not know commercial real estate protocol. Therefore, it is important to educate them up front. It is also important to have a good understanding of everyone's role in a deal, preferably in writing, before any work is done.

- Calling on other brokers' clients. Some brokers call around listing brokers to get information, make a deal, or get a listing. This is unethical and wrong. Do not do it.

- Calling on all the logical prospects of a listing before the listing broker can. When a new listing is coming to market, some brokers will go through the telephone book and call all the logical prospects before the broker who listed it can. The listing broker may have spent considerable time and effort getting the listing, while the other just made a few calls. It is protocol to allow a listing broker to have a short grace period after listing a property in order to make calls on logical prospects.

- Registration. Registration is when a cooperating broker tells a listing broker the name of his or her prospect for protection. Some listing brokers take a registration, some do with conditions, and some don't. Registration is good because it gives a cooperating broker the incentive to put the time and effort in to make a deal. The problem is when the listing broker takes a registration from one broker on a prospect and then another broker brings in the offer from that same prospect. The solution is for registration to protect the cooperating broker from the listing broker only. In other words, if the registered prospect calls the listing broker directly, the registering broker will earn a fee, but if another broker brings in the offer, the registering broker is out.

- Disputes over territory. Large commercial companies often will assign brokers a certain territory or sometimes one broker may just be more active in one area than others.

Disputes often arise over who should handle prospects and listings that come up in that area. Man is, after all, territorial by nature. The solution is to stay in your own territory, cooperate, or work at a firm that does not have territories.

- Disputes over clients. Brokers often build up a relationship with a certain client over time and resist allowing other brokers to call their client. Some companies encourage this because they want to maintain that good relationship with the client. This commonly happens when a new salesperson calls on a more experienced broker's long-time client. This is a real disadvantage to the beginning salesperson. The solution is to cooperate and work with the broker who has the relationship or find a firm that has an open door policy to all prospects. This is more of a practical matter than an ethical one. Generally, all brokers are free to call on all prospects. The obvious exceptions to this would be things such as calling on another broker's exclusive listing or calling when a prospect has asked not to be contacted. Usually, it is more a matter of maintaining good relations with the broker who has the relationship.

Attorneys, Accountants, and Appraisers

You will often find yourself working closely with attorneys, accountants, and appraisers when making commercial real estate deals. It is important to establish a good working relationship with each of them because they are critical to the success of transactions and sources of future business.

Accountants are often the driving force behind the need for, and structure of, investment deals for tax reasons. They often influence things such as the type of property a client buys, the method of ownership, and the payment. When a client is selling property, an accountant is often closely involved with the timing of the sale and the terms of the sale in order to maximize tax savings.

Appraisers are the value gurus. Clients, and especially lenders, lean on them heavily for assurance that prices are in line with market, among other things. Appraisers can kill a sale if they determine the price is too high or too low. The relationship with appraisers is a two-way street. Appraisers rely on brokers for market information and verification of information, and brokers rely on appraisers for advice and information. Helping appraisers is not only a professional courtesy, but also in your best interest because they are sources of business, they help establish your reputation, and you may need their help in the future.

Attorneys are a special case. There is a perceived, historic tension between real estate brokers and attorneys. Brokers often complain of "deal killer" attorneys, and attorneys have been heard to complain about "slipshod" brokers who are more interested in making a commission than in protecting their client's interests. It is true that brokers and attorneys often have slightly different agendas. The broker is trying to bring about a meeting of the minds, which is a process of compromise, and the attorneys are trying to protect their client's interests, which often is an adversarial process. The broker only gets paid if the deal closes, while the attorney gets paid either way. Some attorneys have been known to drag a deal out because they make more money. In spite of these issues, the truth of the matter is that good commercial real estate attorneys make deals happen. These deals also are the best kind because the attorney put them on a sound legal basis. More often than not, the broker who complained of an attorney "killing" a deal, negotiated a deal that needed to be killed.

The important thing about attorneys to remember is to get a good one — preferably one who specializes in commercial real estate transactions. Commercial deals are often complex and require special legal attention. Attorneys, like most professions, specialize in different areas of the law, and some are just better than others on the legal issues and nuances of commercial real estate deals. If you had a heart problem, you would go to a cardiologist and not a proctologist. Similarly, when you need advice on a commercial real estate deal, recommend to your clients that they get a good commercial real estate attorney. Most problems with attorneys occur when they become cautious because they are not familiar with the issues. If there were such things as a "deal killer" attorney, these would be the best candidates. The knowledgeable ones, on the other hand, are usually "deal makers." They know that it is in their client's interests to make the deal, so they endeavor to make it. They quickly spot the problems and rather than kill it, figure out a way to fix it. They will also take you off the hook for any future problems, because they put the transaction on the right legal footing. They help you and your client avoid liability and any future litigation.

Although it has been emphasized elsewhere in this book, one point related to attorneys bears being mentioned again. Do not practice law. There is a fine line in commercial real estate between advising clients on real estate matters and advising them on legal matters. Writing up land sales contracts or mortgages or advising on the legal issues surrounding a condemnation clause in a lease is dangerous stuff. You are not paid to do this and probably not qualified. You should limit your advice to the business terms of the deal and filling in the blanks on preprinted and standardized forms. Let the attorneys do the legal work.

There are many other professionals that you will deal with in the commercial real estate business that have not been mentioned. These may include engineers, environmental consultants, land use consultants, escrow and title officers, general contractors, mortgage lenders and brokers, and surveyors to name a few. Even though their fields may not overlap as much as attorneys, accountants, and appraisers, they are all important to the process. Each offers important skills for the successful completion of deals. Treat them well because they are part of the team that can make or break your chances of success in the business.

CHAPTER 12
Organizations

Do not overlook the many fine local and national commercial real estate organizations. These can include associations, institutes, societies, councils, chambers, and profit and non-profit organizations. They can help you with things such as publications, educational seminars, accruing continuing educational hours for licensing, conventions, current trends and news, governmental affairs, products, and technology. Some organizations involve designations that require rigorous experience and educational standards in order to achieve. These often lend a broker prestige, which can help in getting business. Holding an office and participating in these organizations gives you name recognition that can help your reputation with potential clients, as well as other brokers. You should research the organizations in order to select the one most suitable for your specialty.

Some organizations are sources of leads, prospects, listings, and clients. Some have business trade shows where prospects and brokers with prospects converge to share information and do business. Some also have multiple listing services that you should join. (Multiple listing services were discussed in Chapter 8.) The National Association of Realtors® and its affiliated commercial boards and affiliates provide ethical standards that govern the conduct within the real estate business and provide ways to enforce them.

It generally pays to get involved in these organizations because they throw you into the thick of things and are good sources of referrals, information, and educational programs. They can often offer property sharing and prospect information. Being involved in them can lead to recognition and prestige among prospects, clients, and other brokers. And, it is just good to support your profession and contribute to the organizations that have helped create the circumstances that have allowed you to make a living. However, it is important to remember that being a member of an organization is no substitute for talking with prospects, getting listings, and doing deals. They can be expensive and time consuming, which can distract you from your primary goal of making deals. Be involved, but don't over do it

The following is a summary of some of these organizations and what they do. This list highlights some of the more significant ones in commercial real estate. It is, however, by no means inclusive. There are many national entities whose involvement with commercial real estate is oblique, and local organizations are too numerous to mention.

The National Association of Realtors® (NAR)

The National Association of Realtors® is the national professional organization composed of residential and commercial real estate brokers, salespeople, property managers, appraisers, counselors, and others engaged in all aspects of the real estate industry. It consists of local associations and boards and many institutes, societies, and councils. Members of NAR are termed REALTORS®, which is a registered trademark. REALTORS® subscribe to a strict Code of Ethics and Standards of Practice (see Appendix A). The many products and services NAR offers include education, governmental advocacy, news, policy, meetings, conventions, seminars, technology, and reference information. NAR affiliated institutes, societies, and councils involved with commercial real estate are described below. All offer a designation for that specialty.

Commercial Investment Real Estate Institute (CIREI)

Commercial Investment Real Estate Institute brokers engage in commercial investment real estate. Their expertise is primarily in asset management, valuation, and investment analysis. The institute confers the Certified Commercial Investment Member (CCIM) designation after a rigorous educational process. These are the gurus of commercial investment real estate.

Counselors of Real Estate (CRE)

Members of the Counselors of Real Estate are counselors in real estate matters. Their services include asset and portfolio management, debt restructuring, best use of land studies, and economic and market analysis. They offer the Counselor of Real Estate designation (CRE). Counselors of Real Estate are known for having a broad based knowledge of real estate matters and for providing comprehensive, impartial, and useful solutions to real estate problems.

Institute of Real Estate Management (IREM)

The Institute of Real Estate Management is an educational institute for property management in both commercial and residential real estate. Their main designation is the Certified Property Manager (CPM) for those who have met certain standards in the areas of education, experience, and integrity. Managing commercial property can be complex and often involves difficult problems. Certified Property Managers are experts at dealing with these issues. IREM also offers the Accredited Residential Manager (ARN) designation for on-site managers of multi-family housing and the Accredited Management Organization designation for management companies that want to take that extra step to professionalism.

REALTORS® Land Institute (RLI)

The REALTORS® Land Institute's objective is to improve brokers' professional competence in activities related to land. This includes land brokerage, agri-business, land management, planning and development, appraisals, acquisition, and other land specialty areas. They confer the designation Accredited Land Consultant (ALC) after completing a comprehensive educational program, gaining experience in the field, and having served the institute. Issues surrounding unimproved land are becoming more complex and increasingly require knowledgeable and experienced brokers, such as members of the REALTORS® Land Institute.

Society of Industrial and Office Realtors® (SIOR)

Members of the Society of Industrial and Office Realtors® deal primarily with industrial and office properties. They are dedicated to maintaining high professional standards in those fields through education and experience. The society confers the designation Society of Industrial and Office Realtor® (SIOR) on members who have attained those standards. The society has an extensive referral network and being a member can enhance your brokerage business.

State and Local Boards

In addition to the National Association of Realtors®, there may be numerous state and local associations and boards that are involved with commercial real estate. Often a large metropolitan area will have a Commercial Association of Realtors®, which deals primarily with matters affecting the local commercial real estate market. Typically, they administer the Code of Ethics, provide educational services, arrange social events, and act as advocates for commercial real estate. They also often have methods of sharing information, such as a multiple listing service and e-mail lists for brokers. It is a good idea to join the commercial association in your area that is affiliated with the National Association of Realtors®. It will provide you with considerable information about what is going on in commercial real estate in your area.

Other Organizations

There are many other organizations not directly associated with NAR that deal in commercial real estate. Some are national in scope, such as the National Association of Industrial and Office Properties (NAIOP), which deals with issues surrounding office and industrial parks, and the International Council of Shopping Centers (ICSC), which deals with the same issues in retail. Their members may be industrial park, office park, or shopping center owners, managers, or brokers. These organizations also provide a multitude of other services such as real estate forms, conventions, information exchange, and education.

CHAPTER 13

Striking Out
On Your Own

When you are not the lead dog, the view is always the same. At one time or another, almost all commercial real estate brokers think about becoming independent or starting their own company. Most don't. There is a certain security that comes with working for a large brokerage house. Many remain content working for someone else and letting them deal with the hassles of running a company. Sometimes brokers go to work in some allied field. Commercial real estate is a breeding ground for many allied businesses because the knowledge and training necessary for a commercial broker is easily transferable to other areas. Brokers often become developers, investors, property managers, finance officers, or managers of the real estate assets of wealthy individuals or corporations.

Whatever the case, this chapter is for those who want to go out on their own. This decision is not for everyone. There are advantages and disadvantages to becoming independent. Brokers should carefully weigh the pros and cons of doing so in light of their own personality and abilities and make their own decision. This chapter will first discuss both sides of the issue (the advantages and disadvantages of being independent) and will then present some sales points for those who decide to strike out on their own. The final section of this chapter will summarize the salient points of this book and give some final, concluding thoughts.

Independent or Not

Ernest Hemingway once said, "It is better to die on your feet than live on your knees." This may sound like hyperbole, but there are some individuals who seem compelled to live a free and independent existence. There are many motivating factors for independence. These may include things such as prestige, money, self-determination, dislike of being told what to do, or just wanting more time to play. Whatever the reason, the decision should be carefully weighed.

Large companies can be like gristmills, slowly grinding out robotic-like brokers. They can make one feel like a small cog in a huge, impersonal machine. You must turn faster when someone advances the throttle, or slow down because someone has a hand on the brake. Life in a cube can be like living in a glass house. Everyone overhears what you say, what you do, and what happens to you.

For some brokers, dealing with management and other brokers is a major distraction from their main effort of selling and leasing real estate. Management meetings, evaluation meetings, company-wide meetings, and brokerage meetings are ubiquitous. You are made to deal with broker rankings and the endless paperwork associated with running a large concern. Legal requirements like sexual harassment training and management requirements like dress codes can become unnecessary distractions. Disputes with other brokers over clients, territory, or fee splits are common. You become hamstrung by others who determine who you can call on, where you can work, and how much you will earn in a fee split. Having to deal with other brokers on these kind of issues is perhaps one of the most draining and counterproductive aspects of working in a large company. They are destructive, time consuming, limiting, and rarely lead to making more deals and more money.

Perhaps the single biggest motivation for brokers who go out on their own is money. In large companies there are often many splits of a single fee. If, for example, the fee on a deal is $20,000, an outside cooperative broker could take half, or $10,000. The house (or company) could take 50% of that, or $5,000, and an in-house, co-listing broker could take half of what remains, or $2,500. Thus, on a $20,000 fee, you might make only $2,500. If you are the one who got the listing and negotiated most of the deal, this can be quite frustrating. If you were independent, you would most likely have made $10,000 on the same deal or even $20,000, if there were no cooperative broker. This is a big difference.

There are many more reasons to either remain with a big firm or make the leap of faith. The following is a list of many of the advantages and disadvantages of becoming independent. Some points concern independents only and others those who want to start their own companies. Some of these points overlap.

Advantages of Being Independent

- Independence.

- Freedom.

- Being your own boss.

- More recognition. When your name is on the signs, advertising, and news releases, you will get more recognition.

- Less hassle with management or other brokers. Management makes decisions like who gets what deal or listing, who is promoted, and how disputes are resolved. If you are independent, these decisions are now yours.

- Your listings are between you and the client — not your company and the client.

- Less hype and less intense in-house competition.

- The excitement and challenge of being on your own.

- The opportunity to form alliances with other brokers that would not have happened if you were in a big company. Independents tend to stick together.

- Less liability from other brokers' mistakes. If you are independent, you have more control over your work.

- You do not have to make as many deals because there are fewer splits.

- You may fulfill a lifelong dream of becoming your own boss. It has been said that when people die, their greatest life regrets are not having done what they wanted to do. If you want to be independent and die in peace, become independent.

Disadvantages of Being Independent

- More management responsibility if you have employees and salespeople.

- More risk.

- Possible additional state mandated educational requirements to become a broker, such as those related to office management and client trust accounts.

- Competition for business, especially for listings, with larger firms. This is often a driving concern for those thinking of making the move. Generally speaking, if you got listings on your own in the big house and you are skilled at sales, you will get the business. The large companies, by and large, have a significant part of the national commercial real estate business, which is hard to penetrate. There are, however, many large national, regional, and local prospects available. Also, remember that you do not have to make as many deals as an independent in order to make the same amount of money. Competing with large brokerages will be discussed in the next section.

- More paperwork. You must handle or oversee the books, including client trust accounts, bills, taxes, and so forth.

- You will have overhead such as rent, phone, signs, advertising, secretarial, and so forth. Remember, however, that this overhead is usually much less than the 50% you paid the large brokerage company. If you make $200,000 per year as an independent and your overhead is $30,000 per year, you still have a $170,000 profit. With the large company and a 50-50 split, your income would be $100,000. You just made $70,000 by going out on your own. To be fair, there are some expenses that you will have as an independent that you may not have had with a large company. Some of these include business taxes (such as the portion of FICA your previous employer paid and possibly federal and local business taxes), errors and omissions insurance, and health insurance.

- If you work for a large company and it goes broke, you can lose everything. The same can be said of an independent, but at least in this situation, you have some control over the situation.

- You must find and lease office space.

- You may experience less synergy and camaraderie as an independent.

- You will probably lose some listings and possibly some deals in progress, if you leave a firm.

- When you leave a firm, you may lose future income from things such as renewal options to lease or purchase.

- You will lose any clients who were loyal to the company you left.

- There may be more personal liability if you are an independent contractor doing business in your own name.

- Less structure.

- Start up costs such as furniture, equipment, and miscellaneous. Furniture could include desks, chairs, filing cabinets, and tables. Equipment could include computer, fax, typewriter, phones, and a copy machine. Miscellaneous items include stationary, flyers, envelopes, office supplies, forms, and signs. You are starting from scratch.

Other Considerations

There are other matters to consider if you go out on our own. One is the form of ownership. There are many tax and liability reasons for picking one form over the other. Some types of ownership include sole proprietor, corporation, subchapter S corporations, and partnerships, to name a few. You will also want to decide how big you want to be. Are you going to be independent, a small association of experienced brokers, or a large company with a sales force?

Some additional suggestions that help small brokers succeed and compete are listed below.

- Pick a specific geographic area to work.

- Pick a specialty area and become an expert.

- Be professional and service oriented.

- Be relationship oriented, not transaction oriented.

- Don't try to do all the business, rather try and do an outstanding job for just a few good clients.

- Report regularly to your clients.

Becoming independent is not for everyone. When all is said and done, it really is a very personal matter. A central consideration is whether you will be successful. This requires some honest self-evaluation and hard decisions. If you don't think it is for you, then don't do it. If, however, you are generating more income for your company than you are for yourself; you are getting your own listings; and you love independence and feel that you are being held back, then perhaps you should go for it. If you have managed to become successful in commercial real estate, then the odds are that you will remain successful on your own.

Sales Points for Independents and Small Brokerages

If you decide to go on your own you will find that, more often than not, your biggest competitors are the large local, or national, commercial real estate firms. They are formidable competitors. They have many advantages, including name recognition, money, national connections, and influence. Corporations will often list property with national commercial real estate firms because one of their brokers has a relationship with them in another city or they may have a contract to handle their real estate needs. Sometimes real estate managers of large corporations will list a large real estate company simply because they want the "credibility" of a national firm when reporting to higher management. This is especially true when a property is not moving and higher management questions the real estate manager's methods and abilities. At least in this case, the manager can always say that the property is listed with a national company, rather than with some unknown local entity like you.

National commercial firms are vulnerable in many ways, however, and often lose listing competitions to aggressive and knowledgeable independent brokers. The following are some sales points you can use against large local and national commercial firms to exploit these vulnerabilities. Do not get the wrong idea from this list. There are many fine national commercial brokerage companies with some excellent professional and experienced brokers. This is not an indictment of national firms, but rather a list of points that expose some of their weaknesses. Some of these points were previously discussed in Chapter 5, but are repeated here and tailored to this specific situation.

- Because of the intense competition and rivalry between large commercial firms, there is often less cooperation between them, than between the large firms and "neutral" independent agents, who work with everyone. The independent broker, consequently, is in a better position to gain the cooperation of all brokers in the marketing of a client's property.

- Because of the intense competition and rivalry within large commercial firms, there is often better cooperation between a broker who works with a large firm and an outside independent broker, than between two brokers within the same firm.

- Large firms have high overheads, which include expensive offices, private secretaries, expensive clothes, support staff, self-promoting advertising, and managers. They must naturally, therefore, charge maximum fees in order to survive. Independent brokers have less overhead, so they can do the same job for lower fees and still make more money.

- Large firms like to say that small brokers do not have the horsepower to market large properties. The techniques of marketing commercial real estate (which were discussed in Chapter 8) are the same for large firms and independents. Independents do all of the same things that large firms do to market property, including brochures, mailings, signs, and listing with the multiple listing service. Furthermore, emerging trends in technology make the sharing of information so easy and quick, any advantages large firms may have enjoyed regarding information is rapidly diminishing.

More often than not, small firms and independent brokers do more deals in any one marketplace, than a few large commercial brokerages.

- Large firms are fond of saying that an owner will lose out on national prospects because the independent broker does not have their company's national contacts. In reality, many small firms and independent brokers handle deals for many national corporations. Many referrals of national clients are from other independent brokers in other cities because they prefer to avoid the national brokerages. They know that referrals will be reciprocated by independents and not national companies.

- Brokers in national companies are like any other broker when cooperating with other brokers. They will submit any listing of a small broker to their national client if it fits, because they know if they don't, someone else will. They all understand that a half a fee is better than no fee.

- One national brokerage firm cannot claim an advantage by saying they have national prospects, because all national companies have prospects. What makes one national brokerage with national prospects, better than another national brokerage that also has national prospects? The reality is that they all cooperate as long as the property fits the prospect's requirements, whether the property is listed with a large firm, small firm, or independent brokerage.

- Because national firms tend to be "pressure cooker" environments, they tend to have high broker turnover. Consequently, they often have many neophyte brokers, which causes their representation to be uneven. The client may find themselves assigned to a young, inexperienced broker with only a few years in the business. Further, experienced brokers within the same company do not have the incentive to help inexperienced brokers because they are future competitors.

- Large commercial firms have meetings, reports, broker conferences, strategy sessions, and personal fulfillment programs that detract from making deals. Brokers for large companies often spend more time talking and competing among themselves than they do out in the marketplace working with prospects, pushing their client's listing, and making deals. Independent brokers do not have this handicap.

- Brokers within large firms have less financial incentive to actively work on one property because there are so many splits. For example, if the commission on a property is $9,000, the house would take $4,500, and the balance would be split among the broker "team." If there were three brokers on the listing, which there sometimes are, the experienced broker would earn $1,500, or maybe $750 after tax. If there was an outside cooperative broker, this could be more like $375. Independent brokers make more on each deal and therefore have the incentive to work harder on a single listing.

- Because brokers in large houses make less on each deal, they must work on volume. This causes them to become "order takers." They get used to business coming to them, rather than going to it. For this reason, they often fail to learn the fundamentals of commercial real estate and get lost when business slows down. They also are often over-extended, trying to handle too many listings at one time. Because they must work on volume, they simply do not have the time to work one listing. Also, when there is high volume, it is easier to make mistakes.

- Brokers in large companies, and sometimes the companies themselves, become arrogant. A broker with a prospect may wish to avoid the listing of an arrogant broker in some large firm. This means that a property listed with a large firm may not be exposed to some prospects. This hurts the client's ability to market their property.

- Large brokerage companies are fond of saying that they have the ability to assemble a team and bring the necessary expertise to bear on any special requirements a listing may have. So does an independent broker. A good independent broker can quickly assemble a good attorney, accountant, engineer, environmental consultant, contractor, finance expert, and developer, if needed. Further, this team is often better than the national brokerage company's in-house team because the independent broker can pick the very best that the marketplace has to offer.

- The atmosphere within large brokerages is sometimes one of a cut-throat, directionless, bureaucracy that emphasizes money over people. They do not provide the kind of work environment that helps make deals.

Conclusion

Well, there you have it — an overview of how to succeed in the commercial real estate business. To many of you, the information in this book may have been obvious or even elementary. Perhaps a few were confused, and some even offended, due to the occasional strong opinions. Whatever your reaction, it still seems certain that if you follow the advice presented here, you are bound to succeed. It is amazing how many brokers ignore the fundamentals of success in this business, and no wonder that so many drop out after a short period of time. Certainly, there are different ways to success, but most are just variations on the same fundamentals, which were discussed in this book.

The first steps are to make the decision to enter commercial real estate and then pick a firm with which you are compatible. This should be a place that will succor your success, not detract from it. The next crucial steps are to learn all you can about ethics, contracts, and allied fields. Much of this will come with time and experience, but you need to act like a sponge at the beginning, soaking up all the information you can get. During this early learning period you should take the time to learn how to sell. This is perhaps the most overlooked step by brokers, yet one of the most important things you can do. It simply is hard to fail at anything if you understand the principles of salesmanship. It is not a dirty word. All successful people do it; they just don't know it.

After giving some preliminary thought to organizing yourself and especially your time, you are ready to hit the streets. If you have prepared yourself adequately, you should immediately start seeing results. Prospects will want to talk with you, people will want to do business with you, and owners will want to talk with you about listing their properties. From here on out it is learning on the job. You have now been tossed in with the lions, and there are no safety nets. It is sink or swim time. Without the necessary preparation, at this point many brokers start heading for the depths of the deep blue sea like a lead weight is tied to their leg. Once they start the descent, it is pretty hard to stop.

If you have prepared yourself and continue to follow the practical advice offered in the later part of this book, you are bound to swim. The first step is to get some prospects. They are everywhere. You will soon find that it is not a matter of getting prospects, because you will have so many, but rather a matter of getting the good ones. As you turn these prospects into clients, and especially listings, you are making the crucial step from beginner to experienced broker. You are at the crucial point where good brokers succeed. You understand the importance of getting listings and keeping them, so you automatically have a leg up on competitors who do not understand this. With the listings, you then start the marketing process, spreading the information far and wide in order to get buyers and lessees. This automatically leads to negotiations and eventually deals. Because you have taken the time to learn how to negotiate, they go smoothly and quickly until there is a meeting of the minds. Because you studied contracts early on, you are easily able to reduce the principals' agreement to writing and proceed to closing, or lease execution. You avoid making certain fatal errors because you have learned what to avoid and have learned the important things to know. Before you know it, a commission check rolls in, and you are on your way. As time goes by, you find that success brings you experience and confidence, which makes the business even easier, which causes you to make more deals and earn more commissions.

As your career progresses, you take care to be a professional and maintain professional relationships with those whom you deal. You also join and contribute to the many professional organizations in order to further your professionalism and to give back some of what you have received. After a few years of success in the business, you then are in a position to decide your future. Do you want to go out on your own or remain a part of some successful team? The choice is yours, and your future is nothing but bright.

Living is an art, not a science. There is more to success in life than just succeeding at commercial real estate. Success in the business helps, but it is only one of the legs to a stool that keeps you balanced. The other legs involve our social lives and health. All the money in the world is meaningless without health, and there are many successful commercial real estate brokers who are divorced and lonely. Maintaining each leg is an art. You need to understand and appreciate what each offers you and work to maintain the integrity of that stool.

Good luck!

APPENDIX

Code of Ethics and Standards of Practice of the National Association of Realtors®

The Realtor's® Pledge

I am a Realtor®

I pledge myself...

- to protect the individual right of real estate ownership and to widen the opportunity to enjoy it

- to be honorable and honest in all dealings

- to seek better to represent my clients by building my knowledge and competence

- to act fairly towards all in the spirit of the Golden Rule

- to serve well my community and, through it, my country

- to observe the REALTORS® Code of Ethics and conform my conduct to its lofty ideals

Code of Ethics and Standards of Practice of the National Association of REALTORS®

Effective January 1, 1999. Where the word REALTORS® is used in this Code and Preamble, it shall be deemed to include REALTOR-ASSOCIATES®. While the Code of Ethics establishes obligations that may be higher than those mandated by law, in any instance where the Code of Ethics and the law conflict, the obligations of the law must take precedence.

Preamble

Under all is the land. Upon its wise utilization and widely allocated ownership depend the survival and growth of free institutions and of our civilization. REALTORS® should recognize that the interests of the nation and its citizens require the highest and best use of the land and the widest distribution of land ownership. They require the creation of adequate housing, the building of functioning cities, the development of productive industries and farms, and the preservation of a healthful environment.

Such interests impose obligations beyond those of ordinary commerce. They impose grave social responsibility and a patriotic duty to which REALTORS® should dedicate themselves, and for which they should be diligent in preparing themselves. REALTORS®, therefore, are zealous to maintain and improve the standards of their calling and share with their fellow REALTORS® a common responsibility for its integrity and honor.

In recognition and appreciation of their obligations to clients, customers, the public, and each other, REALTORS® continuously strive to become and remain informed on issues affecting real estate and, as knowledgeable professionals, they willingly share the fruit of their experience and study with others. They identify and take steps, through enforcement of this Code of Ethics and by assisting appropriate regulatory bodies, to eliminate practices which may damage the public or which might discredit or bring dishonor to the real estate profession.

Realizing that cooperation with other real estate professionals promotes the best interests of those who utilize their services, REALTORS® urge exclusive representation of clients; do not attempt to gain any unfair advantage over their competitors; and they refrain from making unsolicited comments about other practitioners. In instances where their opinion is sought, or where REALTORS® believe that comment is necessary, their opinion is offered in an objective, professional manner, uninfluenced by any personal motivation or potential advantage or gain.

The term REALTORS® has come to connote competency, fairness, and high integrity resulting from adherence to a lofty ideal of moral conduct in business relations. No inducement of profit and no instruction from clients ever can justify departure from this ideal.

In the interpretation of this obligation, REALTORS® can take no safer guide than that which has been handed down through the centuries, embodied in the Golden Rule, "Whatsoever ye would that others should do to you, do ye even so to them."

Accepting this standard as their own, REALTORS® pledge to observe its spirit in all of their activities and to conduct their business in accordance with the tenets set forth below.

Article 1

When representing a buyer, seller, landlord, tenant, or other client as an agent, REALTORS® pledge themselves to protect and promote the interests of their client. This obligation of absolute fidelity to the client's interests is primary, but it does not relieve REALTORS® of their obligation to treat all parties honestly. When serving a buyer, seller, landlord, tenant or other party in a non-agency capacity, REALTORS® remain obligated to treat all parties honestly. (Amended 1/93)

Standard of Practice 1-1

REALTORS®, when acting as principals in a real estate transaction, remain obligated by the duties imposed by the Code of Ethics. (Amended 1/93)

Standard of Practice 1-2

The duties the Code of Ethics imposes are applicable whether REALTORS® are acting as agents or in legally recognized non-agency capacities except that any duty imposed exclusively on agents by law or regulation shall not be imposed by this Code of Ethics on REALTORS® acting in non-agency capacities.

As used in this Code of Ethics, "client" means the person(s) or entity(ies) with whom a REALTOR® or a REALTOR'S® firm has an agency or legally recognized non-agency relationship; "customer" means a party to a real estate transaction who receives information, services, or benefits but has no contractual relationship with the REALTOR® or the REALTOR'S® firm; "agent" means a real estate license (including brokers and sales associates) acting in an agency relationship as defined by state law or regulation; and "broker" means a real estate licensee (including brokers and sales associates) acting as an agent or in a legally recognized non-agency capacity. (Adopted 1/95, Amended 1/99)

Standard of Practice 1-3

REALTORS®, in attempting to secure a listing, shall not deliberately mislead the owner as to market value.

Standard of Practice 1-4

REALTORS®, when seeking to become a buyer/tenant representative, shall not mislead buyers or tenants as to savings or other benefits that might be realized through use of the REALTOR'S® services. (Amended 1/93)

Standard of Practice 1-5

REALTORS® may represent the seller/landlord and buyer/tenant in the same transaction only after full disclosure to and with informed consent of both parties. (Adopted 1/93)

Standard of Practice 1-6

REALTORS® shall submit offers and counter-offers objectively and as quickly as possible. (Adopted 1/93, Amended 1/95)

Standard of Practice 1-7

When acting as listing brokers, REALTORS® shall continue to submit the seller/landlord all offers and counter-offers until closing or execution of a lease unless the seller/landlord has waived this obligation in writing. REALTORS® shall not be obligated to continue to market the property after an offer has been accepted by the seller/landlord. REALTORS® shall recommend that sellers/landlords obtain the advice of legal counsel prior to acceptance of a subsequent offer except where the acceptance is contingent on the termination of the pre-existing purchase contract or lease. (Amended 1/93)

Standard of Practice 1-8

REALTORS® acting as agents or brokers of buyers/tenants shall submit to buyers/tenants all offers and counter-offers until acceptance but have no obligation to continue to show properties to their clients after an offer has been accepted unless otherwise agreed in writing. REALTORS® acting as agents or brokers of buyers/tenants shall recommend that buyers/tenants obtain the advice of legal counsel if there is a question as to whether a pre-existing contract has been terminated. (Adopted 1/93, Amended 1/99)

Standard of Practice 1-9

The obligation of REALTORS® to preserve confidential information (as defined by the state law) provided by their clients in the course of any agency relationship or non-agency relationships recognized by law continues after termination of agency relationships or any non-agency relationships recognized by law. REALTORS® shall not knowingly, during or following the termination of professional relationships with their clients:

1) reveal confidential information of clients; or

2) use confidential information of clients to the disadvantage of clients; or

3) use confidential information of clients for the REALTOR'S® advantage or the advantage of third parties unless:

a) clients consent after full disclosure; or

b) REALTORS® are required by a court order; or

c) it is the intention of a client to commit a crime and the information is necessary to prevent the crime; or

d) it is necessary to defend a REALTOR® or the REALTOR'S® employees or associates against an accusation of wrongful conduct. (Adopted 1/93, Amended 1/99)

Standard of Practice 1-10

REALTORS® shall, consistent with the terms and conditions of their property management agreement, competently manage the property of clients with due regard for the rights, responsibilities, benefits, safety and health of tenants and others lawfully on the premises. (Adopted 1/95)

Standard of Practice 1-11

REALTORS® who are employed to maintain or manage a client's property shall exercise due diligence and make reasonable efforts to protect it against reasonably foreseeable contingencies and losses. (Adopted 1/95)

Standard of Practice 1-12

When entering into listing contracts, REALTORS® must advise sellers/landlords of:

1) the REALTOR'S® general company policies regarding cooperation with and compensation to subagents, buyer/tenant agents and/or brokers acting in legally recognized non-agency capacities;

2) the fact that buyer/tenant agents or brokers, even if compensated by listing brokers, or by sellers/landlords may represent the interests of buyer/tenant; and

3) any potential for listing brokers to act as disclosed dual agents, e.g. buyer/tenant agents.

(Adopted 1/93, Renumbered 1/98, Amended 1/99)

Standard of Practice 1-13

When entering into buyer/tenant/agreements, REALTORS® must advise potential clients of:

1) the REALTOR'S® general company policies regarding cooperation and compensation; and

2) any potential for the buyer/tenant representative to act as a disclosed dual agent, e.g. listing broker, subagent, landlord's agent, etc. (Adopted 1/93, Renumbered 1/98, Amended 1/99)

Article 2

REALTORS® shall avoid exaggeration, misrepresentation, or concealment of pertinent facts relating to the property or the transaction. REALTORS® shall not, however, be obligated to discover latent defects in the property, to advise on matters outside the scope of their real estate license, or to disclose facts which are confidential under the scope of agency duties owed to their clients. (Amended 1/93)

Standard of Practice 2-1

REALTORS® shall only be obligated to discover and disclose adverse factors reasonably apparent to someone with expertise in those areas required by their real estate licensing authority. Article 2 does not impose upon the REALTOR® the obligation of expertise in other professional or technical disciplines. (Amended 1/96)

Standard of Practice 2-2

(Renumbered as Standard of Practice 1-12 1/98)

Standard of Practice 2-3

(Renumbered as Standard of Practice 1-13 1/98)

Standard of Practice 2-4

REALTORS® shall not be parties to the naming of a false consideration in any document, unless it be the naming of an obviously nominal consideration.

Standard of Practice 2-5

Factors defined as "non-material" by law or regulation or which are expressly referenced in law or regulation as not being subject to disclosure are considered not "pertinent" for purposes of Article 2. (Amended 1/93)

Article 3

REALTORS® shall cooperate with other brokers except when cooperation is not in the client's best interest. The obligation to cooperate does not include the obligation to share commissions, fees, or to otherwise compensate another broker. (Amended 1/99)

Standard of Practice 3-1

REALTORS®, acting as exclusive agents or brokers of sellers/landlords, establish the terms and conditions of offers to cooperate. Unless expressly indicated in offers to cooperate, cooperating brokers may not assume that the offer of cooperation includes an offer of compensation. Terms of compensation, if any, shall be ascertained by cooperating brokers before beginning efforts to accept the offer of cooperation. (Amended 1/99)

Standard of Practice 3-2

REALTORS® shall, with respect to offers of compensation to another REALTOR®, timely communicate any change of compensation for cooperative services to the other REALTOR® prior to the time such REALTOR® produces an offer to purchase/lease the property. (Amended 1/94)

Standard of Practice 3-3

Standard of Practice 3-2 does not preclude the listing broker and cooperating broker from entering into an agreement to change cooperative compensation. (Adopted 1/94)

Standard of Practice 3-4

REALTORS®, acting as listing brokers, have an affirmative obligation to disclose the existence of dual or variable rate commission arrangements (i.e., listings where one amount of commission is payable if the listing broker's firm is the procuring cause of sale/lease and a different amount of commission is payable if the sale/lease results through the efforts of the seller/landlord or a cooperating broker). The listing broker shall, as soon as practical, disclose the existence of such arrangements to potential cooperating brokers and shall, in response to inquires from

cooperating brokers, disclose the differential that would result in a cooperative transaction or in a sale/lease that results through the efforts of the
seller/landlord. If the cooperating broker is a buyer/tenant representative, the buyer/tenant representative must disclose such information to
their client. (Amended 1/94)

Standard of Practice 3-5

It is the obligation of subagents to promptly disclose all pertinent
facts to the principal's agent prior to as well as after a purchase or lease
agreement is executed. (Amended 1/93)

Standard of Practice 3-6

REALTORS® shall disclose the existence of an accepted offer to any
broker seeking cooperation. (Adopted 5/86)

Standard of Practice 3-7

When seeking information from another REALTOR® concerning
property under a management or listing agreement, REALTORS® shall
disclose their REALTOR® status and whether their interest is personal or
on behalf of a client and, if on behalf of a client, their representational
status. (Amended 1/95)

Standard of Practice 3-8

REALTORS® shall not misrepresent the availability of access to show
or inspect a listed property. (Amended 11/87)

Article 4

REALTORS® shall not acquire an interest in or buy or present offers
from themselves, any member of their immediate families, their firms or
any member thereof, or any entities in which they have any ownership
interest, any real property without making their true position known
to the owner or the owner's agent. In selling property they own, or in
which they have any interest, REALTORS® shall reveal their ownership
or interest in writing to the purchaser or the purchaser's representative.
(Amended 1/91)

Standard of Practice 4-1

For the protection of all parties, the disclosure required by Article 4 shall be in writing and provided by REALTORS® prior to the signing of any contract. (Adopted 2/86)

Article 5

REALTORS® shall not undertake to provide professional services concerning a property or its value where they have a present or contemplated interest unless such interest is specifically disclosed to all affected parties.

Article 6

REALTORS® shall not accept any commission, rebate, or profit on expenditures made for their client, without the client's knowledge and consent. When recommending real estate products or services (e.g., homeowner's insurance, warranty programs, mortgage financing, title insurance, etc.), REALTORS® shall disclose to the client or customer to whom the recommendation is made any financial benefits or fees, other than real estate referral fees, the REALTOR® or REALTOR'S® firms may receive as a direct result of such recommendation. (Amended 1/99)

Standard of Practice 6-1

REALTORS® shall not recommend or suggest to a client or a customer the use of another organization or business entity in which they have a direct interest without disclosing such interest at the time of the recommendation or suggestion. (Amended 5/88)

Article 7

In a transaction, REALTORS® shall not accept compensation from more than one party, even if permitted by law, without disclosure to all parties and the informed consent of the REALTOR'S® client or clients. (Amended 1/93)

Article 8

REALTORS® shall keep in a special account in an appropriate financial institution, separated from their own funds, monies coming into their possession in trust for other persons, such as escrows, trust funds, clients' monies, and other like items.

Article 9

REALTORS®, for the protection of all parties, shall assure whenever possible that agreements shall be in writing, and shall be in clear and understandable language expressing the specific terms, conditions, obligations and commitments of the parties. A copy of each agreement shall be furnished to each party upon their signing or initialing. (Amended 1/95)

Standard of Practice 9-1

For the protection of all parties, REALTORS® shall use reasonable care to ensure that documents pertaining to the purchase, sale, or lease of real estate are kept current through the use of written extensions or amendments. (Amended 1/93)

Article 10

REALTORS® shall not deny equal professional services to any person for reasons of race, color, religion, sex, handicap, familial status, or national origin. REALTORS® shall not be parties to any plan or agreement to discriminate against a person or persons on the basis of race, color, religion, sex, handicap, familial status, or national origin. (Amended 1/90)

Standard of Practice 10-1

REALTORS® shall not volunteer information regarding the racial, religious or ethic composition of any neighborhood and shall not engage in any activity which may result in panic selling. REALTORS® shall not print, display or circulate any statement or advertisement with respect to the selling or renting of a property that indicates any preference, limitations or discrimination based on race, color, religion, sex, handicap, familial status, or national origin. (Adopted 1/94)

Article 11

The services which REALTORS® provide to their clients and customers shall conform to the standards of practice and competence which are reasonably expected in the specific real estate disciplines in which they engage; specifically, residential real estate brokerage, real property management, commercial and industrial real estate brokerage, real estate appraisal, real estate counseling, real estate syndication, real estate auction, and international real estate.

REALTORS® shall not undertake to provide specialized professional services concerning a type of property or service that is outside their field of competence unless they engage the assistance of one who is competent on such types of property or service, or unless the facts are fully disclosed to the client. Any persons engaged to provide such assistance shall be so identified to the client and their contribution to the assignment should be set forth. (Amended 1/95)

Standard of Practice 11-1

The obligations of the Code of Ethics shall be supplemented by and construed in a manner consistent with the Uniform Standards of Professional Appraisal Practice (USPAP) promulgated by the Appraisal Standards Board of the Appraisal Foundation.

The obligations of the Code of Ethics shall not be supplemented by the USPAP where an opinion or recommendation of price or pricing is provided in pursuit of a listing, to assist a potential purchaser in formulating a purchase offer, or to provide a broker's price opinion, whether for a fee or not. (Amended1/96)

Standard of Practice 11-2

The obligations of the Code of Ethics in respect of real estate disciplines other than appraisal shall be interpreted and applied in accordance with the standards of competence and practice which clients and the public reasonably require to protect their rights and interests considering the complexity of the transaction, the availability of expert assistance, and, where the REALTOR® is an agent or subagent, the obligations of a fiduciary. (Adopted 1/95)

Standard of Practice 11-3

When REALTORS® provide consultative services to clients which involve advice or counsel for a fee (not a commission), such advice shall be rendered in an objective manner and the fee shall not be contingent on the substance of the advice or counsel given. If brokerage or transaction services are to be provided in addition to consultative services, a separate compensation may be paid with prior agreement between the client and REALTOR®. (Adopted 1/96)

Article 12

REALTORS® shall be careful at all times to present a true picture in their advertising and representations to the public. REALTORS® shall also ensure that their professional status (e.g., broker, appraiser, property manager, etc.) or status as REALTORS® is clearly identifiable in any such advertising. (Amended 1/93)

Standard of Practice 12-1

REALTORS® may use the term "free" and similar terms in their advertising and in other representations provided that all terms governing availability of the offered product or service are clearly disclosed at the same time. (Amended 1/97)

Standard of Practice 12-2

REALTORS® may represent their services as "free" or without cost even if they expect to receive compensation from a source other than their client provided that the potential for the REALTOR® to obtain a benefit from a third party is clearly disclosed at the same time. (Amended 1/97)

Standard of Practice 12-3

The offering of premiums, prizes, merchandise discounts or other inducements to list, sell, purchase, or lease is not, in itself, unethical even if receipt of the benefit is contingent on listing, selling, purchasing, or leasing through the REALTOR® making the offer. However, REALTORS® must exercise care and candor in any such advertising or other public or private representations so that any party interested in receiving or otherwise benefiting from the REALTOR'S® offer will have clear, thorough, advance understanding of all the terms and the conditions of the offer. The offering of any inducements to do business is subject to the limitations and restrictions of state law and the ethical obligations established by any applicable Standard of Practice. (Amended 1/95)

Standard of Practice 12-4

REALTORS® shall not offer for sale/lease or advertise property without authority. When acting as listing brokers or as subagents, REALTORS® shall not quote a price different from that agreed upon with the seller/landlord. (Amended 1/93)

Standard of Practice 12-5

REALTORS® shall not advertise nor permit any person employed by or affiliated with them to advertise listed property without disclosing the name of the firm. (Adopted 11/86)

Standard of Practice 12-6

REALTORS®, when advertising unlisted real property for sale/lease in which they have an ownership interest, shall disclose their status as both owners/landlords and as REALTORS® or real estate licensees. (Amended 1/93)

Standard of Practice 12-7

Only REALTORS® who participated in the transaction as the listing broker or cooperating broker (selling broker) may claim to have "sold" the property. Prior to closing, a cooperating broker may post a "sold" sign only with the consent of the listing broker. (Amended 1/96)

Article 13

REALTORS® shall not engage in activities that constitute the unauthorized practice of law and shall recommend that legal counsel be obtained when the interest of any party to the transaction requires it.

Article 14

If charged with unethical practice or asked to present evidence to cooperate in any other way, in any professional standards preceding or investigation, REALTORS® shall place all pertinent facts before the proper tribunals of the Member Board or affiliated institute, society, or council in which membership is held and shall take no action to disrupt or obstruct such processes. (Amended 1/99)

Standard of Practice 14-1

REALTORS® shall not be subject to disciplinary proceedings in more than one Board of REALTORS® or affiliated institute, society or council in which they hold membership with respect to alleged violations of the Code of Ethics relating to the same transaction or event. (Amended 1/95)

Standard of Practice 14-2

REALTORS® shall not make any unauthorized disclosure or dissemination of the allegations, findings, or decisions developed in connection with an ethics hearing or appeal or in connection with an arbitration hearing or procedural review. (Amended 1/92)

Standard of Practice 14-3

REALTORS® shall not obstruct the Board's investigative or professional standards proceedings by instituting or threatening to institute actions for libel, slander or defamation against any party to a professional standards proceeding or their witnesses based on the filing of an arbitration request, an ethics complaint, or testimony given before any tribunal. (Adopted 11/87, Amended 1/99)

Standard of Practice 14-4

REALTORS® shall not intentionally impede the Board's investigative or disciplinary proceedings by filing multiple ethics complaints based on the same event or transaction. (Adopted 11/ 88)

Article 15

REALTORS® shall not knowingly or recklessly make false or misleading statements about competitors, their business, or their business practices. (Amended 1/92)

Article 16

REALTORS® shall not engage in any practice or take any action inconsistent with the agency or other exclusive relationship recognized by law that other REALTORS® have with clients. (Amended 1/98)

Standard of Practice 16-1

Article 16 is not intended to prohibit aggressive or innovative business practices which are otherwise ethical and does not prohibit disagreements with other REALTORS® involving commission, fees, compensation or other forms of payment or expenses. (Adopted 1/93, Amended 1/95)

Standard of Practices 16-2

Article 16 does not preclude REALTORS® from making general announcements to prospective clients describing their services and the terms of their availability even though some recipients may have entered into agency agreements or other exclusive relationships with another REALTOR®. A general telephone canvass, general mailing or distribution addressed to all prospective clients in a given geological area or in a given profession, business, club, or organization, or other classification or group is deemed "general" for purposes of this standard. (Amended 1/98)

Article 16 is intended to recognize as unethical two basic types of solicitations:

First, telephone or personal solicitations of property owners who have been identified by a real estate sign, multiple listing compilation, or other information service as having exclusively listed their property with another REALTOR®; and

Second, mail or other forms of written solicitations of prospective clients whose properties are exclusively listed with another REALTOR® when such solicitations are not part of a general mailing but are directed specifically to property owners identified through compilations of current listings, "for sale" or "for rent" signs, or other sources of information required by Article 3 and Multiple Listing Service rules to be made available to other REALTORS® under offers of subagency or cooperation. (Amended 1/93)

Standard of Practice 16-3

Article 16 does not preclude REALTORS® from contacting the client of another broker for the purpose of offering to provide, or entering into a contract to provide, a different type of real estate service unrelated to the type of service currently being provided (e.g., property management as opposed to brokerage). However, information received through Multiple Listing Service or any other offer of cooperation may not be used to target clients of other REALTORS® to whom such offers to provide services may be made. (Amended 1/93)

Standard of Practice 16-4

REALTORS® shall not solicit a listing which is currently listed exclusively with another broker. However, if the listing broker, when asked by the REALTOR®, refuses to disclose the expiration date and nature of such listing; i.e., an exclusive right to sell, and exclusive agency, open listing, or other form of contractual agreement between the listing broker and the client, the REALTOR® may contact the owner to secure such information and may discuss the terms upon which the REALTOR® might take a future listing or, alternatively, may take a listing to become effective upon expiration of any existing exclusive listing. (Amended 1/94)

Standard of Practice 16-5

REALTORS® shall not solicit buyer/tenant agreements from buyers/tenants who are subject to exclusive buyer/tenant agreements. However, if asked by a REALTOR®, the broker refuses to disclose the expiration date of the exclusive buyer/tenant agreement, the REALTOR® may contact the buyer/tenant to secure such information and may discuss the terms upon which the REALTOR® might enter into a future buyer/tenant agreement or, alternatively, may enter into a buyer/tenant agreement to become effective upon the expiration of any existing exclusive buyer/tenant agreement. (Adopted 1/94, Amended 1/98)

Standard of Practice 16-6

When REALTORS® are contacted by the client of another REALTOR® regarding the creation of an exclusive relationship to provide the same type of service, and REALTORS® have not directly or indirectly initiated such discussions, they may discuss the terms upon which they might enter into a future agreement or, alternatively, may enter into an agreement which becomes effective upon expiration of any existing exclusive agreement. (Amended 1/98)

Standard of Practice 16-7

The fact that a client has retained a REALTOR® as an agent or in another exclusive relationship in one or more past transactions does not preclude other REALTORS® from seeking such former client's future business. (Amended 1/98)

Standard of Practice 16-8

The fact that an exclusive agreement has been entered into with a REALTOR® shall not preclude or inhabit any other REALTOR® from entering into a similar agreement after the expiration of the prior agreement. (Amended 1/98)

Standard of Practice 16-9

REALTORS®, prior to entering into an agency agreement or other exclusive relationship, have an affirmative obligation to make reasonable efforts to determine whether the client is subject to a current, valid exclusive agreement to provide the same type of real estate service. (Amended 1/98)

Standard of Practice 16-10

REALTORS®, acting as agents of, or in another relationship with, buyers or tenants, shall disclose that relationship to the seller/landlord's agent or broker at first contact and shall provide written confirmation of that disclosure to the seller/landlord's agent or broker not later than execution of a purchase agreement or lease. (Amended 1/98)

Standard of Practice 16-11

On unlisted property, REALTORS® acting as buyer/tenant agents or brokers shall disclose that relationship to the seller/landlord at first contact for that client and shall provide written confirmation of such disclosure to the seller/landlord not later than execution of any purchase or lease agreement. REALTORS® shall make any request for anticipated compensation from the seller/landlord at first contact. (Amended 1/98)

Standard of Practice 16-12

REALTORS®, acting as agents or brokers of sellers/landlords or as subagents of listing brokers, shall disclose that relationship to buyers/tenants as soon as practicable and shall provide written confirmation of such disclosure to buyer/tenants not later than execution of any purchase or lease agreement. (Amended 1/98)

Standard of Practice 16-13

All dealings concerning property exclusively listed, or with buyer/tenants who are subject to an exclusive agreement shall be carried on with the client's agent or broker, and not with the client, except with the consent of the client's agent or broker or except when such dealings are initiated by the client. (Adopted 1/93, Amended 1/98)

Standard of Practice 16-14

REALTORS® are free to enter into contractual relationships or to negotiate with sellers/landlords, buyers/tenants or others who are not subject to an exclusive agreement but shall not knowingly obligate them to pay more than one commission except with their informed consent. (Amended 1/98)

Standard of Practice 16-15

In cooperative transactions REALTORS® shall compensate cooperating REALTORS® (principal brokers) and shall not compensate nor offer to compensate, directly or indirectly, any part of the sales licensees employed by or affiliated with other REALTORS® without the prior express knowledge and consent of the cooperating broker.

Standard of Practice 16-16

REALTORS®, acting as subagents or buyer/tenant agents or brokers, shall not use the terms of an offer to purchase/lease to attempt to modify the listing broker's offer of compensation to subagents or buyer's agents or brokers nor make the submission of an executed offer to purchase/lease contingent on the listing broker's agreement to modify the offer of compensation. (Amended 1/98)

Standard of Practice 16-17

REALTORS® acting as subagents or as buyer/tenant agents or brokers, shall not attempt to extend a listing broker's offer or cooperation and/or compensation to other brokers without the consent of the listing broker. (Amended 1/98)

Standard of Practice 16-18

REALTORS® shall not use information obtained by them from the listing broker, through offers to cooperate received through Multiple Listing Services or other sources authorized by the listing broker, for the purpose of creating a referral prospect to a third broker, or for creating a buyer/tenant prospect unless such is authorized by the listing broker. (Amended 1/93)

Standard of Practice 16-19

Signs giving notice of property for sale, rent, lease or exchange shall not be placed on property without consent of the seller/landlord. (Amended 1/93)

Standard of Practice 16-20

REALTORS®, prior to or after terminating their relationship with their current firm shall not induce clients of their current firm to cancel exclusive contractual agreements between the client and that firm. This does not preclude REALTORS® (principals) from establishing agreements with their associated licensees governing assignability of exclusive agreements. (Adopted 1/98)

Article 17

In the event of contractual disputes or non-contractual disputes as defined in Standard of Practice 17-4 between REALTORS® associated with different firms, arising out of their relationship as REALTORS®, the REALTORS® shall submit the dispute to arbitration in accordance with the regulations of their Board or Boards rather than litigate the matter.

In the event clients of REALTORS® wish to arbitrate contractual disputes arising out of real estate transactions, REALTORS® shall arbitrate those disputes in accordance with the regulations of their Board, provided the clients agree to be bound by the decision. (Amended 1/97)

Standard of Practice 17-1

The filing of litigation and refusal to withdraw from it by REALTORS® in an arbitrable matter constitutes a refusal to arbitrate. (Adopted 2/86)

Standard of Practice 17-2

Article 17 does not require REALTORS® to arbitrate in those circumstances when all parties to the dispute advise the Board in writing that they choose not to arbitrate before the Board. (Amended 1/93)

Standard of Practice 17-3

REALTORS®, when acting solely as principals in a real estate transaction, are not obligated to arbitrate disputes with other REALTORS® absent a specific written agreement to the contrary. (Adopted 1/96)

Standard of Practice 17-4

Specific non-contractual disputes that are subject to arbitration pursuant to Article 17 are:

1) Where a listing broker has compensated a cooperating broker and another cooperating broker subsequently claims to be the procuring cause of the sale or lease. In such cases the complaint may name the first cooperating broker as a respondent and arbitration may proceed without the listing broker being named as a respondent. Alternatively, if the complaint is brought against the listing broker, the listing broker may name the first cooperating broker as a third-party respondent. In either instance the decision of the hearing panel as to procuring cause shall be conclusive with respect to all current or subsequent claims of the parties for compensation arising out of the underlying cooperative transaction. (Adopted 1/97)

2) Where a buyer or tenant representative is compensated by the seller or landlord, and not by the listing broker, and the listing broker, as a result, reduces the commission owed by the seller or landlord and, subsequently to such actions, another cooperating broker claims to be the procuring cause of sale or lease. In such cases the complainant may name the first cooperating broker as respondent and arbitration may proceed without the listing broker being named as a respondent. Alternatively, if the complaint is brought against the listing broker, the listing

broker may name the first cooperating broker as a third-party respondent. In either instance the decision of the hearing panel as to procuring cause shall be conclusive with respect to all current or subsequent claims of the parties of compensation arising out of the underlying cooperative transaction. (Adopted 1/97)

3) Where a buyer or tenant representative is compensated by the buyer or tenant and, as a result, the listing broker reduces the commission owed by the seller or landlord and, subsequent to such actions, another cooperating broker claims to be the procuring cause of sale or lease. In such cases the complaint may name the first cooperating broker as respondent and arbitration may proceed without the listing broker being named as a respondent. Alternatively, if the complaint is brought against the listing broker, the listing broker may name the first cooperating broker as a third-party respondent. In either instance the decision of the hearing panel as to procuring cause shall be conclusive with respect to all current or subsequent claims of the parties for compensation arising out of the underlying cooperative transaction. (Adopted 1/97)

4) Where two or more listing brokers claim entitlement to compensation pursuant to open listings with a seller or landlord who agrees to participate in arbitration (or who requests arbitration) and who agrees to be bound by the decision. In cases where one of the listing brokers has been compensated by the seller or landlord, the other listing broker, as complainant, may name the first listing broker as respondent and arbitration may proceed between the brokers. (Adopted 1/97)

The Code of Ethics was adopted in 1913. Amended at the Annual Convention in 1924, 1928, 1950, 1951, 1952, 1955, 1956, 1961, 1962, 1974, 1982, 1986, 1987, 1989, 1990, 1991, 1992, 1993, 1994, 1995, 1996, 1997, and 1998.

Explanatory Notes

The reader should be aware of the following policies which have been approved by the Board of Directors of the National Association:

1) In filing a charge of an alleged violation of the Code of Ethics by a REALTOR®, the charge must read as an alleged violation of one or more Articles of the Code. Standards of Practice may be cited in support of the charge.

2) The Standards of Practice serve to clarify the ethical obligations imposed by the various Articles and supplement, and do not substitute for, the Case Interpretations in Interpretations of the Code of Ethics.

3) Modifications to existing Standards of Practice and additional new Standards of Practice are approved from time to time. Readers are cautioned to ensure that the most recent publications are utilizes.

Index